'The Vinx–Zeitlin edition of *Carl Schmitt's Early Legal-Theoretical Writings* is a crucial and long-awaited contribution to the study of Schmitt's political thought, and to legal philosophy more generally. These essays exhibit a young Schmitt grappling with jurisprudential issues from a liberal statist perspective, anticipating and diverging from his later works, both famous and notorious, in often surprising ways.'

John P. McCormick, University of Chicago

'These excellent, long-overdue translations of Carl Schmitt's widely neglected – but hugely important – early contributions to legal thought place his controversial ideas in a new and fresh light. They remind us of a crucial fact too often obscured by recent Anglophone scholarship on Schmitt: Schmitt was a jurist first and foremost, and thus we need to situate his thinking within the context of modern jurisprudence in order to make proper sense of it. With an insightful introduction by two major experts on Schmitt, this volume is essential reading to anyone interested not only in Schmitt and German thought but also in modern legal theory.'

William E. Scheuerman, Indiana University

'This excellent edition of *Statute and Judgment* (1912) and *The Value of the State and the Significance of the Individual* (1914) not only sheds light on two pieces largely ignored in the literature, but also offers a fresh look at Schmitt's constitutional theory. The editors have notably clarified the continuities between these early legal-philosophical writings and subsequent works published after the First World War, which were marked in a completely different context by the social and political instability of their time.'

Sandrine Baume, University of Lausanne

'Lars Vinx and Samuel Zeitlin's meticulous edition of Schmitt's first substantial writings on jurisprudence equip an anglophone readership for the first time to see the trajectory of his thinking over the course of his lifetime, in a balanced and accurate way. It has the singular merit of enabling them to judge soberly just how he chose to use the intellectual resources open to him in deploying them across the drastically changing political contexts of his lengthy life. It is an indispensable resource for judging the weight (and the often erratic bearing) of his contribution to political understanding.'

John Dunn, University of Cambridge

'Carl Schmitt's early jurisprudential engagements in German debates over legal determinacy helped to pave the way for his classic works of political and legal theory. A clear and sophisticated introduction augments the excellent translation that Lars Vinx and Samuel Zeitlin have produced, and the results are indispensable as interest in Schmitt shows no signs of abating.'

Samuel Moyn, Yale Law School

'Lars Vinx and Sam Zeitlin have given us a welcome translation of Carl Schmitt's early – that is, pre-World War I – writings, along with a very informative and analytically important introduction. Why should we care?

Carl Schmitt has in the last thirty years become unavoidable – in political theory, jurisprudence, history and, even, literature. This is despite his well-known and apparently unrepented membership in the Nazi Party.

As Vinx and Zeitlin point out, Schmitt is best known for his opening sentences. "Sovereign is he who decides on the exception." "The concept of the state presupposes the concept of the political." These epigrammatic pronouncements date from the post-World War I period and have served as a springboard for a number of interpretations. For some, these understandings prepare the way for and merge easily with Nazism. For some more sympathetic others, they show that Schmitt was centrally concerned with dealing with the consequences of World War I on German domestic politics. Among those consequences were the "stab in the back" account of Germany's defeat and the vengeful peace imposed at Versailles. Both of these readings, however, understand Schmitt as in the end an ideologue whose thought was primarily shaped by external events.

It is the achievement of this volume to show that neither of these positions is tenable. It shows that, well before World War I, Schmitt was working out the basic elements of what will become his better-known work. The argument in *Statute and Judgment* (*Gesetz und Urteil*) is that "law" (*Recht*) is decision, and that legal decisions are on that which cannot be resolved in a usual manner. *Recht* decides the undecidable. Thus, from his earliest work, Schmitt was working out what becomes a powerful and troubling political theory, and this well before the problems and stresses of Weimar. It is not what becomes Nazism, but it is not incompatible with what Nazism might have been – and that is all the more reason for taking Schmitt seriously.'

Tracy B. Strong, Southampton University

CARL SCHMITT'S EARLY
LEGAL-THEORETICAL WRITINGS

Many of Carl Schmitt's major works have by now been translated, with two notable exceptions: Schmitt's two early monographs *Statute and Judgment* (first published in 1912) and *The Value of the State and the Significance of the Individual* (first published in 1914). In these two works, Schmitt presents a theory of adjudication and an account of the state's role in the realization of the rule of law, which together form the theoretical basis on which Schmitt later developed his political and constitutional theory. This new book makes these two key texts available in English translation for the first time, partnered with an introduction that relates the texts to their historical context, to Schmitt's other works and to contemporary discussions in legal and constitutional theory.

LARS VINX is University Lecturer in Jurisprudence at the University of Cambridge. He is the author of *Hans Kelsen's Pure Theory of Law: Legality and Legitimacy* (2007), and also prepared an English-language translation of the debate between Hans Kelsen and Carl Schmitt on constitutional guardianship (*The Guardian of the Constitution: Hans Kelsen and Carl Schmitt on the Limits of Constitutional Law*, 2015).

SAMUEL GARRETT ZEITLIN is Hong Kong Link Early Career Research Fellow and College Lecturer in Politics at Corpus Christi College, University of Cambridge. His publications include editions and translations of Carl Schmitt's *Land and Sea* (2015) and *The Tyranny of Values and Other Texts* (2018), as well as articles in *History of Political Thought*, *The Review of Politics*, *Politisches Denken Jahrbuch*, *History of European Ideas* and *Modern Intellectual History*.

CAMBRIDGE STUDIES IN CONSTITUTIONAL LAW

The aim of this series is to produce leading monographs in constitutional law. All areas of constitutional law and public law fall within the ambit of the series, including human rights and civil liberties law, administrative law, as well as constitutional theory and the history of constitutional law. A wide variety of scholarly approaches is encouraged, with the governing criterion being simply that the work is of interest to an international audience. Thus, works concerned with only one jurisdiction will be included in the series as appropriate, while, at the same time, the series will include works which are explicitly comparative or theoretical – or both. The series editor likewise welcomes proposals that work at the intersection of constitutional and international law, or that seek to bridge the gaps between civil law systems, the US, and the common law jurisdictions of the Commonwealth.

Series Editors
David Dyzenhaus
Professor of Law and Philosophy, University of Toronto
Thomas Poole
Professor of Law, London School of Economics and Political Science

Editorial Advisory Board
T.R.S. Allan, Cambridge, UK
Damian Chalmers, LSE, UK
Sujit Choudhry, Berkeley, USA
Monica Claes, Maastricht, Netherlands
David Cole, Georgetown, USA
K.D. Ewing, King's College London, UK
David Feldman, Cambridge, UK
Cora Hoexter, Witwatersrand, South Africa
Christoph Moellers, Humboldt, Germany
Adrienne Stone, Melbourne, Australia
Adam Tomkins, Glasgow, UK
Adrian Vermeule, Harvard, USA

Books in the series

Carl Schmitt's Early Legal-Theoretical Writings: Statute and Judgment, and The Value of the State and the Significance of the Individual Edited and translated, with an introduction and notes, by Lars Vinx and Samuel Garrett Zeitlin

Remedies for Human Rights Violations: A Two-Track Approach to Supranational and National Law Kent Roach

Europe's Second Constitution: Crisis, Courts and Community Markus W. Gehring

CARL SCHMITT'S EARLY LEGAL-THEORETICAL WRITINGS

Statute and Judgment
and The Value of the State and the Significance
of the Individual

Edited and translated, with an introduction and notes, by

LARS VINX
University of Cambridge

SAMUEL GARRETT ZEITLIN
University of Cambridge

CAMBRIDGE
UNIVERSITY PRESS

CAMBRIDGE
UNIVERSITY PRESS

University Printing House, Cambridge CB2 8BS, United Kingdom

One Liberty Plaza, 20th Floor, New York, NY 10006, USA

477 Williamstown Road, Port Melbourne, VIC 3207, Australia

314–321, 3rd Floor, Plot 3, Splendor Forum, Jasola District Centre,
New Delhi – 110025, India

79 Anson Road, #06–04/06, Singapore 079906

Cambridge University Press is part of the University of Cambridge.

It furthers the University's mission by disseminating knowledge in the pursuit of
education, learning, and research at the highest international levels of excellence.

www.cambridge.org
Information on this title: www.cambridge.org/9781108494489
DOI: 10.1017/9781108658300

First published in English by Cambridge University Press 2021 as *Carl Schmitt's Early Legal-Theoretical Writings*

This edition is a translation of *Der Wert des Staates und die Bedeutung des Einzelnen*, originally published in German by Duncker & Humblot GmbH (3rd edition, 2014) © Duncker & Humblot GmbH, Berlin, and *Gesetz und Urteil: Eine Untersuchung zum Problem der Rechtspraxis* (3rd edition, 2009) © Verlag C. H. Beck oHG, München.

A catalogue record for this publication is available from the British Library.

Library of Congress Cataloging-in-Publication Data
Names: Schmitt, Carl, 1888–1985. | Vinx, Lars, editor, translator, writer of added commentary. | Zeitlin, Samuel Garrett, editor, translator, writer of added commentary. | Schmitt, Carl, 1888–1985. Gesetz und Urteil. English. | Schmitt, Carl, 1888–1985. Der Wert des Staates, und die Bedeutung des Einzelnen. English.
Title: Carl Schmitt's early legal-theoretical writings : Statute and judgment and the Value of the state and the significance of the individual / edited and translated by Lars Vinx, University of Cambridge; Samuel Garrett Zeitlin, University of Cambridge.
Description: Cambridge, United Kingdom ; New York, NY : Cambridge University Press, [2021] | Series: Cambridge studies in constitutional law | Includes bibliographical references and index.
Identifiers: LCCN 2021000632 (print) | LCCN 2021000633 (ebook) | ISBN 9781108494489 (hardback) | ISBN 9781108714716 (paperback) | ISBN 9781108658300 (ebook)
Classification: LCC K230.S352 A2 2021 (print) | LCC K230.S352 (ebook) | DDC 340/.1–dc23
LC record available at https://lccn.loc.gov/2021000632
LC ebook record available at https://lccn.loc.gov/2021000633

ISBN 978-1-108-49448-9 Hardback

CONTENTS

ACKNOWLEDGEMENTS

I am thankful for the opportunity to continue my studies and teaching, for which I am grateful to Dipesh Chakrabarty, Elisabeth Clemens, Joel Isaac, Sarah Johnson, John P. McCormick, Sankar Muthu, Jennifer Pitts, Nathan Tarcov and Linda Zerilli at the University of Chicago, and to Duncan Bell, Richard Bourke, Christopher Brooke, John Dunn, Marina Frasca-Spada, Shruti Kapila, Christopher Kelly, Duncan Kelly, Charles Read, Lucia Rubinelli, Martin Ruehl, Andrew Sanger, David Sneath, Sylvana Tomaselli, Lars Vinx, Emma Wilson and Harald Wydra at the University of Cambridge.

For *The Value of the State and the Significance of the Individual*, I am particularly thankful to Professor George Schwab for very helpfully checking the translation, as well as to Greg Conti, Adam Lebovitz, Lucia Rubinelli, Joshua Smeltzer, Lars Vinx and Joanna Williamson for their comments and encouragement.

Work on the translation of *The Value of the State and the Significance of the Individual* was completed during a research stay at the Stiftung Maximilianeum in Munich, Germany, and I am grateful to Hanspeter Beisser, director of the Stiftung, for his hospitality and generosity over many years.

To my teachers during my graduate studies, Timothy Hampton, Kinch Hoekstra, Victoria Kahn, Richard Serjeantson and Shannon Stimson, I remain deeply grateful for the example of their teaching and scholarship.

I am thankful for the love of my family: my mother, Elizabeth; my sister, Ellie; and my dear friend and partner, Joanna.

My work on this translation and edition is dedicated to Richard Bourke and Shruti Kapila, with gratitude and intellectual esteem.

Samuel Garrett Zeitlin

I am grateful to David Dyzenhaus, Matthew Kramer and Josh Smeltzer for their extremely helpful input to this project, and to Marianne Nield at Cambridge University Press for her unwavering patience and support.

It was a great pleasure to collaborate with Sam Zeitlin. I hope this will not have been the last of our shared projects.

The preparation of this manuscript received financial support from the Faculty of Law at the University of Cambridge.

Lars Vinx

~

Introduction

Carl Schmitt and the Problem of the Realization of Law

From Political Theory to Jurisprudence

The famous pithy aphorisms that Carl Schmitt used to open his major works – 'the sovereign is he who decides on the exception', 'the concept of the state presupposes the concept of the political', etc. – have become a part of the common discourse of contemporary scholarship on politics and the law. The theoretical framework that animates these slogans, however, has remained somewhat opaque. It has often been argued that there is no such framework – that Schmitt was a situational thinker whose works are best understood as interventions in concrete political debates that do not add up to a grand theoretical vision.[1]

This apparent lack of unity has encouraged a great variety of rather different appropriations. From the left, Schmitt is portrayed as a radical theorist of popular sovereignty, of constituent power and agonistic democracy who aimed to defend popular rule against liberal elitism.[2] Some commentators, by contrast, see Schmitt as a defender of a form of constitutional democracy,[3] even while others interpret him as the prophet of a politically authoritarian neoliberal capitalism.[4] It has been argued that Schmitt's views form the template for populist authoritarianism and that his ideas were, from the beginning, congenial to Nazism.[5] Other scholars have categorized Schmitt as an opponent of

---

[1] Löwith (1995).
[2] Kalyvas (2008); Mouffe (1997); Balakrishnan (2000); Rasch (2016).
[3] Schwab (1989); Bendersky (1983); Schupmann (2017).
[4] Cristi (1998).
[5] Scheuerman (2020); Dyzenhaus (1997), 38–101.

1

legal positivism who rightly objected to a reduction of political legitimacy to mere positive legality.[6]

One reason why it has been so difficult to make sense of the structure and content of Schmitt's overall intellectual project is that its reception and interpretation has tended to focus on Schmitt's political theory and, to a lesser extent, on his constitutional ideas. As a result, the scholarly discussion of Schmitt's work, with some notable exceptions,[7] has lost sight of the fact that Schmitt's key political-theoretical and constitutional ideas grew out of a legal theory – one that forms the implicit background of the political and constitutional arguments one finds in well-known works such as *Dictatorship*, *Political Theology*, *Constitutional Theory* or *The Concept of the Political*.

Schmitt first expounded his legal-theoretical ideas in two early works published before the onset of the Great War – *Statute and Judgment* (1912)[8] and *The Value of the State and the Significance of the Individual* (1914)[9] – which are presented here, for the first time, in full English translation.[10] These texts show, we shall argue, that there is a degree of underlying thematic unity to Schmitt's oeuvre. This is not to say that all of Schmitt's central publications do, in the end, add up to one coherent theoretical edifice or that there is no significant development in Schmitt's thought; rather, Schmitt's early legal-philosophical writings introduce a jurisprudential problem that continued to drive Schmitt's later work, while giving rise to varying responses in different stages of Schmitt's career. To grasp the inner logic of the development of Schmitt's thought, it is necessary to understand how the young Schmitt conceived of that jurisprudential problem.

The problem Schmitt's early legal-theoretical works lay out and engage with is, to adopt Schmitt's own terminology, the problem of *Rechtsverwirklichung*, or of the realization of law. Our aim in this introduction is to

---

[6] Loughlin (2010); Loughlin (2018).

[7] The importance of Schmitt's legal theory is highlighted in some of the German literature on Schmitt. See Hofmann (2002), 34–77; Maus (1980); Kaufmann (1988). Important English-language discussion of Schmitt's legal theory includes Scheuerman (2020); McCormick (1997), 206–248; Croce and Salvatore (2013). On Schmitt's legal theory in the aftermath of the Second World War, see Maier (2019).

[8] Schmitt (1912).

[9] Schmitt (2015).

[10] For commentary on these two texts, see Scheuerman (2020), 19–44; Scheuerman (1996); Neumann (2015), 16–29; Kiefer (1990). There is valuable discussion of Schmitt (2015) in Baume (2003) and Galli (2013). For the biographical context of these two works, see Mehring (2009), 37–40 and 59–65.

lay out the contours of the problem of the realization of law, as Schmitt presented it in his early legal-theoretical works, and to illustrate how these texts can inform interpretation of Schmitt's mature legal, political and constitutional theory.

The Problem of Legal Indeterminacy

We commonly take it that one can meaningfully distinguish between the rule of law and arbitrary, legally unrestrained governance. It is true, of course, that rules of law are made and applied by specific human beings. There is nevertheless a difference between the rule of law and what a contemporary legal philosopher has called a 'system of pure discretion'[11] in which decision-takers are legally free to decide however they see fit. Where there are rules of law and where officials can be counted upon to be guided by those rules, individual subjects of the law will typically be in a position to anticipate how they will be treated by public authorities in the event that they engage in a certain course of action.

One can hold on to the claim that there is a meaningful distinction between the rule of law and a system of mere discretion without denying that general legal rules sometimes fail to determine outcomes in particular cases, whether because legal rules are bound to be confronted with unanticipated factual situations or as a result of the open texture of the terms of natural language that are used to formulate them. The view that general legal rules always allow for determinate solutions to particular cases by way of mechanical application – a view often referred to as 'formalism' – is almost universally rejected as inaccurate in contemporary jurisprudential debate.[12] The prevailing view nowadays is that law is limitedly indeterminate. According to H. L. A. Hart, legal indeterminacy, while undoubtedly real, is peripheral to legal practice. The phenomenon, Hart argued, should not 'blind us to the fact' that the operations of courts are 'unquestionably rule-governed [. . .] over the vast, central areas of the law'.[13]

The young Schmitt found himself in the midst of a heated debate concerning the problem of legal determinacy – one in which formalist

---

[11] See Raz (1999), 137–141.
[12] See Shapiro (2011), 234–258.
[13] Hart (1994), 154. On Hart's theory of adjudication, see Kramer (2018), 110–147. Further to the problem of indeterminacy, see Endicott (2000) and Leiter (2007).

accounts of adjudication still had significant purchase. The orthodox jurisprudential approach in Wilhelmine Germany (scholars usually refer to it as 'statutory positivism') was premised on the assumption of the perfect determinacy of statutory law. Statutory positivists argued that all law is the product of the sovereign will of the state, typically expressed in the form of statutory enactments.[14] What is more, they held that there are techniques of legal interpretation that will enable any trained jurist to decide any possible legal case without resort to teleological consider- ations that might import potentially contentious judgments of value into legal reasoning. The implications of this view for a theory of adjudication were vividly captured, and wittily satirized, by Hermann Ulrich Kantorowicz, a prominent critic of statutory positivism:

> The prevalent ideal conception of the jurist is the following: A higher officer of state with academic training, he sits in his cubicle, armed only with a thought-machine, but one of the very finest sort. The room's only furniture consists in a green table, on which we find the statute book lying in front of the official. One hands him some random case, an actual or perhaps an invented one. In accordance with his duty, the official is able to prove the decision that is predetermined by the legislator with absolute exactitude, with the help of purely logical operations and by the use of a secret technique which is comprehensible to him alone.[15]

By the time Schmitt started his career as a legal scholar, in the first and second decades of the twentieth century, this formalist account of adjudication had come under sustained criticism at the hands of the members of a loose group of legal scholars who referred to themselves as the *Freirechtsbewegung* (the 'free law movement').[16] Kantorowicz published a short monograph in 1906 (under the pseudonym 'Gnaeus Flavius') that was intended to be a manifesto of the free law movement. *Der Kampf um die Rechtswissenschaft* (*The Struggle for Legal Science*) both attacks the assumption of the perfect determinacy of statutory law as descriptively inaccurate and makes suggestions for how judges who have

---

[14] See Wieacker (1952), 430–468. For the political background of statutory positivism, see Caldwell (1997), 13–39. The standard understanding of statutory positivism is challenged by Paulson (2007), who argues that the view is neither wedded to the notion that all law is statutory nor to the claim that law is perfectly determinate, but only to the weaker thesis that statutory law is supreme.

[15] Kantorowicz (1906), 7.

[16] Other notable exponents of the free law school include Eugen Ehrlich and Theodor Sternberg. See Foulkes (1969); Herget and Wallace (1987). For Kantorowicz's theory of adjudication, see Paulson (2019).

abandoned it should go about their business if faced with problems of indeterminacy.

Although the free law movement was perceived as a radical assault on the self-understanding of legal officials, its views have a lot in common with the moderate-indeterminacy thesis espoused by Hart. Statutory rules, Kantorowicz points out, invariably contain terms that are affected by the vagueness of natural language.[17] The application of statute will, at times, have to deal with cases that Hart later described as 'penumbral'[18] – that is, with cases in which the established use of a term that has been employed in the formulation of a legal rule fails to determine whether some state of affairs is to be subsumed under the legal rule. Statutory positivists claimed that there are juristic techniques of interpretation that will enable a judge to deal with indeterminacies in statutory law arising from this problem of the open texture of natural language – but there are no objective criteria, Kantorowicz argues, for deciding which of the available techniques of interpretation (analogy, extensive interpretation, *argumentum e contrario*, etc.) ought to be used in a concrete case so as to remedy the problem.[19] The appeal to such techniques merely serves to rationalize judicial decisions that are driven, however unconsciously, by the will of the interpreter. The belief that decisions are always determined by statutory norms, Kantorowicz concludes, amounts to a kind of false consciousness among legal decision-takers – one that may engender bad decisions that are insensitive to the interests of society and its members.[20]

What would a more defensible approach to adjudication look like? Judges who are faced with statutory norms that fail to clearly determine decisional outcomes, Kantorowicz argues, must resort to normative standards that are not contained in statutory law and which cannot be sourced to the will of the state. Kantorowicz refers to these subsidiary standards as norms of the 'free law'.[21] What endows norms of the free law with legal status, according to Kantorowicz, is their factual acceptance among the members of a legal community.[22] It is here that jurisprudence connects with legal sociology: social-scientific research is needed to determine which expectations of proper conduct and appropriate

---

[17] See Kantorowicz (1906), 15.
[18] See Hart (1958), 606–615.
[19] See Kantorowicz (1906), 23–30.
[20] See ibid., 19–22 and 38–47.
[21] See ibid., 10.
[22] See ibid., 12.

ordering are in fact shared among the members of society.[23] It is to these that a judge is to refer, if possible, when statutory law fails to provide guidance. Even the free law, however, will at times fail to provide sufficient decisional guidance. In such cases, Kantorowicz admits, there is no legal solution to the case at hand[24] and a judge will consequently have to take a decision based on their individual moral opinion, although such opinions are not, in Kantorowicz's view, open to rational justification.[25]

The young Schmitt was clearly impressed by this challenge to statutory positivism. His own theory of adjudication, as developed in *Statute and Judgment*, concurs with the critical conclusions of Kantorowicz's attack.[26] Schmitt refrains, however, from fully endorsing Kantorowicz's response to the problem of the partial indeterminacy of statutory law. In particular, Schmitt rejects the view that there are cases in which the law fails to provide direction, as well as the corollary of this view that judges in such cases are free to make law rather than to apply it.[27] His reaction to the free law movement's challenge to statutory positivism, as a result, takes the form of an attempt to identify an alternative ground of legal determinacy.

A Turn to Legal Practice

Consider again the description of the process of adjudication that Kantorowicz attributes to the statutory positivist: it implies that all legal questions that might arise in a concrete case have a correct answer and that this answer is fully contained in statutory law, assuming that the latter is correctly interpreted. What a judge does, in deciding a specific case, is apply a general decision already taken by the legislator to the concrete situation at hand. This is a purely cognitive process – one that is guided by value-neutral logical techniques of statutory interpretation and which therefore does not require the judge to rely on their own practical judgment. Statutory law, in turn, is portrayed as an instruction or command to the judge – issued by the sovereign – that is binding on judges. The judge, in view of their subjection to the will of the sovereign legislator, is bound by

---

[23] See Kantorowicz (1911), 13–15.
[24] See Kantorowicz (1906), 16.
[25] See ibid., 40–41.
[26] See Schmitt (1912), 11–16, and compare Kantorowicz (1906), 23–32. Schmitt's critique of statutory positivism is also indebted to Sternberg (1904), 123–142.
[27] See Kantorowicz (1906), 42.

statute to decide in a particular way. Accordingly, a judicial decision is to be regarded as correct if and only if it exhibits conformity to statute (*Gesetzmäßigkeit*).[28]

Like the proponents of free law, Schmitt rejects this account of the correctness of judicial decisions as a misdescription of legal practice. His adaptation of the free law movement's critique of statutory positivism, however, emphasizes the question of where this critique leaves our understanding of judicial role. If we abandon the criterion of conformity to statute, how can judges still be said to be subject to the law – to be duty-bound to apply it? It might appear, Schmitt points out, that judges are free to decide for themselves whether to use a statutory norm to decide a particular case, as well as how to use it:

> According to the prevailing opinion, the judge, at each stage of his activity, is to pay obedience to a command whose content he has, in most cases, to determine for himself. This compels the conclusion that the evaluation of this determination, the question of its correctness, cannot be answered by appeal to the command itself. The content of the latter must first be identified through that determination. A 'will' that hovers above the judge is, in all cases, the result of an interpretation, one that therefore cannot, in turn, legitimize itself by appeal to its result.[29]

Note that Schmitt's claim in this passage is not that statutory norms do not bear, often significantly, on how particular cases ought to be decided; rather, the claim is that the process of the application of a statutory norm to a particular case must turn on factors that are not contained in statute itself – which do not themselves derive from a legislative instruction that binds judges. The statute itself, Schmitt points out, does not contain anything more than its 'manifest content'[30] and how the latter is to be understood is what is at issue in difficult cases. It would be futile, Schmitt observes, for a sovereign legislator to try to address this question by issuing a general command to the judiciary to decide in conformity with statute. Such a command would not obviate the need for the interpretation of statutory rules and it could not tell a judge what makes an interpretation correct. But if judges must decide that question for themselves, what difference is there between legislation and adjudication?

Although Schmitt endorses Kantorowicz's rejection of the traditional doctrine of statutory interpretation, he claims that theorists of free law

---

[28] Schmitt (1912), 5–6 and 21.
[29] Ibid., 31.
[30] Ibid.

fail to address the question. Kantorowicz, for one, argues that judges ought to follow statute for as long as it provides clear, unambiguous guidance, that they should plug gaps or resolve ambiguities in statutory law by appeal to the moral opinions factually prevalent among members of society, wherever possible, and that they ought to decide in accordance with their own moral views where conventional morality gives out. But he does not explain why a judge should be seen to be obligated to go down this precise decision tree.[31] The theory of free law, Schmitt argues, remains wedded to the idea that a legal decision, to be legally correct, must be determined by norms that judges can be assumed to have a duty to apply. It merely aims to widen the range of such norms, by attributing subsidiary legal force to conventional morality. But the doctrine of free law, much like the statutory positivist position that it attacks, fails to explain what accounts for the fact that judges and other legal officials are bound to apply the norms in question or to rank them in the suggested way.[32] Unless the question can be answered, even judicial decision-taking that follows the strictures outlined by Kantorowicz must remain a mere exercise of the will of the decision-taker.

To overcome this shortcoming, Schmitt goes on to suggest, we need a conception of the correctness of judicial decisions that lets go of the idea that correct judicial decisions are programmed by legal norms (of whichever kind). To arrive at an alternative, Schmitt turns his attention to the way in which legal practice in fact deals with problems of application. An analysis of legal practice shows, Schmitt claims, that judges approach difficult cases under the guidance of a 'postulate of legal determinacy', which demands of judges that they decide in the way that best fosters and preserves legal determinacy, understood as the 'calculability' and 'predictability' of judicial decisions.[33] As we have seen, Schmitt, like Kantorowicz, rejects the view that judicial decisions do nothing more than implement statutory law and he agrees that legal officials, insofar as they take themselves to be doing nothing more than implementing statutory law, are labouring under a form of false consciousness. But Schmitt also claims, in contrast to the proponents of free law, that existing legal practice is fundamentally sound. Although practitioners often adopt a mistaken self-description, their decision-taking is given sufficient orientation, however unconsciously, by the postulate of legal

[31] See Kantorowicz (1906), 41.
[32] Schmitt (1912), 19–20 and 38–40.
[33] See ibid., 44–67.

determinacy. 'Happily, the method of practice', Schmitt avers, 'is better than what practice takes to be its method.'[34]

Schmitt presents two major lines of argument to sustain the claim that legal practice is in fact governed by a postulate of legal determinacy. The first of these is a general reflection on the function of positive law, which introduces the problem of the realization of law. Schmitt observes that a statute is typically dependent upon established social practices and mores. It usually 'leans against existing orders of life and habits of intercourse', and 'makes use of the moral opinions of the time and the people, of cultural ideas'.[35] The contribution the positive law makes to social order, Schmitt goes on to argue, is to give legal specificity to a society's accustomed form of life. This explains, Schmitt claims, why many positive legal provisions are characterized by an element of indifference of content – why it is often more important that there be some determinate legal regulation, whatever its content may be, rather than none.[36] A society's form of life – the sense of justice shared by its members – may determine, for instance, that there ought to be punishment for murder, but it is unlikely to give an answer to the question of precisely what punishments are to be imposed in the particular circumstances of an individual case. At the limit, it matters more that legal order be capable of settling such questions than how exactly it settles them. This line of thought shows, Schmitt argues, that an appeal to substantive moral standards cannot, by itself, provide a criterion of the correctness of judicial decision. Such standards would fail to tell a judge how to decide in cases in which there are several possible ways of specifying or concretizing those standards.

The main reason why statutory law has gained prominence in modern societies, Schmitt claims, is that it typically (although not invariably) turns out to be a very efficient way of dealing with decisional problems of this sort.[37] As we have seen, Schmitt rejects the view that statutory law can by itself achieve the goal of complete legal determinacy. The claim that statutory law does not always provide clear guidance, however, does not entail that it never does: not all cases are hard. The reason, then, why a judge normally ought to decide in accordance with statute, in cases where statutory law does give clear guidance, is that doing so serves the

---

[34] Ibid., 43.
[35] Ibid., 44–45.
[36] See ibid., 45–53. The theme is likewise discussed in Schmitt (2015), 78–80, and it reappears in Schmitt (1922), 30–31.
[37] Schmitt (1912), 84–85.

aim of achieving legal determinacy. This interpretation of the point and purpose of statute, Schmitt holds, can be extended into a general account of the way in which legal officials deal with difficult problems of interpretation and application.

In this vein, Schmitt's second line of argument is to point out that many features of legal practice that would otherwise be difficult to account for – that judges are required to provide reasons for their decisions; that important cases are decided not by a single judge, but rather by a collegium of several judges; that there is usually a possibility of appeal to a higher instance; that judges are more likely to invoke conventional morality than their own ideas of justice as a subsidiary standard; that they show anticipatory deference to the judicature of higher courts – can plausibly be understood to serve the purpose of legal determinacy.[38] All of these practices enhance the predictability of judicial decision and thus serve to realize legal determinacy.

The claim that legal practice is governed by a postulate of legal determinacy is introduced as a descriptive claim about 'contemporary legal practice'. Schmitt's interpretation of legal practice is nevertheless intended to yield normative conclusions and practical effects. If judges were to self-consciously adopt the description of legal practice offered in *Statute and Judgment* and let go of the myth that they do nothing more than to implement decisions already contained in statute, their decision-taking would be more likely to achieve legal determinacy.[39] And that practice is, as a matter of fact, committed to the achievement of legal determinacy entails, Schmitt suggests, that an individual judge is duty-bound to decide in the way most conformable to the postulate of legal determinacy.

Schmitt's Criterion of Correctness

That assumption finds expression in Schmitt's aim to provide an alternative criterion of the correctness of judicial decision, which is intended to replace the criterion of conformity to statute (or of norm-conformity more generally). Schmitt formulates his practice-based criterion of the correctness of a judicial decision as follows: 'A judicial decision is correct, today, if it is to be assumed that another judge would have decided in the same way. "Another judge", in this context, refers to the empirical type of the modern,

---

[38] See ibid., 68–79.
[39] See ibid., 73.

legally trained jurist.'[40] Schmitt makes it clear that this criterion is not to be understood as an invitation to engage in sociological or psychological research that might allow judges to offer causal predictions of one another's behaviour.[41] The guiding idea behind the 'formula of correctness', as Schmitt calls it, is that the cause of legal determinacy is best advanced if a legal community's judges rely on the same reasons for their decisions and use them in the same way when they decide similar cases. An individual judge is to ask how another judge is likely to approach the task of arguing about the case at hand. To answer that question, the judge must know what reasons another judge would likely invoke, as well as how the other judge would likely interpret and apply them. In other words, Schmitt's claim is that legal practice will have formed customs and conventions as to how one is to interpret statute and to deal with gaps in the positive law, as to what subsidiary norms may be invoked apart from statute and in what order, as to what weight is to be given to precedent, and so forth. A correct decision is simply one that conforms to the prevailing customs and conventions of legal practice and which is, as a result, calculable and predictable.[42]

Schmitt argues that this approach adopts what is valuable in the free law movement's critique of statutory positivism, while avoiding what he sees as its shortcomings. Schmitt's practice-oriented theory of adjudication, like the doctrine of free law, dispenses with the idea that judicial decisions merely implement general decisions already taken by the legislator. Statutory rules retain their status as a paradigmatic form of law because an appeal to statute is often apt to render decisions predictable. But departures from or additions to statute are permissible – even required – on the condition that they are to be expected, given the established customs and conventions of legal practice. While collective practice determines how legislative input will be interpreted and used, the individual judge is duty-bound to make their decisions conformable to established practice – that is, to adhere to the postulate of legal determinacy.[43]

The rejection of statutory positivism, Schmitt concludes, will neither undermine the regularity of legal decision-taking nor improperly endow individual judges with a power to make law. The statutory positivists, in other words, were quite right, in Schmitt's view, to argue that legal

[40] Ibid., 68.
[41] See ibid., 17–19 and 74–75.
[42] See ibid., 79–114.
[43] Schmitt affirms this point repeatedly. See ibid., 40, 42, 75, 96 and 99.

decisions are (and ought to be) fully predictable and that legal officials ought, at all points, to be subject to the law – although they were wrong to portray legal determinacy as the result of a mechanical application of statutory law, imposed on legal practice from the outside by a sovereign legislative will. The proponents of free law, meanwhile, were correct to point out that legal practice is not exclusively governed by statute in the way statutory positivists claim. But they overlooked that legal practice has its own resources to bind judges and to achieve legal determinacy.

Homogeneity and Legal Determinacy

Schmitt is willing to go much further than Kantorowicz in loosening judicial subjection to statute. He demands, as we have seen, that judges rely on statutory rules as long as doing so will enhance the predictability of decisional output, but he argues that they may be justified in departing from the guidance of statutory law if the pursuit of the goal of legal determinacy so requires. Schmitt explicitly allows for, while Kantorowicz denies, the possibility that judicial decisions that go against a clear statutory provision may sometimes be correct – namely, in cases where a judge has reason to assume that other judges would likewise choose to decide *contra legem*.[44] Imagine a case in which statutory law appears to provide unambiguous guidance, but where it would strike participants in legal practice as patently unreasonable to apply statute, or where to do so would go against a sense of justice that is shared by the community of judges (and perhaps by society at large), so that an individual judge has strong reason to assume that other judges would take a decision *contra legem* if faced with a relevantly similar case. Given such circumstances, the judge, Schmitt argues, is required to take a decision that contravenes statute.

And yet, Schmitt defends a rather demanding understanding of legal determinacy: one that combines the claim that the law (as used in practice) speaks to every case that may have to be adjudicated with the view that it is always predictable, with a fair degree of accuracy, how a typical judge is going to decide. If legal determinacy, thus understood, is to obtain, judges must have arrived at a stable, undisputed and coherent set of customs and conventions of adjudicatory practice. What is more, they must share, and know that they share, a strong intuitive sense of how it would be proper to 'go on' in cases where grounds of decision that have

---

[44] See ibid., 106–109, and compare Kantorowicz (1911), 13.

already been recognized in past legal practice either fail to pinpoint a unique solution or lead to outcomes that are perceived to be unacceptable. Schmitt concedes that, in such cases, judges may have to take resort to *Rechtsgefühl* – that is, to a sense or feeling of what decision would be just or appropriate in the circumstances of the case. But he adamantly denies that judges are permitted to decide difficult cases by appeal to their personal moral convictions; to preserve legal determinacy, they must instead rely on moral convictions they can assume to be prevalent among the members of the judiciary, even if these differ from their own.[45]

What is necessary for legal determinacy to obtain, Schmitt implies, is not merely that all participants in legal practice have mastered a scientific method of the correct interpretation and application of legal rules; it is also necessary that they form a sufficiently homogeneous group.[46] Only thus will judges share a *Rechtsgefühl* – or at least understand what *Rechtsgefühl* is shared in their community – and be enabled, as a result, to render predictable decisions even in difficult cases. Where homogeneity does not obtain, the determinacy of legal practice is bound to break down and the question of how another judge would decide will often have no clear answer. It would perhaps be too dramatic to describe such a situation as one in which there would no longer be any law. It is quite likely, after all, that there would still be legislative and adjudicative institutions, and that their decisions would still be enforced by the use of the organized power of society. But, at least from Schmitt's point of view, the decisions of judges could, under such circumstances, no longer be seen to be realizing the law as opposed to imposing the decision-taker's personal conception of proper social order.

Schmitt on the Idea of Law

Schmitt argues that modern legal practice is committed to achieving legal determinacy. He also argues that the insight that modern legal practice is

---

[45] See Schmitt (1912), 91–93.

[46] The importance of homogeneity in Schmitt has been emphasized by Scheuerman (2020), Scheuerman (1996) and Dyzenhaus (1997). Schmitt does not use the term prominently in *Statute and Judgment*, but there are passages, for instance, that argue that judges must share a common understanding of conventional morality for legal determinacy to be possible (see Schmitt [1912], 94), or that portray 'the judgment of the medieval juror, who was certain that his decision would find the agreement of all his legal associates' as a paradigmatic example of a correct decision (see ibid., 86).

so committed gives rise to a normative demand: judges ought to decide in the ways most conducive to the realization of legal determinacy. This normative demand cannot be defended, at the end of the day, by appeal to the mere fact that a concrete practice is committed to determinacy. It might be argued, after all, that the practice in question would be improved by loosening or shedding the commitment. Why, then, is the achievement of legal determinacy to be regarded as the paramount aim of judicial activity? What is the value of legal determinacy? Why should we take it that legal officials ought to consider themselves bound, when they apply the law, to submit to the postulate of determinacy?

Schmitt's understanding of legal determinacy is tied to the problem of the realization of law. In *Statute and Judgment*, both positive legal norms and judicial decisions, as pointed out above, are understood as elements of the legal concretization of an underlying form of social life. As far as judges are concerned, this concretization is to take place in accordance with firmly established customs and conventions of adjudication, so as to make judicial decisions predictable. However, Schmitt dismisses the view, which he associates with Bentham, that the predictability of judicial decisions is valuable merely because it serves individual economic interests.[47] What makes suitably determinate positive law authoritative or legitimate, Schmitt suggests instead, is that it gives legal specificity to a form of social life that is assumed to be valuable. Schmitt must explain, then, what would make a form of social life valuable, so that its authoritative legal concretization by officials will enjoy a presumption of legitimacy. The second of the two works translated here, *The Value of the State and the Significance of the Individual*, engages with this substantive normative question.

We need to begin with a terminological clarification. Schmitt's argument in *The Value of the State* focuses on the notion of *Recht*, which is best rendered as 'the law', in the sense that contrasts with 'a law', or alternatively as 'right', in the objective sense of 'what is right'. Schmitt also occasionally refers to the *Rechtsgedanke* ('the thought or idea of law/right'). The term *Recht*, although central in *The Value of the State*, is hardly ever used in *Statute and Judgment*. The terminological focus of *Statute and Judgment* is on *Gesetz* – that is, on positive statutory rules. Statutory positivists, as we have seen, held that the law, *Recht*, in the objective sense of the term, consists in large part of the statutory rules enacted by the sovereign will of the state. The use of the notion of *Recht* in

---

[47] See Schmitt (1912), 61–62.

The Value of the State is best understood as an implicit repudiation of this tendency to identify law with statute.[48] The primary reference of the term is to that which is concretized by the enactment of positive statutory rules and in judicial decisions. In other words, Schmitt's terminology in *The Value of the State* intimates that what gives legitimacy to positive legal decisions, whether they be legislative or judicial, is the fact that they implement a meta-positive idea of law. This suggests, in turn, that a form of life must conform to, or be structured by, that idea if its legal concretization is to carry a presumption of legitimate authority.

The core thesis of *The Value of the State*, accordingly, is that it is the state's essential function to realize *Recht*, the meta-positive idea of law – that is, to translate it into determinate and enforceable positive law. One telling passage in *The Value of the State* explicitly distinguishes, in this vein, between *Recht* as an abstract standard that pre-exists the state, and the positive law enacted by the state, which latter is described by Schmitt as a 'serving' and 'mediating' form of law whose sole purpose it is to make *Recht* effective in the empirical world.[49] The state's value and its authority, Schmitt argues, derive exclusively from this function of the realization of *Recht*. Indeed, Schmitt defines the state as the task (*Aufgabe*) of realizing law in the world.[50] These claims are expressed in a language that readers of Schmitt's later works might find quite surprising. Schmitt argues that the only principled way of giving content to the concept of state is to 'assign the state a place in a system of values, one from which its authority follows'. The state, Schmitt claims, 'is not the creator of law [*Recht*], but rather the law is the creator of the state: the law precedes the state'.[51] A little later, Schmitt's reader is informed that 'the law is not in the state, rather the state is in the law'.[52] Schmitt describes a *Rechtsstaat* – that is, a state committed to the rule of law – as one that 'wants wholly to become a function of the law' and recognizes that it should subject itself to its own positive norms only 'because they are law [*Recht*]' – that is, because they are right or correct.[53]

It seems difficult to imagine a more thoroughgoing disavowal of the idea – so prominent in Schmitt's *Political Theology* – that a sovereign

[48] On the distinction between *Recht* and *Gesetz*, see Berman and Zeitlin (2018), xiii–xiv.
[49] Schmitt (2015), 77.
[50] See ibid., 56: 'The state is accordingly the legal construct whose sense consists exclusively in the task of realizing law.'
[51] Ibid., 50.
[52] Ibid., 52.
[53] Ibid., 54.

does not have to have legal authority to make law.[54] But we should note that the notion of sovereignty makes an early appearance in *The Value of the State*. Schmitt points out that law as *Recht* must be 'formulated with precise content' if it is to be implemented and enforced in the empirical world: 'The legal idea ... must become positive, that is, its content is set by an act of sovereign decision.'[55] The claim that Schmitt makes here, it would seem, is that the state must be guided, in making positive laws, by the meta-positive idea of law. But its decisions as to how to specify that idea are not only materially indifferent but also final and, in that sense, sovereign. The relation of the state to *Recht*, in other words, is somewhat akin to that of the Hobbesian sovereign to the practical standards that Hobbes refers to as the 'laws of nature'.[56] The sovereign, for Hobbes, is the sole interpreter of those laws, but the sovereign does not create them and the sovereign's decisions can be critically assessed in their light.

In contrast to Hobbes, however, who expended significant intellectual energy on the attempt to outline the content of the laws of nature, Schmitt does not offer an extended discussion of the content of *Recht*. *The Value of the State*, as Schmitt concedes in his introduction to the book, does not provide a full analysis of the content of the idea of law;[57] rather, Schmitt's main concern is to defend a negative claim about *Recht* – namely, that *Recht*, by contrast to the sanction-backed positive laws that implement it, cannot be a product of mere *de facto* power (and thus cannot derive from the will of the state understood as a mere *de facto* power).

There are some intimations that the young Schmitt understood *Recht* in religious terms. He describes *Recht* as a *Gebot*[58] – a term that, in the original German, evokes the idea of divine law in making implicit reference to the Ten Commandments. Later in the work, Schmitt, in discussing the Catholic Church as an exemplar of an institution that is given over to the realization of *Recht*, refers to the *ius divinum*, the divine law, as a form of *ius* or *Recht* properly so-called. Indeed, Schmitt asserts that the *ius divinum*, as Catholic doctrine understands it, is a 'true *ius*' – that is, a true law.[59]

---

[54] Schmitt (1922), 13.
[55] Schmitt (2015), 79.
[56] See Hobbes (1996), 91–111, and Dyzenhaus (2001).
[57] Schmitt (2015), 15: 'Should the legal-philosophic inquiry find a specific definition of the state, then this is a result, in any case, for scientific inquiry, even if the definition of law remains restricted, for the time being, to a few necessary [but] negative claims [...].'
[58] See ibid., 43.
[59] See ibid., 82: '... a *jus divinum*, which is a true *jus* and not an ethics.'

However these intimations are to be understood, what is clear is that Schmitt is once more opposing the statutory positivists, who argued not merely that law depends on the will of the state, but also that it is meaningless to ask where the state gets the authority to command. From the statutory positivist viewpoint, the state is seen to have the power to make law simply by virtue of its effective coercive control of the population of a certain territory. Whether such power is justified or exercised in ways deserving of the deference of subjects was not regarded, by the statutory positivists, to be a question jurisprudence is competent to ask or to answer.[60]

Schmitt's argument for the claim that the law cannot be the product of a *de facto* power starts out from the correct observation that any theory that portrays law as the product of the state's overwhelming *de facto* power will be unable to vindicate the claim that the positive law is essentially authoritative.[61] For some *de facto* power to be rightful, and thus to be able to generate binding rules or decisions, that power must be suitably related, Schmitt claims, to a prior legitimating standard. Schmitt goes on to identify *Recht* with that standard, whatever its precise content may be, and thus arrives at the conclusion that *Recht* cannot have been produced by the state's power. The positive rules enacted by a state, in turn, make out their claim to be law, and thus to be authoritative, only by serving the realization of *Recht* in the empirical world.[62] The statutory positivists stand accused, implicitly, of taking the view that the sanction-backed commands of a brute, but preponderant, power are invariably binding even if they fail to conform to any antecedent normative standard that carries legitimating force. This is the infamous reduction of legitimacy to legality – of *Recht* to *Gesetz* – of which Schmitt accused his positivist opponents.[63]

Such a reduction would clearly be confused, but there can be no doubt that the main proponents of modern legal positivism are not guilty of such confusion. Schmitt's argument about the reduction of legitimacy to legality arises from the concatenation of two theses: first, the claim that positive law is essentially authoritative or binding; and second, the claim that positive rules have the quality of law simply because they were enacted by a factually supreme power. The second of these two theses might be imputed to some positivist authors, but positivists, needless to

[60] See Anschütz (1933), 1–8.
[61] See Schmitt (2015), 22–43.
[62] See ibid., 44–56.
[63] See Schmitt (1932a).

say, invariably reject the first.[64] What positivists claim about the legitimacy or authoritativeness of positive law is simply that positive legal rules can or cannot be legitimate, depending on whether or not they happen to conform to the practical standards, whatever they may be, that properly ought to guide our critical moral assessment of laws. There is no reason whatsoever why a positivist should be disbarred from making the claim that some valid law is illegitimate or why a positivist should be disbarred from making the normative demand that positive laws ought to conform to the practical standards that are relevant for assessing the practical quality of those laws. One can, of course, decide, like Schmitt, to call these standards *Recht* and then claim that (a kind of) natural law theory has been vindicated against positivism.[65] But this is mere wordplay that does not mark any interesting difference from positivist conceptions of legality – at least if it is to say no more than that laws must conform to moral standards to be legitimate.

Schmitt on the Relation of Law and Morality

Might there be a way of interpreting Schmitt's claim that the state is 'in the law' in a more charitable way – a way that makes it out to be an interesting and distinctive jurisprudential thesis? When Schmitt proclaims that the state is 'in the law', he does not mean to argue that every observable state-like institution that exercises *de facto* control over some territory is credibly committed to the goal of the realization of law or successful in its pursuit; rather, Schmitt claims that a purely empirical concept of the state – one formed by simple abstraction of the common features of a large number of empirical instances of organized, large-scale social control – must be unsatisfactory. If one wants to explain why it is essential to the state to, say, have a territory or to exercise a monopoly of force, one must show, Schmitt argues, that these features are necessary for the state to fulfil its essential function or purpose. That purpose or function, Schmitt goes on to claim, can only be the realization of law.[66] To say that the state is in the law or that every state is wholly governed by the idea or by the thought of law, then, is to say that an institution that does not aim to realize *Recht*, or that is wholly

---

[64] See Kelsen (1934), 15–19; Hart (1994), 185–212.

[65] Schmitt (2015), 83, refers to this standard as *jus divino-naturale*, or that law which is natural and divine. For discussions of this view as being one that Schmitt affirmed repeatedly, see Taubes (2017); Meier (1994).

[66] Schmitt (2015), 77.

unsuccessful in the task, is a defective instantiation of statehood or no state at all and that its laws are defective or, in the extreme case, no laws at all.

An approach of this kind might come to something jurisprudentially distinctive and interesting, but only if more can be said about the content of *Recht* and about the state's relation to *Recht*.[67] What are the normative standards comprised in the idea of law and how do they differ from other, non-legal, normative standards? Why is the peculiar institution that we call the state necessary to realize *Recht* in the empirical world? While Schmitt does address the latter question about the state – by pointing to the inability of *Recht* to realize itself[68] – he has little to say, beyond the religious intimations mentioned above, about the content of *Recht*. In the text of *The Value of the State*, he rests content to remark that his theory of *Recht* is a theory of 'natural law without naturalism'.[69] Instead of further describing the content of *Recht*, Schmitt, besides claiming that *Recht* is prior to the state, merely offers a few additional negative clarifications as to what *Recht* is not.

One such clarification concerns the relation of law and morality. Although *Recht*, in its original form, is supposed to be a purely normative standard, it is nevertheless wholly distinct, Schmitt proclaims, from morality. The pure norms of law that are to be implemented by the state are to have nothing to do with the rules of morality. Schmitt's claim that *Recht* and morality are wholly distinct and unrelated practical standards is developed in a lengthy discussion of neo-Kantian conceptions of the relation of law and morality that cannot be analysed in detail here.[70] Suffice it to say that Schmitt opposes the Kantian view that legal duties concern external behaviour, and not inner motive, and are thus apt to be enforced by the coercive power of the positive law.[71] In this Kantian

---

[67] For a contemporary attempt to do just that, see Finnis (2011).

[68] Schmitt (2015), 40. Although neither *The Value of the State* nor *Statute and Judgment* make explicit mention of Hobbes, the argument has clear Hobbesian undertones. On Schmitt's (and Schmittian) interpretations of Hobbes, see Stanton (2011); Mastnak (2015); Zeitlin (2017); Freund (2017); Taubes (2017).

[69] Schmitt (2015), 76, Schmitt speaks of 'the element of originary, non-state law, the further determination of which is not the task of this treatise and of which (in order to be concise, for once, at the risk of paradox) we wish to say no more than that it must emerge as a natural law without naturalism'. The context makes it clear that 'naturalism', in Schmitt's terminology, designates the methods of empirical social sciences concerned to offer causal explanations of social phenomena.

[70] See ibid., 60–69. Schmitt discusses Stammler (1911); Natorp (1913); Cohen (1904).

[71] See Kant (1996b), 383–385.

picture, Schmitt complains, the role of positive law is merely to secure the 'external conditions for internal morality'.[72] For Schmitt, this amounts to an intolerable 'debasement of the law', in that it portrays the law as 'ideal housewife, who, by way of her circumspection and noiselessness, keeps the house in order and therewith fulfills the external conditions for the undisturbed professional activity of her husband'.[73] The proper approach, Schmitt proclaims, is not to derive morality and law from the same principle: 'They cannot come into contradiction with one another because they have nothing to do with one another.'[74]

Although Schmitt's distinction of *Recht* and morality remains rather opaque, it seems clear enough that it does not align with a Fullerian distinction between the internal and the external morality of law.[75] Schmitt's notion of *Recht* does not concern the way or form in which the state uses the positive law to pursue its substantive policies – that is, whether the state abides by principles of legality; rather, it would appear that *Recht*, for Schmitt, is to be understood as providing the outlines of a substantive conception of good social order. This comes out in several passages of *The Value of the State*, perhaps most clearly in a short discussion of the rights of the criminally accused at the end of the first chapter. Schmitt observes that any 'normal' person would rightly demand to be judged by their equals – that is, by other 'normal' people. He goes on to claim that everyone would, by contrast, reject a criminal's demand only to be judged by their equals – that is, by other criminals. The principle of equality before the law is itself premised, Schmitt claims, on the substantive content of *Recht* – that is, on a preference for non-criminal behaviour – and this entails, Schmitt rather brusquely concludes, 'that this right to equal treatment does not exist for those who', like the criminal, 'are abnormal in the legal sense'.[76]

At first glance, Schmitt's claims about *Recht* in *The Value of the State* appear to carry a Kelsenian flavour.[77] Like Schmitt, Kelsen claims that law is normative, but that its normativity is altogether distinct from

---

[72] Schmitt (2015), 67.

[73] Ibid., 70.

[74] Ibid

[75] See Fuller (1964), chs I and II.

[76] Schmitt (2015), 41. The claim that equality before the law assumes homogeneity recurs in Schmitt's later work. See Schmitt (1934), 48–52; Schmitt (1942), sections 1, 3 and 17.

[77] See Neumann (2015), 16–29. For a comparative analysis of Kelsen's and Schmitt's legal theories, see Paulson (2016), 510–546. Schmitt refers to Kelsen respectfully in both *Statute and Judgment* and *The Value of the State*: see Schmitt (1912), 53–55; Schmitt (2015), 78.

moral normativity. Like Schmitt, Kelsen rejects the view that law can be a product of brute *de facto* power. To interpret an exercise of *de facto* power as the exercise of a legal power, one must presuppose an empowering meta-positive *Grundnorm* that cannot be validated by psychological or sociological facts.[78] Despite these superficial similarities, the views of the young Schmitt on the relation of law and state differ fundamentally from those of Kelsen. Whereas Schmitt's *Recht* is a substantive ideal of good order, Kelsen's *Grundnorm* is a blanket authorization of the first legislator, and Kelsen consequently claims that the positive law can receive any content.[79] Like Schmitt, Kelsen affirms that every state is a *Rechtsstaat*, but he does not want to claim, in putting forward his thesis of the identity of law and state, that an institution of power must be committed to the realization of a substantive and legitimating idea of law to count as a state, but rather that any large-scale, rule-based organization that exercises a coercive monopoly of force in a territory is a *bona fide* state, irrespective of the content of its rules.[80] Kelsen rejects the idea, as has already been emphasized, that positive law is endowed with intrinsic practical authoritativeness.

Schmitt's Anti-individualism

The last chapter of *The Value of the State*, in which Schmitt presents his views on the 'significance of the individual', contains a final attempt to clarify the notion of *Recht* – one that helps to explain the motivation behind Schmitt's separation of law and morality. The claim that it is the task of the state to realize the law is not, in itself, a terribly surprising thesis. Schmitt is aware, of course, that authors who stand in the tradition of social contract theory – such as Hobbes, Locke, Rousseau or Kant – would have agreed with that view in the abstract, but he rejects the understanding of the content of the idea of law that prevails in the social contract tradition. That tradition, to paint with a broad brush, takes it that the task of the state consists in the realization and protection of individual rights or fundamental individual interests in – as a Lockean might have it – life, liberty and property. Schmitt repeatedly affects contempt for the idea that it could be the purpose of law to deal with such mundane and unedifying matters, and

---

[78] For a concise overview of these themes in Kelsen, see Paulson (1992).
[79] See Kelsen (1934), 55–60.
[80] See ibid., 97–106, and compare Kletzer (2018), 21–52.

that the value of the state could consist in being an instrument of the satisfaction of individual desires;[81] rather, Schmitt proposes a reversal of the view that the state's value derives from the way in which it serves individual interests (including the interest in the moral life). The value of the individual, at least from a legal point of view, he claims, depends on the way in which the state's positive law integrates the individual into the collective task of *Rechtsverwirklichung*. Individuals become valuable, from a legal point of view, by being instruments of the state, while the latter, in turn, derives its value from the fact that it realizes the meta-positive ideal of *Recht* in the empirical world.[82] The position of the individual towards the law is therefore one of heteronomous determination: the state, to which Schmitt refers as the 'only subject of the legal ethos',[83] imposes the task of *Rechtsverwirklichung* on individuals, thus giving the individual an opportunity to participate in a higher calling than the satisfaction of individual preference.[84] Whatever *Recht* (understood as *Gebot*, i.e. as commandment) may be, its realization, for Schmitt, must involve more than the provision of the institutional conditions that will delimit and protect individual rights.

Schmitt's arguments for the view that the legal value of individual human beings derives from the way in which they serve the purposes of the state are not entirely convincing. He points out, for instance, that it would be a mistake to think that value attaches to individuals as mere empirical creatures or biological particulars. Even Kant, Schmitt claims somewhat tendentiously, held that the individual human being has value only insofar as it conforms to the moral law, which has no regard for the empirical differences between individuals.[85] A more plausible reading might hold that, for Kant, the capacity to act on the moral law is sufficient to endow the human being with the dignity of a moral agent. Kant would certainly have rejected the claim that the individual carries that dignity only once it becomes the instrument of a purpose that stands above the individual's own law-giving practical reason. Schmitt's intent in putting forward his unorthodox interpretation of Kant, however, is apparent enough: he aims to separate the law

---

[81] See Schmitt (2015), 67, 86 and 99.

[82] See ibid., 85–93.

[83] Ibid., 10, 57, 86 and 100.

[84] This emphasis on heteronomy is equally present in Schmitt (1912), 73, in the context of a description of the individual judge's subjection to practice-based law.

[85] Schmitt (2015), 89.

from moral discourse because the latter might be taken to express a concern for individual human dignity, whereas the dignity of the law, for Schmitt, consists precisely in its repudiation of the inherent value of the individual.

Although the arguments offered in *The Value of the State* are at times inconclusive and gesture towards questions that the young Schmitt had not yet answered, the text is nevertheless of great interest for understanding Schmitt. It expresses a number of normative convictions that Schmitt will, in the further course of his scholarly career, repackage in several different ways, but never abandon. These convictions are best summarized by focusing on the deeply ambivalent conception of the state that emerges from *The Value of the State*. In one sense, the state is demoted from the paramount position that statutory positivists attributed to it. The sovereign, legislative will of the state as a positive institution endowed with de facto control of a certain territory and population, in Schmitt's account, is no longer the source of all law; rather, the state's legislative enactments can claim the quality of law (which Schmitt assumes to go along with normative authoritativeness) only as long as they realize a normative idea of *Recht* that is prior to the will of the state. The central case of a state is an institution that is wholly given over to the task of *Rechtsverwirklichung*, and empirical states can therefore fail to live up to their essential task and degenerate into illegitimate mechanisms of oppression that serve the partial interests of those who happen to control the levers of institutional power. And yet the state is elevated to a position far above its individual subjects or citizens. Individuals derive their own worth and significance from the service they render to the state. A state that does live up to its idea, by serving the purpose of the realization of law, is entitled to expect the absolute loyalty of its subjects to the point of denial of the individual's most fundamental interests. This claim is only made more ominous by the fact that the content of Schmitt's notion of *Recht* – of that which is to be realized by the state, and thus to legitimate the state's law-making and decision-taking – remains elusive. Those who hold the reins of power in the state are to make the final judgment, apparently, as to its content.

From Jurisprudence to Political Theory

In an influential study on Schmitt's legal and political theory, German legal scholar Hasso Hofmann argued that Schmitt's intellectual development was 'governed by the question of the legitimation of public power'.[86] *The Value of the State* answers, as we have seen, that the state draws its legitimacy from providing an authoritative and determinate concretization of a transcendent idea of law that is the sole source, as far as legal philosophy is concerned, of all practical value. We would now like to offer a very brief account of how this conception of the legitimacy of positive law came to be transformed in works that Schmitt published after the Great War.[87]

At first glance, the decisionist conception of legal order that Schmitt began to defend in *Dictatorship* and which is perhaps most clearly expressed in *Political Theology* seems to differ dramatically from the picture given in *Statute and Judgment* and *The Value of the State*. In *Political Theology*, Schmitt famously claims that the sovereign is the one who decides on the state of exception and he appears to portray sovereign power as unrestricted by any prior normativity.[88] Closer inspection, however, reveals clear elements of continuity with the early legal-theoretical works. Although Schmitt's terminology in *Political Theology* tends to conceal the fact, the thesis that sovereignty consists in the power to altogether suspend the law must obviously refer to the positive law, not to the idea of *Recht* that, according to *The Value of the State*, political authorities are called upon to realize. The claim that the sovereign decision is born of normative nothingness, then, need not be understood as a manifestation of normative nihilism. What Schmitt argues is simply that sovereign authority is neither constrained nor constituted by positive law. He clearly does not give up the view that it is the task of the state, in making law, to implement some principle of legitimacy that is antecedent to positive law.[89]

The thesis that any legal norm requires an 'homogeneous medium' – that is, 'a normal, everyday frame of life to which it can be factually applied'[90] – constitutes another clear element of continuity between the argument of *Political Theology* and the views expressed in Schmitt's early

---

[86] Hofmann (2002), 11.

[87] On Schmitt in Weimar, see Kennedy (2004). For an overview of the mature constitutional theory, see Vinx (2019a).

[88] See Schmitt (1922), 5–15.

[89] Schmitt accordingly describes dictatorship as the realization of law. See Schmitt (1921), xlii–xliii. The realization of law (*Rechtsverwirklichung*) likewise reappears in the German text of *Political Theology*: see Schmitt [1996], 35. The English translation (Schmitt [1922], 28), rather misleadingly, renders *Rechtsverwirklichung* as 'the self-evolving law', although Schmitt emphasizes that law needs the authority of the state to be implemented in the empirical world. See Schmitt (2015), 39–41.

[90] Schmitt (1922), 13.

legal-theoretical works. Schmitt observes, in effect, that legal decision-taking will necessarily lack calculability and foreseeability – it will fail to be guided in any meaningful way by the application of positive statutory norms – unless the social circumstances to which the norms in question are to be applied conform to the expectations – to the conception of normal social order – which the legislator had in mind in making them.

This observation is a perfectly natural extension of the argument of *Statute and Judgment*. Differences in emphasis and presentation result from the fact that Schmitt's early work, published before the Great War, speaks to a condition of normality, while the theory of the Weimar period responds to an experience of deep political and social upheaval. As a result, Schmitt now highlights the claim that it is the sovereign's task to reconstitute the social conditions of legal determinacy, of the predictable and calculable applicability of positive legal norms. What is more, we see the beginnings of an important shift in how that task is portrayed.

In *The Value of the State*, sovereign authority is to concretize a transcendent idea of law that is assumed to be beyond sovereign choice. At one point, Schmitt even describes *Recht* as timeless (*zeitlos*)[91] – although he declines, as we have seen, to offer an explicit account of its content. One might plausibly surmise that Schmitt felt entitled to defer that task because he believed that the form of life that had been successfully concretized by the legal practice of the Wilhelmine Empire did, at any rate, conform to the timeless idea of *Recht*.[92] *Political Theology*, by contrast, responds to a situation characterized by profound societal disagreement about the right or proper form of social life. It has now become a point of political contention what form of life, what notion of *Recht*, the state's positive law is to legally specify. The sovereign's authority, Schmitt suggests, must come to be correspondingly more capacious. In deciding to suspend the positive law so as to reconstitute a situation of normality, the sovereign of *Political Theology* does not merely respond to a perception of abnormality; rather, the sovereign decides what is to count as normal or abnormal in light of a prior choice for one or another of the competing and incompatible conceptions of social order that now have currency in society.[93] It might be argued that this portrayal of the sovereign's role does not yet leave the theoretical framework set up in *The*

---

[91] Schmitt (2015), 81.

[92] For nostalgic post-WWII remarks on 'the old [Wilhelmine] monarchy' in Schmitt's correspondence, see Schmitt's letter to Armin Mohler dated 14 April 1952, in Schmitt (1995), 119; Taubes (1987), 36.

[93] See Schmitt (1922), 6.

Value of the State behind. The sovereign, Schmitt could have claimed even now, is still morally (although not legally) bound to make a choice for the one form of social order that best conforms to the timeless idea of *Recht*. Schmitt rejected this option, however, and came to claim, in his *Constitutional Theory*, that any sovereign choice for one form of order or another is to be regarded as legitimate as long as it is successful in creating and maintaining the social underpinnings of a stable legal order.

Note that this move, although it discards the view that the state is bound to realize a transcendent idea of *Recht*, preserves the claim that the positive law is legitimated by the fact that it implements a conception of order that is prior to it – one that Schmitt, in his *Verfassungslehre*, somewhat confusingly, refers to as the 'positive constitution'. He describes the latter as the result of a fundamental political decision for a certain form of social life and distinguishes it sharply from constitutional laws – that is, from the positive legal norms contained in a written constitution.[94] In line with this basic idea, Schmitt's attacks on the constituted political system of the Weimar Republic typically boil down to some version of the claim that the legislative decisions produced by that system fail adequately to express the positive constitution.[95] But if *Recht* is not merely to be authoritatively concretized but also to be given content by a sovereign decision, we face the question of why the sovereign – the one who can decide on the exception – should be taken to have the power to define the content of *Recht*: what is it that gives legitimacy to that more radical form of sovereign decision?

Schmitt's answer to that question, throughout the Weimar years, is to appeal to the notion of the constituent power of the people.[96] The sovereign's decision for some form of social order must be supported by the people, Schmitt concedes, so as to prevail. In a democratic age, such support will be forthcoming only if the sovereign succeeds in presenting their choice as the people's choice – that is, if the people (or enough of them) affirm and are committed to the positive constitution chosen by the sovereign.[97] Successful exercises of sovereign authority that establish a situation of normality and validate a particular form of social order as the basis of positive law are legitimate, then, because they amount to exercises of the constituent power of the people. And Schmitt presents the view that a people is entitled, in a democratic age, to

[94] See Schmitt (1928), 75–88.
[95] See, e.g., Schmitt (1932a).
[96] See Schmitt (1928), 125–135; Rubinelli (2020), 103–140.
[97] See Schmitt (1928), 136–139.

determine its own form of life – the underlying substance of its positive law – as an unchallengeable bedrock assumption.[98]

Schmitt's theory of constituent power assumes that the sovereign's choice for one or another conception of *Recht* is not restricted by antecedent normative criteria. Whatever positive constitution the constituent power sees fit to endorse will, by virtue of that choice alone, have to be regarded as legitimate.[99] The constituent choice, as we have seen, is to settle disagreement about the proper form of social order. It does that in a rather peculiar way: not by arriving at a compromise between contending groups and their respective ideas, or by using some organized democratic procedure that gives voice and standing to all members of society, but rather through an act of exclusion. The constituent decision takes the form of an acclamation of a proposal put forward by a charismatic leader[100] and it is itself polity-defining: the constituent decision puts all those who support and identify with the positive constitution chosen by the sovereign on the inside of the political community, and all those who reject that choice on the outside, as enemies who are not to be granted the protection of the law.[101] A successful exercise of constituent power homogenizes society and thus creates the conditions for the determinate (and therefore legitimate) applicability of positive law.

We are as far away as we could be, then, from the view that the state draws its legitimacy from implementing a universal ideal of legality. A sovereign's task is no longer to make positive laws that give determinate and executable form to a transcendent idea of *Recht*, but to create and maintain a community – if necessary, by the use of dictatorial force – that is united by an homogeneous form of life and a shared attachment to a community-specific idea of law. Where legal governance does not rest on an antecedent social consensus, in belief and practice, the legislative and judicial decisions to which it gives rise cannot express a united will of the people. They must instead, Schmitt argues, reflect the rule, unaccountable and 'indirect', of one part of society over another.[102] Where legal determinacy obtains, on the other hand, the operation of the positive law expresses and concretizes an antecedent normative consensus, and it is only where this is the case that positive legality – whether in the form of

[98] See ibid., 75–77.
[99] See ibid., 139.
[100] See Schmitt (1927), 48–83.
[101] See Schmitt (1932b), 25–27 and 46–47.
[102] See Schmitt (1938), 65–77.

a formal constitution, of positive statutory enactments or of judicial decisions based thereon – can claim to be legitimate.

The thesis that the legitimate applicability of positive legal norms presupposes homogeneity makes understandable the otherwise puzzling position that Schmitt adopted, in the early 1930s, in the dispute with Hans Kelsen over who should be the 'Guardian of the Constitution' – a constitutional court or the head of the executive.[103] Schmitt, arguing against the former and for the latter option, was accused by Kelsen of putting forward a view inconsistent with the theory of adjudication he had defended in *Statute and Judgment*.[104] In *The Guardian of the Constitution*, Schmitt held that judicial decisions are legitimate only as long as they take the form of straightforward subsumption under statutory rules. What is more, Schmitt portrayed decisions in hard cases that give rise to problems of application, especially in constitutional matters, as inherently political and thus not fit for courts to adjudicate.[105] This position, as Kelsen pointed out, appears to stand in direct conflict with the theory of adjudication developed in *Statute and Judgment*, which had emphasized, as we have seen, that judicial decisions need not conform to statutory law to be correct.

The impression of inconsistency, however, can be dispelled easily enough once we pay attention to Schmitt's understanding of the problem of the realization of law. Schmitt is willing, in *Statute and Judgment*, to accord to judges a power to go beyond and against statutory law on the assumption that there exists a coherent practice of adjudication – one that is grounded in a homogeneous form of life and thus affords legal determinacy. Where this condition is satisfied, judicial decisions remain calculable and predictable, even if they are not always guided by statutory law, and judges need not decide upon politically contested questions. Where, by contrast, the conditions of legal determinacy fail to obtain and adjudication would consequently have to settle politically contested issues, judicial power ought to be restrained as much as possible, so as to make room for acts of sovereignty that restore a condition of normality and thus secure the legitimate applicability of statutory norms.[106] This

---

[103] See Schmitt (1931), 79–173; Paulson (2016).

[104] See Kelsen (1931), 189–191.

[105] See Schmitt (1931), 79–124.

[106] Schmitt's critique of parliamentary democracy proceeds along similar lines: parliamentary legislation is legitimate only if it expresses antecedent consensus; in all other cases, it amounts to a mechanism of arbitrary oppression at the hands of a mere numerical majority. The conditions of the possibility of legitimate legislation, in other words, are the same as those of legitimate adjudication. See Schmitt (1932a), 39–47, and compare Dyzenhaus (1997), 56–70.

pattern of argument continues through the subsequent stages of Schmitt's career. In the Nazi era, Schmitt is once again disposed to countenance judicial activism,[107] which is to creatively reinterpret or override inherited statutory law to give effect to the 'concrete order' of Nazi society, whereas he reacts to the natural law jurisprudence of the postwar West German Constitutional Court with vigorous denunciations of supposed judicial overreach.[108]

Homogeneity Restored

The idea that homogeneity functions as a condition of the possibility of legitimate governance is likewise central to Schmitt's work in the early years of the Nazi period. Schmitt's decision to support the National Socialist regime after its *Machtergreifung* in 1933 has often been portrayed as a purely opportunistic choice that amounted to a departure from the constitutional theory he had developed in the Weimar years.[109] It is true that Schmitt was not a Nazi before the *Machtergreifung* and that he had his apprehensions about National Socialism, like many German conservatives at the time. He expected the sovereign choice that would define Germany's constitutional identity more clearly than the Weimar Constitution to proceed from the President of the Republic.[110] But the claim that Schmitt's writings in the initial years of the Nazi regime stand in stark conflict with his earlier constitutional theory overlooks the flexibility of Schmitt's theoretical framework. Schmitt would hardly have been able to capitalize on the opportunities for the advancement of his career afforded by the demise of democracy if his jurisprudential approach had not been adaptable to the new circumstances.

One thing that Schmitt did have to offer was a reading of the transition from democracy to dictatorship that was eminently suitable for National Socialist purposes. At first glance, this claim might appear surprising. During Weimar, Schmitt, like some other legal scholars, had put forward the view that the Weimar Constitution contained material limits to amendment, although its text made no mention of any such limits.[111] This thesis, let us note, is an implication of Schmitt's account of the

[107] See Schmitt (1933), 42–46.
[108] See Schmitt (1967). On this text, see Zeitlin's editorial commentary and notes, ibid., 3–41.
[109] See Schwab (1989); Bendersky (1983); Balakrishnan (2000); Kalyvas (2008).
[110] See Berthold (1999); Seiberth (2001); Mehring (2009), 281–302.
[111] See Schmitt (1928), 150–154.

realization of law: if positive laws can be legitimate – that is, enjoy full
legal quality – only if they express an underlying 'positive constitution', it
follows that the constituted powers – the legislative authorities that
operate under the rules of competence defined by a constitutional
document – must lack the authority to enact laws that conflict with
that positive constitution, even if they use the procedure for constitutional amendment to do so. Some scholars argue that it follows that the
Machtergreifung must have been illegitimate, from the perspective of
Schmitt's constitutional theory, and conclude that his willingness to
throw in his lot with the Nazis could only have been a result of rank
opportunism that has no bearing on the viability of his constitutional
analysis. What lends a degree of superficial plausibility to this interpretation is the fact that the Enabling Act that endowed Hitler with dictatorial
power was passed, by the *Reichstag*, in the form of an amendment to the
Weimar Constitution, giving Hitler's rise to power an appearance of
legality.[112] Since Schmitt had argued that the procedure of amendment
could not validly be used to bring about a fundamental change in
constitutional identity, his constitutional theory should be taken to
entail, it is claimed, that the *Machtergreifung* was both illegal and
illegitimate.[113]

Schmitt himself took a somewhat different tack. He adamantly denied
that the validity of Nazi law was in any way dependent on the Weimar
Constitution. The Enabling Act, Schmitt was only too happy to concede,
did indeed violate the positive constitution, the constitutional identity of
the Weimar Republic.[114] But since Schmitt had claimed that a successful
exercise of constituent power has the authority to redefine a polity's
constitutional identity and not merely to rewrite its constitutional
laws – a point he emphasized in his *Constitutional Theory*, even while
arguing that the authority of all constituted powers, of parliament and the
judiciary, was constrained by material limits to amendment implied by
the positive constitution[115] – the concession did not in any way commit
Schmitt to the view that Hitler's seizure of power had been illegitimate.

---

[112] Whether this amendment was in fact passed in accordance with the relevant constitutional procedures is open to question: see Evans (2004), 552–558. For a (sceptical)
assessment of the supposed legality of the *Machtergreifung*, compare Gusy (1997),
459–467.
[113] For a recent statement of this view, see Schupmann (2017), 201–220, who portrays
Schmitt's Weimar constitutional theory as a staunch defence of 'constrained' democracy.
[114] See Schmitt (1933), 5–6.
[115] See Schmitt (1928), 75.

Instead, the claim that the positive constitution is subject to constituent power opened the door for a justification of the *Machtergreifung* that was entirely consistent with the constitutional theory Schmitt had developed in Weimar and Schmitt avidly embraced it. The passage of the Enabling Act, according to Schmitt, was part and parcel of an extended plebiscitary affirmation of a new constitutional founding that had supposedly been accomplished by what Schmitt was happy to refer to as the 'German Revolution'.[116] If the *Führer*, Schmitt argued, had chosen to have the Act passed under a procedure provided by the Weimar Constitution, he had done so for purely pragmatic reasons, to maintain administrative continuity.[117] But the process through which the Act was enacted, Schmitt claimed, had nothing to do with its legitimacy or, consequently, with the Act's standing as a fundamental constitutional law of the Third Reich. The laws enacted by Hitler pursuant to the Act did not, according to Schmitt, derive their legal validity from the Weimar Constitution, but from the fact that Hitler had succeeded, despite the legalistic appearances, in orchestrating an exercise of the constituent power of the German people.[118]

To be sure, Schmitt could have chosen to apply his theory in a different way. He might have denied, that is, that the supposed National Socialist Revolution was an authentic exercise of constituent power. But it is nevertheless hard to see how the way in which Schmitt adapted his views to the new regime can be said to have stood in deep conflict with his previous jurisprudential approach. Schmitt's notion of the positive constitution, as we have seen, was intended to impose material restrictions on legislative and judicial, but not on constituent, power. And it would be wrong to assume that constituent power, for Schmitt, is a form of legislative or judicial authority. As should be clear by now, Schmitt's theory of the realization of law implies a rejection of that view. Constituent power, for Schmitt, is not manifested in the

---

[116] See Schmitt (1933), 8.

[117] See ibid., 7–8.

[118] See ibid., 5–9. Schmitt claims that the enactment of the Enabling Act merely implemented the result of the elections of 5 March 1933; these elections, in turn, 'were in truth, regarded from a legal-scientific point of view, a popular referendum, a plebiscite, through which the German people recognized Adolf Hitler, the leader of the national-socialist movement, as the political leader of the German people' (ibid., 7). See also Huber (1939), 44–52. After the war, Schmitt changed his tune and claimed that an insistence on formal legality had been Hitler's 'strongest weapon' in taking power, while he blamed the supposed positivist reduction of legitimacy to mere legality for having made that weapon available. See Schmitt (1950a), 450; Schmitt (1954); Schmitt (1970), 202.

authoritative issuance of positive statutory rules or in their authoritative application, but rather in the successful production, by dictatorial means, of a situation of normality that makes legitimate legislation and adjudication possible in the first place. Schmitt argues that constituent power, so understood, nevertheless serves the task of the realization of law, since it produces the social conditions under which positive laws become legitimately applicable. Constituent power, however, is restrained neither by an objectively valid conception of the content of *Recht* – which Schmitt, as we have seen, was either unwilling or unable to deliver – nor by the idea of order that is expressed by an existing constitution. The restraints on a sovereign who claims to exercise constituent power, in Schmitt's mature theory, are purely political. They derive from the fact that the sovereign, to commit the polity to this or that 'concrete order', must find or generate sufficient political support to be factually successful.

Some scholars argue that Schmitt came to reject his decisionist theory of sovereignty, in the course of the 1930s, in favour of an institutionalist theory of law or, as Schmitt himself preferred to put it, a theory of 'concrete order'.[119] But the introduction of the term 'concrete order' was evidently little more than an attempt to rebrand the condition of social normality or homogeneity that Schmitt had always taken to be a precondition of the legitimate applicability of positive law.[120] From 1933 to 1936 (and indeed afterwards), Schmitt argued, in effect, that Hitler's sovereign decision had re-established a condition of normality capable of undergirding stable and legitimate legality.[121] The latter, in Schmitt's view, had come to be undermined by the chaotic disorder of a liberal and pluralist democracy that seemed to want to avoid a clear choice for one form of social life or another.[122] It is not surprising, then, that Schmitt's interest in the foundational capacity of sovereign decision should have receded in favour of a focus on the further implementation,

---

[119] See Croce and Salvatore (2013). Schmitt introduced 'concrete order thought' in Schmitt (1934). Croce and Salvatore's claim that this work constitutes a new departure in Schmitt's legal thought overlooks that all three elements of legal order Schmitt distinguishes in this work – positive norms, sovereign decisions that contravene such norms and a concrete order that underpins the legitimate applicability of norms – are already present in the early legal-theoretical works.

[120] The same holds for Schmitt's later talk of a 'nomos'. See Schmitt (1950b), 67–79; Schmitt (1942), 59–60. For an account of the systematic continuity of Schmitt's constitutional theory and his account of international law, see Vinx (2013).

[121] See Schmitt (1933).

[122] See Schmitt (1931), 125–160.

in legal practice, of the form of social order that had supposedly animated the National Socialist *Machtergreifung*.[123]

It was here that Schmitt's institutional jurisprudence – his 'concrete order thought' – was particularly useful to the Nazis, as Bernd Rüthers demonstrated in his landmark study on adjudicative practice in Nazi Germany.[124] Schmitt's institutionalism did not aim to restrict the extra-legal powers of the sovereign; rather, it was intended to facilitate the judicial reinterpretation of inherited statutory norms so as to make them conformable to the new regime's racist assumptions about the proper order of German society.[125] Schmitt's 'concrete order thought' was frequently invoked by the courts of Nazi Germany to justify decisions that were issued in clear contravention of statutory law, for example in cases that denied welfare benefits to Jewish claimants, cases that permitted landlords to terminate rental agreements with Jewish tenants, or cases that allowed 'Aryan' spouses to divorce Jewish husbands or wives.[126] In the light of this context, one cannot plausibly maintain that Schmitt's call to cleanse German legal scholarship of all Jewish influence was simply a morally regrettable personal lapse that need not deter us from accepting the substance of his jurisprudential ideas.[127] Schmitt's idea of the realization of law does entail that those who are (or are defined as) enemies of a society's 'concrete order', as affirmed by constituent power, must not be permitted to hold legal office or to participate in legal practice. To extend such permission would compromise the homogeneity that Schmitt regards as the indispensable prerequisite of legal determinacy and thus of the legitimate applicability of positive norms.[128] Once Schmitt had

[123] See Hofmann (2002), 172.
[124] Rüthers (2017); De Wilde (2018).
[125] See Schmitt (1933), 42–46, and compare for the context Pauer-Studer (2014); Meierhenrich (2018), ch. 5.
[126] See Rüthers (2017), ch. 3.
[127] See Schmitt (1936).
[128] Schmitt, using language that clearly echoes that of *Statute and Judgment*, is commendably explicit in Schmitt (1933), 43: 'The fiction that a judge is normatively bound to a statute has today become untenable, theoretically and practically, for key areas of legal life. Statute is no longer capable of assuring the calculability and security which, according the ideal of the rule of law, belongs to the definition of statute. Security and calculability are not grounded in normative regulation, but in a situation that is presupposed to be normal.' Schmitt then adds (ibid., 44): 'If adjudication by independent courts is to continue to exist, even while a mechanical and automatic subjection of the judge to norms determined in advance is no longer possible, then everything must depend on the kind and type of our judges and public servants. [...] The essential substance of [the judge's] "personality" must be secured with all rigour, and it consists in being bound to one's people and in the similarity in kind [*Artgleichheit*] that every human being

chosen to accept the legitimacy of the *Machtergreifung* and to describe it as an exercise of constituent power, his call for an expulsion of Jewish influence from German law was all but compelled by his account of the conditions of the possibility of legitimate legal order.

Homogeneity, Determinacy and the Legitimacy of Law

Does Schmitt, in the end, succeed in offering a compelling explanation for why legal determinacy, as it supposedly results from social homogeneity, should be regarded as the supreme condition of the legitimacy of law? To answer this question, we need to clarify how Schmitt conceives of the relationship between legal determinacy and social homogeneity. Is Schmitt's fundamental argument concerning the conditions of the legitimacy of positive law meant to run from legal determinacy to social homogeneity, or the other way around?

Let us consider the first possibility. The claim would then be that social homogeneity is desirable on instrumental grounds as the causal precondition of legal determinacy. Legal determinacy, in turn, ensures that addressees of the law are subject to the rule of law. Suppose that positive law was not determinate, as a result of the absence of homogeneity. Judges (or, for that matter, parliamentary legislators) would have to take decisions that are political, in the sense that they would have to appeal to judgments of value that might turn out to be controversial both within the judiciary and among addressees of the law. Such decisions, Schmitt argues, cannot legitimately be taken by judges (or parliamentary legislators) who are to apply the law (or the constitution) and not to make it. They are to be reserved to a sovereign who has the political authority to set aside the positive law in order to restore the social conditions of legal determinacy. A sovereign, in doing so, may of course resort to violence against those it declares to be enemies of the people, but an exercise of sovereignty cannot be accused of being an example of discretionary rule, hypocritically disguised by appeal to mere formal legality. One either identifies with the polity-defining choices of a sovereign or one does not. If one does, the sovereign's decisions will be in line with one's own view of the proper order of social life; if one does not, one is an enemy. The

entrusted with the exposition, interpretation and application of German law must exhibit.' The context makes it clear that Schmitt is calling for the expulsion of Jews from the legal profession. The German word *Artgleichheit* carries racial connotations: *Art* is the German term for a biological species. On Schmitt's use of this terminology, see Gross (2005); Zeitlin (2020).

powers a sovereign may use to deal with enemies are undoubtedly awesome (in the literal sense of the term), but they are justified, according to Schmitt, by the fact that acts of sovereignty are required to create the social preconditions of determinate, and therefore legitimate, legal order.

This is a rather quaint conception, to put it gingerly, of the rule of law and of its value.[129] It implies that any legal decision, whether it be judicial or legislative, that rests on a contestable judgment of value must always be illegitimate *vis-à-vis* all those who disagree with that judgment. There would be little reason, it seems, to embrace a conception of the rule of law that carries that radical, almost anarchic, implication or to accept the call for perfectly determinate positive law unless one were already committed to perfect homogeneity as one's real ideal of social order. Perhaps, then, Schmitt's argument about the legitimacy of law should be taken to run not from determinacy to homogeneity, but rather from homogeneity to determinacy. Determinacy is desirable, on that view, only because it is indicative of homogeneity, which is held to be intrinsically valuable. So understood, Schmitt's legal, constitutional and political theory boils down to a simple rejection of plurality and diversity, and of the political and legal compromises they might require. We have seen that the trajectory of Schmitt's thought lends some credence to this interpretation. The transcendent idea of law invoked in *The Value of the State* comes to be replaced with an exclusivist conception of political identity – the task of the realization of law shrinks to the coercive creation and preservation of homogeneity.

It is hard to avoid the conclusion that Schmitt tried to clothe what is in effect a call for social uniformity in the more genteel language of a concern with the creation and preservation of legitimate legal and constitutional order – a gambit that, as a piece of rhetoric, continues to be spectacularly successful.[130] But if Schmitt's master argument is really driven, at the end of the day, by a simple preference for homogeneity over plurality and diversity, it must be mistaken to portray that argument as a sober and insightful reflection on the conditions of the existence of legitimate legal order. Homogeneity is itself a contested ideal. And if homogeneity is a contested ideal, then attempts to bring it about through the use of extra-legal sovereign power cannot be justified by appeal to a conception of the rule of law – as perfect legal determinacy – which is

[129] For further discussion, see Vinx (2015) and Vinx (2019b).
[130] For studies of Schmitt as a political rhetorician, see Kahn (2003); Kahn (2014); Smeltzer (2018); Zeitlin (2015); Zeitlin (2018).

itself dependent on a prior endorsement of the ideal of homogeneity. Even if one were to grant that perfect social homogeneity does engender complete legal determinacy, one might prefer to embrace a conception of legal order that does not promise that legal decisions will always be perfectly predictable. One might, after all, be interested in having the opportunity to co-exist peacefully with others in a diverse society. If Schmitt's argument about the legitimacy of law is not to be regarded as blatantly circular, it must therefore be understood as a blunt call for social homogeneity. What remains of it, in that case, is little more than a distaste for social plurality, coupled with an educated contempt for legality. Although Schmitt presents his key works in the guise of reflections on the realization of law, they are really nothing of the sort.

Statute and Judgment

A Note on the Text and the Translation

The following translation is based on Carl Schmitt, *Gesetz und Urteil. Eine Untersuchung zum Problem der Rechtspraxis*, 2ⁿᵈ edition (Munich: C. H. Beck, 1969). The first edition of *Gesetz und Urteil* appeared with Otto Liebmann in Berlin in 1912. The second edition does not reproduce the original pagination, but otherwise offers the same text as the first, with an introductory note that Schmitt appended to the second edition.

The references in the notes to the German text are often extremely abbreviated and do not follow a consistent style. This translation imposes a uniform style and aims, wherever possible, to give a full bibliographical reference the first time a work is cited in a note. In the original text, the numbering of the notes restarts on every page. In our translation, all notes are numbered continuously and cross-references have been added. All parts of the text, whether in the main text or in the notes, that are enclosed in square brackets in boldface are editorial additions. These additions include the page numbers of the German edition of 1969, which are given in the main text below, translations into English of passages that appear in languages other than German in the original and some editorial comments. Citations within editorial additions refer to the bibliography at the end of this volume.

The translation faces some terminological obstacles. The most pressing concerns the word *Gesetz*, which, in the original, is typically used to refer to statutory norms. At times, however, Schmitt employs it in a wider sense to refer to legal norms in general, so that *Gesetz* comes to include customary norms, norms of conventional morality and norms of natural law. The English word 'statute' is thus too narrow to cover all uses of *Gesetz* in the source. It would have made systematic sense, given Schmitt's argument, to translate *Gesetz* as 'legal norm', as Schmitt himself suggests in the note he added to the second edition in 1968. But Schmitt employs the terms *Norm* or *Rechtsnorm* very rarely in *Gesetz und Urteil* and their indistinct use in the translation would have concealed the evident focus of much of the discussion on statutory law. The indistinct use of 'law', on the other hand, invites confusion between '*a* law' and '*the* law', which latter, as *Recht*, is sharply distinct, in German, from *Gesetz*. We have therefore chosen to adopt a flexible approach: the large majority of occurrences of *Gesetz* in the original clearly refer to statutory norms. In these cases, *Gesetz* has been rendered as 'statute'. This usage has also been adopted in translating the title of the work. In the few cases in which the context suggests that *Gesetz* is used in a wider sense, we depart from that default and render *Gesetz* as 'legal norm'. This latter term has also been used as the equivalent of the German *Rechtssatz*, which occasionally appears in the text.

The German terms *Rechtsgefühl*, *Rechtsbewusstsein* and *Gerechtigkeits-gefühl*, which do not appear to have well-established English equivalents, pose another thorny problem. Schmitt appears to use these terms inter-changeably and to translate them too literally – rendering them, respectively, as 'legal feeling', 'legal consciousness' and 'feeling of justice' – would conceal the fact that they are rather close to one another in meaning. They all refer to something like a sense of what is legally appropriate – of what it would be just and fitting for the law to determine. Indeed, at times, Schmitt associates these terms with the notion of substantive justice. We have therefore chosen to translate them all as 'sense of justice'.

Schmitt's text contains a number of expressions and statements that we would regard as ethnic slurs or that indicate racist attitudes. We have decided, in the interest of historical accuracy, not to 'sanitize' Schmitt's language in these instances. Needless to say, this choice should not be construed as approval of Schmitt's attitudes on the part of the editors.

Statute and Judgment

An Investigation into the Problem of Legal Practice

DR. JUR. CARL SCHMITT

Dedicated, with full veneration, to Professor Dr. Fritz van Calker in Straßburg

The treatise *Statute and Judgment*, published in the year 1912, is concerned with the judicial decision and its independence from the norm to whose material-legal content it appeals so as to justify itself. Further reflection on the independent significance of the decision as such (*Dictatorship* 1921, *Political Theology* 1922, *The Guardian of the Constitution* 1931, *On the Three Types of Juristic Thought* 1934) later led me to the general insight that the domain of law as a whole is structured not merely by norms, but also by decisions and institutions (concrete orders).

The thought of the independence of the decision, however, also had state-theoretic consequences. It led to a definition of the sovereignty of the state as political decision and to the insight that dictatorship is the end of discussion. In vigorous polemical attacks against this insight, others have distorted the decision into a fantastical act of arbitrariness, portrayed decisionism as a dangerous worldview and turned the word *decision* into a mere slogan and term of abuse. Compared to all this, the treatise of the year 1912 retains something of the simplicity of the beginning. It makes the original sense of judging and deciding immediately evident. A reconsideration of this beginning might contribute to the clarification of a polemically confused debate and help to lead it to acceptable conclusions.

October 1968
Carl Schmitt

FOREWORD

The present treatise asks itself the question of when a decision taken in legal practice is correct and it answers that it is legal practice itself that decides on the matter. The true endeavour of any judge, according to this treatise, is to decide the case at hand in the way that contemporary practice in general would have decided it. The demand for regular and uniform practice, hence, is the basis of all efforts to reach a correct decision. The positive law, considerations of equity, the interests of legal intercourse and the results of theory are mere means for attaining such uniformity, although the pre-eminent position of positive law admittedly requires special attention. Legal practice thus is to have its own standards of correctness for its decisions. It is something more, in particular, than applied legal doctrine – in as much as it uses the results of the latter in rather independent and unique ways. It becomes its own master, so to speak, and the evaluation of a decision as practically correct means not only that the decision is conformable to the needs of legal intercourse – that it is 'practical' – but also that the correctness of a decision taken within practice is to be judged according to special criteria, which are to be determined here.

Since the investigation arrives at some unfamiliar conclusions, particularly in emphasizing the difference in kind of the interests of theory and practice, it had to be concerned, above all things, with securing itself against numerous obvious objections and attaining unambiguous clarity in expression. Needless to say, clarity is not to be equated, in a topic of this nature, with effortless levity; this applies in particular to the rather abstract arguments of the first chapter, which were unfortunately necessary. The reader is entitled to judge how far the desired determinacy in the positioning towards other opinions has been achieved, and likewise to assess the scientific value, as well as the practical significance, of the work and of its result. *This book addresses itself to the practice* that it has as its object. Many important things, to be sure, have been said in recent years on legal science and legal practice, but the discussion of the topic has not yet reached the point at which the attempt to offer a novel solution could no longer hope for benevolent interest, even if the solution itself were to find no assent.

I must not omit, in this place, to express my reverent gratitude to Herr Professor VAN CALKER. Two important preconditions for the value and effectiveness of a book such as this, should they have been fulfilled here, are to be credited to him: a strong desire for methodological clarity and an interest directed towards the reality of the life of the law.

Düsseldorf, in May 1912
Carl Schmitt

TABLE OF CONTENTS

Chapter I

The Problem

The decisive question is this: when is a judicial decision correct?

In order to provide a clear delimitation, from the beginning, to this polyvalent question, the sense of which is to reveal itself, step by step and in hopefully unambiguous determinacy, in the course of our further presentation, it is to be specified as follows: which normative principle lies at the basis of modern legal practice?

The investigation is a juristic one. It asks when a decision that has been taken in today's legal practice is to be regarded as juristically correct. It does not ask how decisions are taken in fact or whether the average of decisions is correct. Of course, every decision will normally aim to be correct. What meaning is to be attributed to this tendency and what correctness consists in: that is the theme. Not, however, whether more correct than false judgments are rendered today. It is likewise not of decisive significance, for a theme like this, what opinions on the correctness of a decision are dominant in contemporary practice and are articulated within it. The investigation will have to confront these opinions – but a finding that certain views on the matter are *dominant* today will not answer the question as posed.

The theme is not: when is a decision nowadays regarded as correct, i.e., when is it generally held to be correct? The empirical fact, after all, that something is held to be correct is no proof of its correctness. By the same token, the interest is also not in the question of how it came about, historically, that certain ideals, for instance concerning the relation of the judge to statute, are followed today. Rather, it is asked: which decision ought to be *regarded* as correct today? [2]

It is contemporary practice that is at issue, in the first place, and therein lies a historical concretization. An answer to the question of the absolute, timeless correctness of a decision, as it might be derived from the 'idea' of

47

judicial decision, is not to be sought here; it would, in any case, have no immediate practical value. It is the task of the doctrine of the method of the application of law to find the guiding idea of *contemporary* practice, and to be of use to the latter by helping it to become aware of its own purposes and means. There is scientific progress in a practice becoming aware of its own sense. If, therefore, modern practice is taken as the object of investigation, this object is therewith historically delimited. But the inquiry does not therefore turn into a historical one, as though it aimed to ascertain how our modern practice has developed historically, what causal factors were effective in its genesis and which of these continue to be so today. It is not a causal explanation that is sought, but rather the principle that must be regarded as the underlying basis of modern legal practice. What is the criterion of correctness specific to legal practice? The presupposition of a definite historical condition – a definite class of subjects of the state professionally applies mostly written statutes – is not meant to intimate any methodological dependence of this criterion on the historical genesis of our legal practice. It is not to be claimed, for instance, that since the application of law developed in intimate connection with the exegesis of Roman law, the after-effects of the latter, still felt today, stand in need of investigation. Such an investigation would be a problem for itself. Its dignity and significance are located in another sphere, and it does not pertain to our theme, since we can never draw an inference as to the correctness of a decision from the empirical effectiveness of such factors. It does matter, however, that we be able to show how the criterion, once it is found, can be applied to events in actual practice, how the postulate from which the criterion [3] is derived in fact governs the life of the law and is not deduced down from an ethereal region of concepts – is not a *norma coelitus hausta* ['a norm drawn from the heavens']. From what happens, one certainly cannot infer what ought to happen. But the investigation is not therefore compelled to search for a timeless standard of correctness hostile to all content – one that would be useless to practice. Neither is it to determine the categories of juristic thought. Rather: the evaluative consideration of existing practice is to connect with a postulate that enjoys actual effectiveness, so as to use the latter as a starting point from which to determine the correctness of a judicial decision in existing practice. This linkage with an effective postulate, which neither turns the theme into a historical nor into a natural-scientific one, is conditioned by the task, which is to determine the correctness of a decision in contemporary legal practice. The empirical validity of the presupposed postulate forges a connection between evaluative contemplation, which is in itself independent of empirical factors, and the empirically determined complex of appearances 'modern legal practice'. This means to say: what is correct cannot be derived from what actually happens in modern practice. Neither, however, can one choose any postulate whatsoever as the point of departure, in answering the question of what is to be regarded as correct in modern practice, but only one that is empirically valid within it. The deduction of the standard against which decisions are to be measured thus proceeds from a *postulate*, not from empirical processes; the empirical validity of the postulate merely provides its legitimation to be regarded as an immanent evaluation of modern legal practice as an empirically determined object – it guides the choice from among several postulates that might come under consideration. In the event that there are several available postulates, it is therefore not the scope of their empirical validity but rather their suitability to offer a unified explanation of legal practice, and of the 'sense' of its endeavour to find the correct decision, that is decisive. [4]

The goal is thus to condense the method of modern legal practice into a formula that expresses the answer to the question: when do we have to say of a judicial decision, today, that it is correct?

The practitioner will hopefully excuse that some further preliminary remarks will be added, in the interest of methodological clarity, so as to delimit the topic. This work will lead to the result that the formal validity of a positive statute does not have the significance for the evaluation of legal practice that is usually attributed to it. That a decision conforms to statute does not, by itself, offer a sufficient answer to the question whether it is correct. The criterion of the correctness of a decision that is to be regarded as valid in practice, on the one hand, and what the legal-scientific interpretation of the legal material produces as 'valid law', on the other hand, oppose each other as two distinct validities. What is in question here, therefore, is not the opposition of validity and being, of norm and empirics, of abstractly valid statute and 'daily life', of normative jurisprudence and explicative social science, but rather the opposition of two different validities within one and the same domain of knowledge, of which the one validity – that of practice – is to be found. We do not, for example, mean to present new facts or to amass statistics in order to attempt to deduce therefrom, by way of induction, natural-scientific regularities that govern judicial decision-taking, or assessments of the larger or smaller probability of the conviction of a defendant. Just as little will we offer collective- and social-psychological observations of the judges as a social group, or of this group's relations to the members of the bar,[1] or of a statute's effects on the people, or of the processes in the soul of the judge. The present investigation is neither a social-scientific nor a psychological one. It is juristic, although it does not therefore refuse to recognize the significance of sociology and psychology for the life of the law, [5] as should hopefully become clear from the work itself. (But one ought not to charge it with not having chosen to address the one theme that the evaluator would have been most interested in.) This treatise is not a sociological investigation, in particular, because it is not concerned with explaining causal interactions of human beings with one another, or offering a morphology of human society, or describing the sociological peculiarities of the group of judges or lawyers. Its subject, rather, is the method of a practical activity – the principle from which the activity of a determinate class of human beings ought to proceed. The expression 'class of human beings', in this context, is meant only to bring about a preliminary individualization of the activity in question. It does not contain any pointer towards a decisive significance of sociological or social-psychological factors.

When is a judicial decision correct? It is usually held to be correct in the event that it 'conforms to statute' – if it is in line with valid positive law. To postulate that a decision's conformity to statute is the criterion of its correctness is to take as one's point of departure the view that judges are bound to statute. The jurist would, consequently, arrive at an answer to the question of the correctness of a decision most easily where a statute made an unambiguous prescription to the judge to evaluate a certain definite matter of fact in some definite way. If, for example, there were a positive legal prescription that commanded the judge to keep strictly to the wording of statute, and to the linguistic usage of everyday life, and never to decide any case that is not indubitably regulated by some statute, this would ground the highest possible likelihood that all judicial decisions will turn out to be correct. But a statute of this kind would contain its own refutation, since it would, in effect, boil down to a command to the judge to decide only in cases in which he is quite sure to decide correctly, but to refuse a decision in doubtful cases. Little would thus be gained by such an 'ideal' of the conformity of practice to statute, for the obvious reason [6] that the scientific, as well as the practical, interest stems precisely from cases that are open to doubt.

---

[1] In private conversations, I have often heard excellent practitioners relate the conflict between so-called conceptual jurisprudence and so-called sociological adjudication to the antagonism of judges and lawyers.

There is one single case, however, in which the correctness of a decision can be brought into immediate connection with a positive legal prescription and which, in any case, needs to be mentioned here. According to § 565 ZPO,[i] a judgment that has been voided by the court of appeal is to be referred back to the court from which the appeal was made, for renewed consideration and decision. The court of first instance is then bound to base its own novel decision on the legal evaluation that led the court of appeal to void the original decision. This case is an example for a direct derivation of the evaluation of a decision from a positive statute; it contains the desired 'positive' answer to the question of the correctness of a decision. If the court of first instance now bases its decision on the legal opinion of the court of appeal, then its decision is doubtless correct according to the positive law.[2]

This single case, however, does not suffice to prove that the subjection of judges to statute is a suitable starting point for answering the question of the correctness of the decision. Section 565 of the ZPO, which grounds the conformity to statute of the novel decision of the court of first instance, does not, after all, tell us anything about whether the content of the decision conforms to statute. It is, of course, conceivable that the content of the court of appeal's decision may not conform to statute. That of the court of first instance does not, in that case, become conformable to statute merely in virtue of the fact that it accords with § 565 ZPO. It only contains a formal correctness – one that does not refute the key objection that ought to be raised against the criterion of 'conformity to statute': namely, that the latter does not, by itself, answer the essential questions and that it is therefore unusable on account of the problematic of its content.

The only norm of positive law that addresses the relation of statute and judge, [7] is § 1 GVG,[ii] which reads: 'The judicial power is exercised by independent courts that are subject only to statute.'[3]

This paragraph, as is well known, contains a recognition of the doctrine of the separation of powers and particularly of the independence of adjudication from administration. Whether it also prescribes that the judge is bound to statute, in the sense that the judge may do no more than

---

[2] The Roman judge, who received the formula from the *praetor* and thereafter simply condemned or acquitted, found himself in a similar position.

[3] Section 48 of the Colonial Civil Service Statute is likewise to be mentioned here. For this topic and for the many ministerial decrees that refer to § 1 GVG, compare FRIEDRICH DOERR, 'Begriff und Grenzen der richterlichen Unabhängigkeit', in *Rheinische Zeitschrift für Zivil- und Prozeßrecht* 3 (1911), pp. 425–466, which occupies itself mainly with the independence of judges in matters of administrative supervision (and which contains extensive documentation of the recent literature on the issue), while here the interest is solely in the question of the juristic correctness of a decision.

to apply a clear statute, so that he is to be regarded, as it is put in Montesquieu's famous saying, as nothing more than '*la bouche qui prononce les paroles de la loi*', ['the mouth that pronounces the words of the law'],[iii] and whether and to what extent certain methods of legal interpretation are therewith officially recognized, is a different question. When the aforementioned paragraph refers to 'statute', this is to be understood negatively, in the first place, as drawing a contrast with extra-legal limitations of the judge's decisional latitude. The latter are to be rejected: a cabinet-justice, to speak practically, ought no longer to exist. The judge, thus, ought to be subject to statute – but § 1 GVG does not say anything about what this subjection consists in, or, for that matter, about what is to be regarded as a statute and what as its content. If one approaches the paragraph with the means of historical interpretation, one will have to conclude that it was the 'will of the statute' or the 'will of the legislator' to bind the judge to the clear meaning of the statutes. The judge was to do nothing further than to subsume under statutes. And this, in turn, would seem to imply that a judicial decision is correct if, and only if, it presents itself as the result of a subsumption under a statute – if it is (this is the sense in which the expression is used here) in conformity with statute. If one understands this sentence in the way in which it must reasonably be understood, this entails that only the manifest content of a statute [8] is to be taken account of by the judge; everything else does not concern him. But this clear content of statute, so understood, could regulate only very few of the cases that are put to a judge for decision. It is unthinkable that life, in all of its facets, could find an exhaustive regulation in a few paragraphs, which one would merely have to read out of the statute in concrete cases. The result was a practical situation that entitled an English jurist to declare that the proposition that the judge is bound to statute was a 'childish fiction'.[4/iv] It is a matter of fact that there is 'effective' and 'ineffective' law, that legal practice understood the content of statutes at times in wider and at times in narrower terms, and that it consequently conceived of a decision's 'conformity to statute' as a relation to a content that did not lie open in a statute, without further ado, but which had to be read into it through

---

4 AUSTIN, *Province of Jurisprudence*, vol. II, p. 265, cited in JULIUS HATSCHEK, *Englisches Staatsrecht*, in *Handbuch des Öffentlichen Rechts der Gegenwart*, vol. IV.II.4.I (Tübingen: Mohr Siebeck, 1905), p. 101. The distinction drawn in the following sentence between 'effective' and 'ineffective' law is to be found in EUGEN EHRLICH, 'Über Lücken im Rechte', in *Burians Juristische Blätter* 17 (1888), pp. 447–630, at p. 484. See also EUGEN EHRLICH, 'Soziologie und Jurisprudenz', in *Die Zukunft* 54 (1906), pp. 231–240, at p. 236.

complicated constructions. This was necessary, since the subjection of the judge to statute, together with the prohibition of a refusal of justice, according to which a judge may not appeal to the silence or darkness of the statutes, gave rise to a 'judicial state of emergency' – a conflict that received its definitive presentation in RADBRUCH.[5]

In the last few years, it has been pointed out innumerable times that a judge can, under no circumstances, rest content with the positive law alone – how the demands that arise in the course of legal intercourse often require a decision even though the problem at hand has not yet found its special statutory regulation, so that the judge must be something other than the mouth that pronounces the words of the statute, than a machine of subsumption, a statute-automaton, or whatever one called it when one wanted to deliver a contemptuous description of the role. [9] No one, at any rate, can now escape from the insight that one must understand, by the statute to which § 1 GVG refers the judge, something other than its clear wording. Indeed, the voluminous revisions of the words of a statute, their modifying penetration with a thousand scientific concepts, their reshaping into a system, the mountains of books that often weigh on one single word in the statute, the libraries of precedents: elements of all of these are effective in a decision that is to be gathered from the 'statute'. If one still sees in this a 'conformity to statute' – if one still regards the postulate of the subjection to statute as fulfilled, in the face of the 'unavoidable departures from statutory law on the part of the law that comes to the fore in adjudication'[6] – then one has the scientific obligation to explain what one understands by the content of statute and by the claim that a judge is bound to this content. The reference to § 1 GVG says nothing about this. Since there are obviously but few cases that permit a smooth subsumption under the statutory text, even he who holds fast to the requirement of 'conformity to the statute' is compelled to make use of certain methods so as to elucidate the 'essential' content of a statute, which, from the perspective of the manifest content, must appear to be inessential. And the whole question revolves around

[5] GUSTAV RADBRUCH, 'Rechtswissenschaft als Rechtsschöpfung', in *Archiv für Sozialwissenschaft und Sozialpolitik* 22 (1906), pp. 355–370. The expression 'judicial state of emergency' is used by SIEGMUND SCHLOSSMANN, *Der Irrtum über wesentliche Eigenschaften der Person und der Sache nach dem Bürgerlichen Gesetzbuch: zugleich ein Beitrag zur Theorie der Gesetzesauslegung* (Jena: G. Fischer, 1903), p. 63, and by RUDOLF SOHM, 'Begriffsjurisprudenz', in *Deutsche Juristen-Zeitung* 15 (1910), cols. 114–118, at col. 115.
[6] OSKAR BÜLOW, *Gesetz und Richteramt* (Leipzig: Duncker & Humblot, 1885), p. ix.

these methods: it is asked what justification there is for referring to the content of a statute that has been determined with their help as the 'statute' and for claiming that a judgment built on that content is still in 'conformity to statute'. It would be of the utmost importance, consequently, to prove why the judge is subjected to these methods of interpretation by § 1 GVG.[7] The paragraph, after all, does not say a word about this, which leaves us with no way of reading it as an answer to the question: when do we have to regard a judicial decision as correct? **[10]**

The traditional hermeneutics, then, cannot refer to § 1 GVG, or even first interpret it according to its method, in order to go on to prove that its method exhibits 'conformity to statute'. It is hard to see how this provision, assuming that one wants to make use of it for determining the correctness of a judicial decision, contains anything more than a pointer towards the positive prescriptions of the civil and criminal law of procedure that are to be followed in the writing of judgments, such as the obligation to provide the judgment with reasons of decision, whereby § 1 GVG, with a view to its suitability to provide a criterion of the correctness of decision, would take its place alongside the abovementioned § 565 ZPO. It does not contain a material criterion of correctness any more than the prescriptions of civil and criminal law that determine that a judge is liable for 'unstatutory' decisions. It does not say how the judge is bound to statute nor whether the obligation of the judge may cease under certain circumstances. As far as the methods of exegesis are concerned, nothing can be derived from it without committing an obvious *petitio principii*. One therefore cannot expect it to provide an answer to the fundamental question.[8]

---

[7] Therein lies the answer to the latest appeal to § 1 GVG by ERNST NEUKAMP, 'Der gegenwärtige Stand der Freirechtsbewegung', in *Deutsche Juristen-Zeitung* 17 (1912), cols. 44–50, at col. 47, who declares every departure from the traditional hermeneutics to be a violation of statute – a breach of § 1 GVG.

[8] This is the conclusion that discussions of § 1 GVG arrive at, insofar as they are relevant for our topic. Compare DOERR, 'Begriff und Grenzen' (see n. 3), p. 443 sqq. The same holds for the appeal to the oath of service: ZITELMANN [Schmitt does not give a title here]; compare SCHLOßMANN, *Der Irrtum* (see n. 5), p. 39. Article 3 of the Italian *Codice Civile* would not be of help to us either. The article (in the translation of DONATO DONATI, 'Review of: Hermann Kantorowicz, *La lotta per la scienza del diritto*', in *Archiv für Rechts- und Wirtschaftsphilosophie* 3 [1909], pp. 286–288, at p. 287) states that: 'In the application of the statute the latter is not to be endowed with any other meaning than that which results from the true significance of the words, taken in their context, and understood according to the intention of the legislator (?). If a case cannot be decided by appeal to any precise statutory norm, then norms that concern analogous (?) cases or issues are to be taken into consideration. If the case nevertheless remains doubtful, the decision is to be

The traditional remarks on interpretation that are found in text-books and commentaries limit themselves to offering a presentation of the methods of exegesis as they are actually in use. [11] Accordingly, the 'true' content of a statute is to be brought to light by the use of different methods: extensive (widening) and restrictive (narrowing) interpretation, analogy and the proof from the contrary (*argumentum e contrario*). This method, which is to be criticized in more detail later, regards two presuppositions as self-evident, without any proof: (1) that its different means of exegesis will yield the 'true' content of a statute; and (2) that a judicial decision is correct whenever the statute that it applies has been interpreted correctly. This mistake is to be avoided here and it must be emphasized here already, in setting out the problem, that one must not identify the question of when a correct decision has been taken with the question of when an interpretation is correct.

The view that all decisions exhibit 'conformity to statute' can today be regarded as overcome.[9] The 'Struggle for Legal Science' that took its start from the unsatisfactory results of the traditional method of exegesis and in which the 'modern' or 'free law' movement, at least in Germany, initially bore a purely oppositional character,[10] emphasized, in challenge to the doctrine of the 'logical closure' of the law, the gaps and imperfections of the law, the 'poverty' of the material of the traditional doctrine of exegesis, and the psychological fact that emotional and irrational factors, as opposed to the strained deductions and constructions oriented towards the wording of statute, are often, in truth, what is decisive for the judge when settling upon a judgment. It was pointed out that the method that had hitherto been used was an undignified jugglery with concepts and constructions that concealed the real way [12] in which a decision is found and must be found: by

---

taken in accordance with the (!) general principles of law.' [The question- and exclamation marks in the quotation appear to be Schmitt's additions.]

[9] 'I believe one can now claim that the dogma that the law is gapless or logically closed, or that all law is source-based, is done for', says ERICH JUNG, *'Positives' Recht. Ein Beitrag zur Theorie von Rechtsquelle und Auslegung* (Gießen: A. Töpelmann, 1907), p. 41, who was also one of the first to expound the logical mistakes and the arbitrariness of the traditional hermeneutics, in his essay 'Von der "logischen Geschlossenheit" des Rechts', in the *Festschrift* of the Faculty of Law in Gießen for Heinrich Dernburg (Berlin: H. W. Müller, 1900), pp. 131–157.

[10] As is emphasized by HEINZ ROGGE, *Methodologische Vorstudien zu einer Kritik des Rechts* (Berlin and Leipzig: W. Rothschild, 1911), p. 3.

appeal to a sense of justice, by the weighing of interests, by paying attention to the needs of actual intercourse and by appeal to social considerations. Extensive or restrictive interpretation, the analogy from an (always problematic) 'equality', or even the 'similarity' of the equally problematic 'legal rationale', arguments *e contrario*: all of these techniques are used in disorderly succession and without any methodological clarity, so as to reach a result prescribed by an altogether different determining ground. The initiate knows very well that the 'construction' is bold, perhaps even correct, but, in any case, inevitable. As a result, the new movement had an easy game. The method of analogy and the *argumentum e contrario* have (and rightly so) fared the worst in recent years. It was shown what logical mistakes and misconceptions are implicit in the attempt to derive, by way of analogy, a host of new legal propositions from the 'principle' of a legal proposition, supposedly in 'logical stringency' and by means of a pure 'relation of ground and consequence'.[11]

The intention of this procedure was to offer a purely logical deduction from concepts, but it was overlooked that while one can indeed order one's knowledge in purely logical ways, one cannot increase it in content, as well as that while there is a firm relation between the premise and the conclusion of a syllogism, there is none between the conclusion and the premise.[12] Now, it would indeed be justified [13] to infer individual

---

[11]   This is how analogical reasoning is usually described. The phrases enclosed in quotation marks in the text are in HEINRICH THÖL, *Einleitung in das deutsche Privatrecht* (Göttingen: Dieterich, 1851), pp. 154–155.

[12]   That both analogy and the *argumentum e contrario* are forms of teleological reasoning has been made clear, in particular, by JUNG, 'Von der "logischen Geschlossenheit" des Rechts' (see n. 9), p. 140. See also HERMANN KANTOROWICZ (Gnaeus Flavius), *Der Kampf um die Rechtswissenschaft* (Heidelberg: C. Winter, 1906), p. 29. Compare ALEXANDER GRAF ZU DOHNA in *Juristisches Literaturblatt* 18 (1906), p. 157, who, in this respect, wishes to endorse K[ANTOROWICZ]'s discussion 'in every sentence of this thoughtful piece'. See also PHILIPP HECK, in *Goldschmidt's Zeitschrift für das gesamte Handels- und Wirtschaftsrecht* 37 (1890), p. 278, and, in special depth, LORENZ BRÜTT, *Die Kunst der Rechtsanwendung. Zugleich ein Beitrag zur Methodenlehre der Geisteswissenschaften* (Berlin: J. Guttentag, 1907), p. 79. What these authors have achieved, at any rate, is that the belief in the logical fecundity of juristic concepts and in their promiscuous tendency to generate a large offspring has, apparently, come to an end now. Among the earlier discussions of this question, we would like to point to the remark in ADOLF WACH, *Handbuch des deutschen Civilprozessrechts*, vol. I (Leipzig: Duncker & Humblot, 1885), p. 256, according to which analogy does not serve pure logic, but rather helps to 'determine what is reasonable'. Compare also JOSEF SCHEIN, *Unsere Rechtsphilosophie und Jurisprudenz* (Berlin: C. Heymann, 1889), p. 158 sqq. – Likewise of interest, in this context, are the remarks in THEODOR STERNBERG, *Einführung in die Rechtswissenschaft*, vol. I (Leipzig: G. J. Göschen, 1912), p. 119 sqq., on the word 'logical'.

decisions from an ultimate *purpose* of all law.[13] But the traditional doctrine always operated with logical 'concepts' – it was constantly passing off what was, in truth, its teleological perspective as purely logical – and it then went on to commit the additional logical mistake of believing that one can validly infer the general from the particular, the *genus* from the *species*.[14] The argument *e contrario* was just another purposive consideration: one that was used to draw conclusions from the silence of a statute. Such arguments may at times hit the mark, but it was wrong to portray them as logical arguments of general validity, and their illogical character became manifest in the fact that one argued now analogically and now *e contrario*, [14] without being able to identify the logical principle at the ground of these substitutions. In truth, the grounding principle was teleological, a consideration of purpose, for which the 'logical' argumentations were nothing but tools to justify results that had been found in a different way. Legal concepts are no

---

[13] GEORG SIMMEL, 'Weibliche Kultur', in *Archiv für Sozialwissenschaft und Sozialpolitik* 33 (1911), pp. 1–36, at p. 4: 'If there was an objectively ascertainable final purpose of all law, then it would, of course, be possible in principle, with a view to that purpose, to construe every individual legal provision in a purely rationalistic manner. However, such a purpose, for its part, could be posited only by a meta-logical deed, a deed that would be nothing other than a different form of the sentiment of justice, its crystallization into a firm and special logical entity.' FRITZ VAN CALKER's theory of perfection is an example of such a determination of a highest purpose and one to which SIMMEL's proposition applies in all its details. Compare *Politik als Wissenschaft* (Leipzig 1899) [There seems to be no edition of this text that came out in Leipzig in 1899. Schmitt may be referring to Van Calker (1898)], and *Ethische Werte im Strafrecht* (Berlin: O. Liebmann, 1904).

[14] I have discussed a specific instance of this mistake, the derivation of the concept of culpability from its 'kinds', in my treatise *Über Schuld und Schuldarten: Eine terminologische Untersuchung* (Breslau: Schletter, 1910), § 1. (The occasional methodological remarks in this study, see for instance p. 130, find their correction in the work presented here.) Let me also mention, in this context, the formulation with which ARISTOTLE (*Metaphysics* 28, 1024b) refutes the error in question: ἔτι ὡς ἐν τοῖς λόγις τὸ πρῶτον ἐνυπάρχον ὃ λέγεται ἐν τῷ τί ἐστι τοῦτο γένος, διαφοραί λέγουται αἱ ποιότητες (*item ut in rationibus quod primum inest, quod dicitur in eo quod quid, hoc genus, cuius differentiae dicuntur qualitales*). [Again, in formulae their first constituent element, which is included in the essence, is the kind, whose differentiae the qualities are said to be.' Schmitt cites the Greek original and a Latin translation, without identifying the editions used. English translation from Aristotle (1995), 1617–1618.] and ibid., 998b: κἂν εἰ ἔστι τὴν τῶν ὄντων λαβεῖν ἐπιστήμην νὸ τῶν εἰδῶν λαβεῖν, καφθ᾽ ἃ λέγονται τά ὄντα, τῶν γέ εἰδῶν ἀρχαὶ τά γένη εἰσίν (*cum autem singular cognoscamus per definitiones, principia vero definitionum genera sint, necesse est definitorum etiam principia vero genera esse*) [' … but in so far as we know each thing by its definition and the genera are the principles of definitions, the genera must also be the principles of definable things'. Aristotle (1995), 1577.]. Also compare RUDOLF STAMMLER, *Theorie der Rechtswissenschaft* (Halle: Buchhandlung des Waisenhauses, 1911), pp. 6–7.

more 'fertile' than concepts of any other kind.[15] Only the purpose is fertile. It had become evident: 'The understanding can serve good as well as evil.'[16] What had shown itself, to use HEGEL's inspired turn of phrase, was the 'eternally deceptive method of the understanding and its mode of ratiocination' [Hegel (1991), 32].[17]

With such arguments, the free law movement[18] refuted the traditional hermeneutics of valid law. One can only call this critique decisive. Its success, accordingly, was unusual, especially compared to earlier endeavours with comparable aims,[19] **[15]** and we have now happily come so far that Bergbohm's sentence[20] – 'he who fills the supposed gaps of a positive

---

[15] The most succinct formulation of this point in OTTO FRIEDRICH GRUPPE, *Antaeus. Ein Briefwechsel über spekulative Philosophie in ihrem Konflikt mit Wissenschaft und Sprache* (Berlin: Naucksche Buchhandlung, 1831), p. 276, cited in HANS VAIHINGER, *Die Philosophie des Als Ob. System der theoretischen, praktischen und religiösen Fiktionen der Menschheit* (Berlin: Reuther und Reichard, 1911), p. 392: 'Concepts spring from linguistic practice and only suffer practical employment; nothing theoretical can be derived from concepts themselves, one can draw nothing from them; they are only means, not content, only abbreviations and auxiliary expressions.' – The reality of concepts has recently been defended by JOSEF KOHLER, 'Die Geschichte im System des Neuhegelianismus', in *Archiv für Rechts- und Wirtschaftsphilosophie* 3 (1909/1910), pp. 321–325, at 324, but in a different context.

[16] FRANZ SYLVESTER JORDAN, 'Bemerkungen über den Gerichtsgebrauch, dabey auch über den Gang der Rechtsbildung und die Befugnisse der Gerichte', in *Archiv für die civilistische Praxis* 8 (1825), pp. 191–260, at p. 219, who also casually anticipates a number of other points that are strongly emphasized today (see, for example, p. 208). ERNST LANDSBERG, *Geschichte der deutschen Rechtswissenschaft*, vol. III.2 (Munich and Leipzig: R. Oldenbourg, 1910), p. 187, rightly highlights this essay.

[17] GEORG WILHELM FRIEDRICH HEGEL, *Grundlinien der Philosophie des Rechts* (Berlin: Nicolai, 1821), p. 11. Compare the example in Note I. [A reference to the first note in the appendix at the end of the text.]

[18] We will, for now, keep this designation for what is, in itself, a very diverse movement. Its name is derived either from the fact that it points towards a free, i.e. a non-positive, law (EHRLICH and KANTOROWICZ) and thus positions itself alongside the free religion movement (KANTOROWICZ), or else from the fact that it desires liberty from a Romanism that is alien to life as well as from the reactionary tendencies of natural law (ROGGE). The position this work takes towards the different opinions that the movement puts forward will become clear from the further course of discussion in the following chapters.

[19] Compare, for this point, the remarks contained in Note II at the end. This is not to raise the objection of a lack of originality. To do so is far from my concerns, because it would be beside the point, to begin with, to evaluate such a movement by reference to the question of originality or non-originality. Compare the discussion in EDUARD ROSENBAUM, *Ferdinand Lassalle. Studien über historischen und systematischen Zusammenhang seiner Lehre* (Jena: G. Fischer, 1911), pp. 2–3: '[T]he concept of originality, in its essential meaning, cannot at all be grounded on the priority or the independence of someone's thoughts.'

[20] CARL BERGBOHM, *Jurisprudenz und Rechtsphilosophie. Kritische Abhandlungen* (Leipzig: Duncker & Humblot, 1892), p. 134.

legal system with parts of a non-positive one, deduced from somewhere, he who is at all willing to conceive of norms that are supposed to be legal and yet do not belong to the law that is currently under consideration, but to some other, is a believer in natural law' – will no longer frighten anyone. Today, it is possible to talk about the natural law[21] without being held for an ideologue or believer in phantasms, and the sentence *fiat justitia, pereat mundus* ['let justice be done, though the world perish'], which is simply a particularly striking expression of the aspiration to base all decisions on acknowledged sources, has declined in popularity as well as motivating force and is not even accepted as an excuse anymore.[22] But let this be enough of this issue. The merits of the new movement in highlighting new problems, such as the position of jurisprudence in the methodology of science, the relation of psychology and jurisprudence, and that of sociology and jurisprudence, likewise do not belong here. The only thing that is of interest to us is this: legal practice cannot be explained with reference to positive [16] statute alone. This error was superseded, henceforth, by a view that UNGER formulated as follows: statute contains gaps; *the law* is gapless. It remained unexplained or contested, however, what was to be understood by 'law'.

Now to return to the delimitation of the problem: some of the opponents of the traditional view proceeded from the psychological fact that 'voluntarist' factors tip the scale, for the judge, in arriving at a judgment. The verdict is often settled before its justification – that is, the juristic derivation from a statute – has been found. From this observation, one came to draw conclusions for the question of when a decision is correct.[23]

---

[21] EUGEN EHRLICH, *Freie Rechtsfindung und freie Rechtswissenschaft* (Leipzig: C. L. Hirschfeld, 1903), p. 23: 'The natural law as such may have lost its power over our thought, but its seed has opened up: German legal science is in many ways the unconscious bearer of its content.' Or KANTOROWICZ, *Der Kampf um die Rechtswissenschaft* (see n. 12), p. 10, in which there is talk of a 'resurrection of natural law in a modified form'. STAMMLER, as is known, refers to his 'correct law' as a 'natural law with changing content'.

[22] BURKHARD WILHELM LEIST, *Über die dogmatische Analyse römischer Rechtsinstitute* (Jena: F. Frommann, 1854), p. 68, already pronounced the verdict on it: 'The sentence "*fiat justitia, pereat mundus*", which often helped to euphemize a resistance (against the "nature of things"), simply turns around by itself; it is not the world but those who resist against it that perish.' – It must not be overlooked, however, that LEIST, in this passage, opposes empirical reality to the norm. The refutation of the sentence is valid only for the case in which one presents the results of an exegesis undertaken in accordance with the art of interpretation, as it is taught in the schools, as the content of '*iustitia*'.

[23] MAX RUMPF, *Gesetz und Richter. Versuch einer Methodik der Rechtsanwendung* (Berlin: O. Liebmann, 1906), ch. IV, in particular, proceeds in this fashion. He found his refutation in BRÜTT, *Die Kunst der Rechtsanwendung* (see n. 12), p. 182. SCHLOẞMANN, *Der Irrtum* (see n. 5), p. 35, likewise wanted to pay attention to the path 'on which we actually

It was pointed out that the interpreter or judge, in the end, allows himself to be guided by his sentiment, wherefrom it was supposed to follow, more or less explicitly, that it was superfluous to continue to offer the juristic argumentation as an intermediate link. It was held to be more reasonable and more honest openly to appeal to one's sense of justice, as well as to one's healthy common sense, rather than to engage in a 'comedic art of camouflage'. According to this view, what a judge is really doing, as a matter of (psychological) truth, in finding a decision is supposed to determine the correctness of the decision. It was often pointed out, with great vehemence, how frequently judgments are determined by extra-legal considerations, from which it was then concluded that the aimless detour through the words of a statute could not lead to a correct result. [17]

This conclusion is incorrect, at least if offered without any further qualification. One cannot gain a criterion of the correctness of a decision by analysing its psychological genesis. And no practising jurist would think it was a good idea to attempt to do so. Everyone knows that the judgment of a judge who has been bribed may be correct, although it comes about in an incorrect way, while that of an incorruptible judge may be false. A decision taken by a judge who has sat through a session of six hours will, in all psychological probability, turn out otherwise than if it had been taken at the beginning of the session. But what criterion of the correctness of the decision could be derived from these observations? The justification of the *judgment* is not to be confused with the causal-psychological explanation of *judging*. To give an example: a young lad concluding from the fact that he has skewed heels that the earth is round would have made no noteworthy discovery. The justification belongs to the judgment and a correct opinion is not yet knowledge. Assume a scholar of the seventeenth century had been able to show that all those who, at the time, believed in the roundness of the earth had come to their belief as a result of looking at the

walk', without, however, aiming to describe the psychological genesis of the decision. – The abovementioned arguments are found especially frequently in the work of ERNST FUCHS, for instance in *Die Gemeinschädlichkeit der konstruktiven Jurisprudenz* (Karlsruhe: G. Braun, 1909), pp. 30–31 and 38. For another example, compare JULIUS FRIEDRICH, *Die Bestrafung der Motive und die Motive der Bestrafung. Rechtsphilosophische und kriminalpsychologische Studien* (Berlin: W. Rothschild, 1911), as reported in JULIUS FRIEDRICH, 'Psychologische Rechtsforschung', in *Archiv für Rechts- und Wirtschaftsphilosophie* 3 (1909/1910), pp. 200–209, at p. 207. – H. U. KANTOROWICZ does not belong in this context, because he poses the problem of legal practice psychologically and no longer asks for any criterion of 'correctness', as should be clear after his treatise *Zur Lehre vom richtigen Recht* (Berlin and Leipzig: W. Rothschild, 1909).

skewedness of their heels. Would he have proved, thereby, that the earth is flat or that it is a cube? Or has the young lad's opinion become noteworthy in virtue of the fact that his discovery came to be affirmed by science at a later stage? Can he now claim that his way to that conclusion was much simpler and more immediate, and that it yielded a now-recognized result without any artifice? The one as little as the other. – The psychological argument, moreover, will always be faced with the question of why inter- preters or judges do not immediately follow their sense of justice, but feel that they are legally bound (and this, too, may be a manifestation of the sense of justice) to 'construct' and to present the logic of their constructive jurisprudence, as opposed to considerations of sentiment, as what is decisive for the justification of their judgment. Why judges are supposed to be mistaken if they proceed in this way is not at all as self-evident as is sometimes claimed today. [18] One might, after all, think of the following parallel: the fact that a hypocrite, in front of all the world, explains his actions by appeal to moral reasons, even though these actions are caused by immoral motives, will lead no one to conclude that it would be false to act from moral motives, because this hypocrite is evidently using the latter as a mere pretext and would do better to avow his true reasons. On the contrary, one will perceive a triumph of morality in the fact that the hypocrite feels compelled to pay it tribute through his hypocrisy. What is at issue here, naturally, is only the relation between real and pretended reasons, together with the consequences that result therefrom for the evaluation of the one or the other. The possibility of deriving any conclu- sions whatsoever as to the evaluation of the motives themselves from this psychological relationship is precisely to be denied.[24] An experimental- psychological investigation of the processes in the soul of the judge can yield nothing as to the conditions under which his judgment is to be regarded as juristically correct. The argument that it is a fact that one would not hold any judgment to be correct, these days, unless it conformed to one's sense of justice commits the grave mistake of confusing the opinion of correctness with a criterion of correctness.[25] As soon as there

---

[24] And even if a psychoanalyst of the school of FREUD were to prove of some judicial decision, completely and without any objection, that it was based, in its psychological genesis, on the reproduction of infantile affects, on the transfer of emotions and on introjections, judicial activity would not thereby have been shaken in its foundations (which FREUD himself does not assume).

[25] HEGEL, *Grundlinien der Philosophie des Rechts* (see n. 17), p. 5 [Hegel (1991), 27]: 'But this concept as it is for itself in its *truth* may not only be different from our *representation* of it: the two must also differ in their form and shape. If, however, the representation is not also false in its content, the concept may well be shown to be contained in it and

is a decision – regardless of how it came about – it is subject, together with its justification, [19] to special norms that no longer have anything to do with the individual- or social-psychological genesis of the concrete decision, or with the prevalent opinion about decisional correctness. They are located in an altogether different sphere.

But one thing is common to all opponents of the old doctrine of exegesis,[26] most of whom probably do not fail to recognize the contrast between a genetic explanation and a normative assessment: they all replace the old interpretation, which remains within the confines of positive statute, at least theoretically, with another. They seek to identify 'supra-positive' norms that are more encompassing and adaptable, and which leave the judge with more decisional latitude. The 'law' that the judge applies receives new contents from the outside, and these 'meta-statutory' factors are supposed to be of significance for every individual decision and to be readily available for use as reasons of decision. If, for instance, one takes one's start from a 'cultural ideal', one can develop individual norms with pretty determinate content out of it, so as to evaluate existing positive law in their light, and so as to refer the judge to these standards in order to fill the gaps and uncertainties in the positive law. The complex of norms on which a judge can rest his decision is thus extended, and the difficulties and practical impossibilities that arise from the view that the judge is bound to the strict wording of statute, as well as to an outdated method of exegesis, are remedied. It is, of course, easy to produce judgments, in this way, that conform to our sense of justice – to the 'legal sentiment of a cultural epoch' (BEROLZHEIMER). After all, to find a way of doing so was precisely the guiding consideration that motivated the appeal to such extra-positive sources. How far this approach is justified is not to be determined here, where we discuss the structure of the problem. It merely needs to be emphasized that even these views, [20] at the end of the day, postulate a kind of 'conformity to

---

present in essence within it; that is, the representation may be raised to the form of the concept. But it is so far from being the measure and criterion of the concept which is necessary and true for itself that it must rather derive its truth from the concept, and recognize and correct itself with the help of the latter.' These sentences will keep their meaning, just like those ibid. on p. 8, even if one understands under 'concept' something other than HEGEL.

[26] Let it be repeated that no history of the free law movement shall be written here. Likewise, it is unnecessary, in the given thematic context, to offer a thorough discussion of opinions that put forward comparisons with and parallels to other branches of knowledge (such as natural science or medicine) as proofs. Yet the reader is referred to Note III at the end of the book.

statute' as the criterion of the correctness of a decision. They differ from the old doctrine of interpretation merely in understanding the word 'statute', in the phrase 'conformity to statute', in a different way, but still as referring to something that is to be interpreted and applied. This view therefore likewise draws no distinction between the criterion of the correctness of interpretation and that of the correctness of decision. However strongly all investigations of the question may take this indistinctness to be self-evident, another perspective is nevertheless possible. As a preliminary, it ought to be repeated that the concern is only with the correctness of the decision.

Chapter II

The Will of Statute

Contemporary legal practice wants to apply statute. It regards the 'will of the legislator' or the 'will of statute' as its controlling standard and it therefore answers the question of the correctness of a decision as follows: a judicial decision is correct in the event that it has been provided for by the legislator in the positive law – if a decision is taken in the way that has been prescribed by the relevant legislative authority, or at least (as one unreflectively adds, as though this were not something altogether different) in the way that this authority would have decided had it anticipated the case at hand. The decision, accordingly, like the statute itself, takes its force and, what is apparently seen to come to the same thing, its conformity to statute – that is, its correctness – from the same will whose content is contained in the statute. To use the imagistic language that is popular in discussions of this matter: the decision is drawn from the source of statute.[27] [22]

Because everything now depends on a 'will', it seems natural to regard the real will of the author of a statute, or else that of the empirical and concrete 'legislator', as decisive and to try to apprehend the concrete notional content of the psychological processes that transpired, during the drafting of a

---

[27] In what follows, a critique will be attempted of the dominant conception of juristic method, with a steady view to the result of this investigation. This is also the point of view of the presentation of the 'will' of the statute or of the legislator, which therefore does not intend to be a history or a comprehensive overview of the theories that are under consideration here. The luminous critique of traditional hermeneutics by THEODOR STERNBERG, *Allgemeine Rechtslehre*, vol. I (Leipzig: G. J. Göschen, 1904), § 12, is, in its own type, complete and there would be nothing to repeat or to add here if there were not such a large difference between STERNBERG's claims ('the ascertainment of the objectively correct law alone must today be the sole guideline for all juristic operations' and 'the general ethical will, with consideration for its psychological progression, is the true legislator' [ibid., p. 139, note I]) and the results of this work that an authentic presentation of the dominant doctrine of a measure-giving 'will' becomes justified. (On the second edition of STERNBERG's book, compare the introductory note to the third chapter.)

statute, in the human beings one is able to designate as factors of legislation.^{v}
One assumes that the concrete matter of fact to be decided upon is contained in that concrete notional content and that the decision does nothing
more than express what the historical 'legislators' have already decided. If
the decision does not straightforwardly follow from the wording of the
statute, one initiates inquiries to determine whether statements made by the
originators of the statute that dissolve the doubt may be found somewhere.
If such statements imply that the wording of the statute does not align with
the legislator's real volition, this real will is to be given preference. Imagine
the case of a petty prince of the eighteenth century having enacted the
following statute: 'The Roman law of dowry is to be the statutory regime of
matrimonial property in my realm', and that it turned out, without any
historical doubt, that he understood the Roman law of dowry to mandate a
general community of goods. The application of the statute would, according to the view now under discussion, have to hew to the prince's real will
and to regard the general community of goods as the statutory regime of
matrimonial property. Naturally, this is an example that has not occurred, in
this exaggerated form, in history, but it would be hard to see how the view
that takes the actual will to be the sole standard could decide the case
differently. – The so-called materials of the statute; the 'motives' of a draft
statute; the utterances of representatives of government in statutory commissions: all these acquire a great importance for this 'pragmatic' view, since
it not only lumps together the juristic legislator and the historical bearer of
this function, but also, in addition, frequently confuses the historical 'legislator' with the drafter of the statute. To the naive person, it is all 'completely
clear': the statute is what the legislator (that is, he who [23] 'makes' the
statute) wills (that is, what he actually willed) and it must be possible, in
some way, to 'determine' what that was – by asking him, if he is still alive. If
he is dead, it will of course become more difficult – but, given the development of modern historical science, not altogether impossible – to discover
something new. The following comparison, for instance, was used in a
textbook of juristic 'hermeneutics':^{28} if someone receives an illegible letter

---

28 JOHANN JAKOB LANG, *Beiträge zur Hermeneutik des römischen Rechts* (Stuttgart: Cotta,
    1857), p. 64, who appeals here to the 'thoughtful theological hermeneuticist' GERMAR,
    and for whom theological and juristic interpretation are straightforwardly the same. The
    quote from PLINY mentioned further below is also to be found in this book on pp. 64–65.
    LANG, by the way, deserves to be mentioned for his desire to achieve methodological
    clarity. But that is all. As his 'solid principles' (ibid., p. i), he presents the whole traditional
    doctrine of exegesis, and he complains that statutes are turning into 'changelings in the
    hands of the exegete' (ibid., p. xv); he warns against IHERING's 'siren song' (having in
    mind the latter's introductory essay to *Jahrbücher für die Dogmatik des heutigen*

and is trying to decipher it, he will put himself into the sender's mind – perhaps the addressee is acquainted with the sender's character, his manner and form of speaking, his handwriting and the purpose of the letter, and with other useful indications that may help in deciphering it – and he thus will succeed in reading the letter. The interpreter of a statute and the judge are said to be in the same position if they are faced with an unclear statute. We might come to the point, thus, at which we would find we have to rely, in all seriousness, on the facial expressions of a member of Parliament during the debate on a statute, on the tone of his voice and the character of his gestures, as means of interpretation. If the comparison to the letter were to be regarded as correct, we could, after all, cite Pliny: '*Nam sermonem vultus, gestus, vox ipsa moderatur: epistola omnibus commendationibus destituta malignitati interpretantium exponitur*' ['In speech, the tone is set by the expression, gestures and voice of the speaker, whereas a letter lacks such recommendations and is liable to wilful misinterpretation': Pliny the Younger (1969), 356–367] – a quotation to which one has indeed made appeal. Certainly, this way of proceeding is unlikely to be implemented in practice. An appeal to what the redactors of a statute 'had in mind', however, is found so often[29] that it may excuse the long-windedness of the presentation [24] we have given so far. This understanding of the legislator, which STERNBERG has called 'fetishistic', rests on a crude confusion of the organs of state with the concrete human beings who function, respectively, as the state's organs; it employs the expression 'will' in the most naive way and it is perhaps to be historically explained by the fact that the judge of an absolutist state regarded himself as a servant of the prince, in every decision he took, who was bound to execute the prince's concrete will.[30] Of course, one did not overlook here that decisions are taken, and on a daily basis, that one could not possibly regard as manifestations of the conscious will of the legislator. But departures from that conscious will were taken to be

---

römischen und deutschen Privatrechts 1 [1857], pp. 1–52) and makes light of the 'storm birds of the jurisprudence of the future', while failing to see the methodological problem.

29 Even in the work of a scholar like LENEL we find the argument (in his 'Abhandlung über den Irrtum', in *Ihering's Jahrbücher*, XLIV) that one must pay attention to SAVIGNY's and the pandectists' doctrine of error, because the latter influenced the authors of § 119 BGB. [This appears to be a reference to Lenel (1902).] Against this view, see SCHLOßMANN, *Der Irrtum* (see n. 5), p. 23.

30 See FRANZ ADICKES, *Stellung und Tätigkeit des Richters: Vortrag gehalten in der Gehestiftung zu Dresden am 27. Oktober 1906* (Dresden: v. Zahn & Jaensch, 1906), p. 10, who refers to ADOLF FRIEDRICH STÖLZEL, *Brandenburg-Preußens Rechtsverwaltung und Rechtsverfassung, dargestellt im Wirken seiner Landesfürsten und obersten Justizbeamten*, vol. II (Berlin: F. Vahlen, 1888), pp. 137–138.

grounded in the *presumptive* will of the prince, as were the results of the interpretation of a statute, for the reason that interpretation, likewise, was considered to be the exclusive preserve of the legislator. This line of thought is thoroughly consistent and it manifests a better understanding of the essence of interpretation than the view according to which interpretation does not create any new contents but merely unveils what is already present. One appealed to the sentence, '*Tam conditor quam interpres legum solus imperator juste existimabitur*' (C. I. 12. C. 1. 14) ['The emperor alone is justly to be regarded as the maker and interpreter of laws': Codex Iustiniani 1.14.12]. And the theses XLIII and XLIV of the *Positiones Juris*,[vi] which GOETHE presented as his dissertation, state: '*Omnis legislatio ad Principem pertinet. Ut et legum interpretatio*' ['All legislation pertains to the prince, as does all interpretation of laws']. All of this was completely consistent. In practice, however, one constructed the ideal legislator, who only ever wills what is reasonable and who pushes aside the historical legislator. This approach suggested itself as a result of the changes in the procedure of legislation that went along with the introduction of constitutionalist constitutions and the argument against giving consideration to the factual historical will of the legislator that is most popular today is to point out that there simply is no personal legislator in the German Empire. [25] Nowadays, one therefore no longer speaks of the will of the legislator, but only of the will of statute.

The contradictions and inconsistencies of the doctrine of the will of the legislator had their ground in the fact that one did not wish to admit to oneself that one was operating with a mere fiction. Had one been consciously aware of the fact that one treated a number of 'transpositive' moments and contents as though they were the will of the legislator, and had one – always remaining conscious of this fiction and proceeding from it – tried to develop a theory of interpretation, one would have arrived at theoretically and practically valuable results. Instead, the fiction was transformed into a dogma.[31] One then strained to prove that what one treated as

---

[31] VAIHINGER, *Die Philosophie des Als Ob* (see n. 15), pp. 220–221: 'The soul has the tendency to bring all contents of representation into equilibrium and to create an uninterrupted connection between them. However, hypothesis (and, as will be explained on p. 221, fiction even more so) stands in hostile opposition to this tendency, insofar as it contains the representation that it is not yet to be put alongside the other objective representations. [...] Once it has been assumed to be objective, a representation has a *stable* equilibrium, while a hypothesis only has a *labile* one: The psyche, however, tends towards making every psychological content more and more stable [...].' In the case of fiction, the soul is likewise inclined to make an end to the uncomfortable condition of

though it were the will of the legislator was his real will and thus invented a legislator that fit that assumption. The further development of the theory subsequently set out from this 'legislator', and further engaged in the latter's piecemeal construction and repair, instead of taking its start from the insight that this legislator was a simple fiction, an 'as-if contemplation', the peculiar character and content of which was the real issue. The more recent phrase 'will of statute' is modelled on the talk of the 'will of the legislator' and unthinkable without the latter, both formally and with regard to its content. It is dependent on it in virtue of opposing it. This novel approach argues, first, that it is practically impossible to ascertain the real psychological content of the will of a particular human being, for instance Justinian's or Frederick the Great's, [26] in some specific period of time. The whole project sinks into obvious absurdity if one is dealing with the 'will' of a legislative assembly, such as the *Bundesrat*[vii] or some other many-headed assembly. Second, the theory of the 'will of the legislator' is said to contain a misapprehension of the essence of a statute. A statute is not a content that is unchangeably fixed, but rather a 'constant, living force' (WACH). All that is made into statute, after all, is what is published as statute. For this reason alone, the materials of a statute, the deliberations of the commissions, this or that private opinion, cannot be regarded as having statutory force. – Apart from that, however, the novel approach took over the tools of trade of the old doctrine of interpretation. The latter had never really been serious about its inquisition of the mind of the legislator, but had developed a number of different methods to process the material of the valid law: the will of the statute is at times narrower, at times wider, than its literal meaning; at times (the details are left to the judge's tact), an inference to the contrary will is drawn from the silence of the statute; at times, the silence of the statute is taken as an indication that one ought to look for a factual situation that resembles the case at hand and that has already found a statutory regulation, and apply the determinations that are valid for that other situation 'analogically'. In the extreme case, one is to interrogate the spirit of legal order as a whole so as to come up with an analogy, which method, however, introduces a degree of indeterminacy so high that someone already called the method of analogy an 'excess of interpretation' almost a hundred years ago.[32] Using such artful means, one can, of course, [27] 'take' from a statute whatever one may wish to find in it; instructions

<hr>

tension that results from the fact that something which is not present is treated as though it were present: 'Thus, the fiction turns into dogma: The "as if" turns into a "because".'

[32] IGNAZ VON RUDHART, *Das Recht des Deutschen Bundes: Ein Lehrbuch zu dem Gebrauche bei Vorlesungen and deutschen Universitäten* (Stuttgart: Cotta, 1822), p. 9. JORDAN,

on when one is to employ one or another of the different methods of interpretation are, after all, altogether unavailable, although a certain degree of regularity in the use of the arguments provided by the different methods has developed over time. The large number of juristic controversies already suffices to show how far the arguments in question fall short of being compelling demonstrations.[33]

With regard to both opinions, that focusing on the will of statute and that focusing on the will of the legislator, we are interested, first and foremost, in the following: the point of view of both concerns the correctness of interpretation only, not the correctness of the decision in practice, although both approaches assume that these two questions are 'self-evidently the same'. They both want to interpret – that is, they want to determine the content and the scope of applicability of a legal norm. The criticism that has, in the last few years, been levelled against both approaches was concerned with proving that they are in no way capable of providing that determination. The critics conceded, therewith, that the task at hand is to offer a determination of the content and the scope of applicability of legal norms and that correct interpretation is identical with correct decision. *But that is precisely*

'Bemerkungen über den Gerichtsgebrauch' (see n. 16), p. 227, cites him and claims that 'one cannot determine by appeal to general rules' when reasoning by analogy is to be employed. He goes on to claim that 'astuteness and correct judgment (!) are going to find analogy where a superficial mind looks for them in vain', and he does not forget to add, *astutely*, 'and conversely'. In discussions of this topic, and not only in proponents of the established view, one again and again encounters statements such as this, which answer the request for a clear and methodological engagement with the cheap retort that 'it is all the worse for healthy common sense if it does not tell us enough'.

33 The degree to which traditional hermeneutics is insecure and unstable when it comes to explaining its own method shall be demonstrated with reference to GUSTAV RÜMELIN's seemingly clear sentence in *Kanzlerreden* (Tübingen: Mohr Siebeck, 1907), p. 67: 'A sense of justice no longer has anything to do with the question what is or what was actually valid law. This question is altogether under the sway of a scientific technique, of the laws of hermeneutics and of historical critique, though it may be claimed that, even here, a sympathetic identification with the rightful intention of the legislator may supplement the grammatical-logical interpretation of the words.' (See also ibid., p. 275.) The way in which 'sympathetic identification' is connected with scientific technique, by the phrase 'though it may be claimed', contains the following unsolvable riddles. (1) What matters, apparently, is the intention of the legislator (probably of the historical legislator). (2) Whence does scientific technique obtain the ability to ascertain this intention? (3) What connection is there between scientific technique and sympathetic identification, so that the latter may supplement the former? This ability to supplement presupposes a homogeneity, and then one has to ask (4) why the sense of justice, nevertheless, is not supposed to 'have anything to do with' the question of what is factually (?) valid law. And (5) is it indeed the case that valid law is nothing other than the content of the 'rightful intention of the legislator'?

what is to be put in question here. [28] The content of the statute, which is presumed to be valid, enters into a different sphere, its function turns into another, in virtue of the fact that it is applied by a judge, just as the abstract content of a valid statute, in fact, is immediately transformed into a different content once it is referred to the concrete case. Whatever one may think about the phenomenon, the connection between a legal norm that is valid in abstraction from and untouched by real life with its concrete application to an individual case is lacking as soon as the correctness of interpretation (which is concerned merely with the abstract content of a norm and which employs concrete cases only to ascertain that content) and the correctness of concrete decision are declared to be one and the same. Theories that refer to the will of a legislative authority are therefore to be tested with reference to this most general presupposition. We aim to examine whether it is really the case that to interpret correctly and to decide correctly are one and the same, or whether it is perhaps the case that the correctness of an interpretation, while it is a presupposition of the correctness of decision, does not exhaust the latter, so that other factors need to be taken into account before the decision can be called correct. We ask, furthermore, whether this will not change the role of interpretation in such a way that it has its own area for itself and is no longer at all to be regarded as a general presupposition of the correctness of a decision.

Three famous scholars have rejected the decisiveness of the will of the legislator and, in particular, of the materials of a statute.[34] What they have achieved therewith is that the 'dominant opinion' now declares 'the objective thought-content' of statute to be decisive, while it [29] avoids mention of the will of the legislator.[35] Instead, one refers to the 'will of statute'. Of course, it would now have been as necessary to overcome, or at least to clarify, the altogether nebulous concept of 'will' as it was to

---

[34] KARL BINDING, *Handbuch des Strafrechts*, vol. I (Leipzig: Duncker & Humblot, 1885), pp. 471–472; WACH, *Handbuch* (see n. 12), p. 254 sqq.; JOSEF KOHLER, 'Über die Interpretation von Gesetzen', in *Grünhut's Zeitschrift für das Privat- und Öffentliche Recht der Gegenwart* 13 (1886), pp. 1–61. Since these publications contain full references to the literature that had appeared up to that point, we will make further special mention only of ANTON FRIEDRICH JUSTUS THIBAUT, *Theorie der logischen Auslegung des römischen Rechts* (Altona: J. F. Hammerich, 1806), who, like OSKAR KRAUS, 'Die leitenden Grundsätze der Gesetzesinterpretation', in *Grünhut's Zeitschrift für das Privat- und Öffentliche Recht der Gegenwart* 32 (1905), pp. 613–636 (compare the following chapter), invokes considerations of legal security, and SCHLOßMANN's treatise *Der Irrtum* (see n. 5), § 7, which we have already cited repeatedly.

[35] Still, even the impressive voices of BINDING, WACH and KOHLER did not suffice to free practice of the constant appeals to the materials, as well as of the great indeterminacy of their relation to the statutory text. Compare Note IV at the end of this book.

offer a brilliant attack on the spectral 'legislator'. One got rid of the latter, but the 'will', the more dangerous spectre,[36/viii] remained. Just as before, one corroborates the result of an interpretation by offering the assurance: it is the true will of statute. One also spoke of the 'purpose' of a statute and, with this objectivation of the notion of purpose, one could only want to refer to the purpose that a reasonable person would pursue through the enactment of the statute in question. In this way, it also became possible to connect the doctrine of the correctness of a judicial decision with the exegesis of private declarations of will,[37] which, in truth, already suffices to prove that the theory of the 'will of statute' is unsuitable as a basis for the application of law. Like the theory of the 'will of the legislator', it inevitably results in a construction of the reasonable legislator and it truly does not matter whether one impresses on one's argumentations the seal of the 'indubitable will of the legislator' or that of the 'indubitable will of statute', [30] given that the competence of any such 'will' has not yet been clearly established. One looked for the command to which the judge was obedient in case he decided correctly and one closed oneself to the insight into the fact that one was trading in a fiction. One merely treated the recognized results of exegesis as if they were statute (and thus, as one usually assumed, command). One tried to identify a fixed will so as to evaluate the application of law. This alien will, which was to be identified by the use of certain methods, was taken to be the one to which judges are bound; the decision was regarded as an individual instance of this will; the correct decision must then be the 'true will'. The will commands; the judge obeys. Thus statute and judge were juxtaposed to each other. It may well be appropriate, in state law, to understand the position and activity

---

[36] BACON DE VERULAM would classify the 'will of the legislator' as a combination of *idolum fori* and *idolum theatri*, and would regard it as a *suppositio phantastica*. (FRITZ MAUTHNER, *Wörterbuch der Philosophie. Neue Beiträge zu einer Kritik der Sprache*, vol. I [Munich and Leipzig: G. Müller, 1910], p. 75 sqq., translates *idolum* as 'spectre'; hence the use of the term in the text above. GEORG WILHELM BARTOLDY, in his translation of the *Novum Organum* annotated by Salomon Maimon [Berlin: G. C. Nauck, 1793], instead uses the somewhat too feeble 'prejudice'.) The will of the legislator is indeed a peculiar creation: it is a 'will' that always wants the good (RGZ, vol. 67, p. 70), that has always considered the most important issues (RGZ, vol. 67, pp. 66, 68, p. 329) and that always expresses itself as concisely as possible (RGZ, vol. 73, p. 137), a will that is incapable of behaving like a 'weak-willed person' (KULEMANN, 'Platonische Gesetze', in *Deutsche Juristen-Zeitung* 16 [1911], cols. 570–573, at col. 572) and which is supposed to be endowed with an 'organic striving for purpose', and a will that, last but not least, is said to be extremely fertile – he who avails himself of such magical creatures …

[37] In particular ERICH DANZ, *Die Auslegung der Rechtsgeschäfte: Zugleich ein Beitrag zur Rechts- und Tatfrage*, 3rd edition (Jena: G. Fischer, 1911).

of a judge who is a public servant from the perspective of a relation of this kind. As soon, however, as we ask for an evaluative standard to guide the application of law, for a criterion of the correctness of a judicial decision, we are contemplating the matter under an altogether different category – one that must be distinguished, at least conceptually, from the former. Although an overlap in content is likely to result in most cases, a jurist, at least, ought to possess enough methodological skill and capacity for abstraction to distinguish the question of what a judge is personally obligated to do, as a public servant, from the question of which judicial decision is to be regarded as juristically correct. Both of these two questions, after all, do not become identical in virtue of the fact that the judge, as a public servant, is obligated to decide in a way that is juristically correct. Such a command to decide correctly would presuppose a criterion of correctness, but not contain one. It will be replied at this point that the statute itself is the command – that it contains the command. First, however, the 'imperative nature' of the legal norm is not at all self-evident. Second, if the correctness of the decision is supposed to rest on the command, it will have to be a command to the judge (and not to the people). And what might the content of that command be? Manifestly, that the judge ought to decide in the way provided for by statute. But to decide correctly contains at least [31] two activities; first, to bring the right statute into connection with the matter of fact that is to be evaluated; and then to achieve a correct understanding of what is written in the statute (leaving aside, for now, the cases that have not been envisaged in the statute). How are we to infer from the content of the command that both activities have taken place according to prescription? The statute itself, after all, does not contain more than its manifest content.

According to the dominant view, the judge, at each stage of his activity, is to obey a command whose content he has, in most cases, to determine for himself. This compels the conclusion that the evaluation of this determination, the answer to the question of its correctness, cannot be given by appeal to the command itself. The content of the latter must first be identified through that determination. A 'will' that hovers above the judge is, in all cases, the result of an interpretation – one that therefore cannot, in turn, legitimize itself by appeal to its result. (The practical usefulness of the result, at any rate, is not a legitimation derived from the content of the relevant command.) Every act of interpretation is an act of independent creative synthesis of a 'legislator', no matter whether it is an extensive or intensive interpretation, an analogy or an 'argument from the contrary'. The legislator is constructed, not reconstructed. Every jurist who creates a new system transforms older thoughts and introduces new ones. One does not have to be a great philosopher to come to understand that this has always been a process that a practitioner of the civil law would refer to as a kind of 'specification' – the processing of some matter into a new construct:

> The exegesis, whether it be explanatory, extending, limiting, or modifying always brings forth a new legal norm. If one denies this, by arguing that the norm was already contained in the wording of the statute, then one overlooks that the scientific exegesis made it clear, in the first place, that it is contained in it, in this and no other way.[38]

---

[38] Thöl, *Einleitung in das deutsche Privatrecht* (see n. 11), p. 144, in which he criticizes GEORG FRIEDRICH PUCHTA (*Pandekten*, § 16) [see n. 39] and emphasizes that the science of the law is necessarily productive, not receptive. That he then fell into the error of turning science into a 'source of law' was a consequence of the assumption that anything by which a decision is measured must be a statute – an error that is to be dealt with at a later point, in discussing the view that turns the judge into a legislative organ because he also draws from 'sources' other than statute. By contrast, it is unobjectionable for STERNBERG, *Allgemeine Rechtslehre* (see n. 27), § 12 (p. 138), to claim: 'A material difference between interpretation and legislation does not exist.' Here, the question is of the logical process of the application of law; it is not whether the judge creates formally valid law or whether a steady practice might be said to give rise to customary law. It is emphasized, herewith, that the 'subjection to statute' or the 'conformity to statute' are not suitable criteria of the correctness of decision, for the reason that statute acquires a new content with every decision. SCHLOßMANN's sentence in *Der Irrtum* (see n. 5), p. 34 (which is directed against *Binding, Handbuch des Strafrechts* [see n. 34], p. 456), deserves to be mentioned here: 'It seems to me to amount to a ὕστερον πρότερον [*Hysteron proteron*, 'later earlier', a reversal of the natural order of explanation] to ask how one is to interpret and apply a statute, if one understands by a statute everything that realizes itself in the life of the law as a consequence of the existence of the statutory text as well as of the constitutional norms that endow it with force on the one side and of the spiritual dispositions of the human beings who are psychologically influenced by it on the other.' It would nevertheless be a misunderstanding to therefore declare the present work to be a 'legal-sociological' one (HERMANN KANTOROWICZ, 'Rechtswissenschaft und Soziologie', in *Verhandlungen des Ersten Deutschen Soziologentages vom 19.-22. Oktober 1910 in Frankfurt am Main* [Tübingen: Mohr Siebeck, 1911], pp. 275–309, at pp. 276–277), for the reason that it opposes the law that is factually effective to the law that is valid. Here, the intention is merely to demonstrate the insufficiency of a certain criterion of the correctness of decisions. Although this demonstration makes use of psychological facts, the many internal logical contradictions of the theory of 'conformity to statute' are the factor that shifts the balance of the argument in its disfavour. (Let it be repeated that legal-sociological investigations contain their very own problems.) – It is a misrecognition of practical legal doctrine, as well as of legal practice, and a confession of allegiance to the old hermeneutics, for RUDOLF STAMMLER, *Die Lehre von dem richtigen Rechte* (Berlin: J. Guttentag, 1902), p. 4, to say that 'they (technical discussions of legal doctrine) always delimit themselves as a reproduction of the content of a will, one that is present, and that we have an interest to expound because it is there.' Or ibid., p. 607: 'It is beyond doubt that there are very many cases in which one can reliably ascertain the real

In light of these facts, how can the 'will of statute' [33] still provide a yardstick and 'conformity to statute' still be a criterion of correctness? Whoever makes a serious attempt to think through the consequences of the doctrine of the will of statute immediately finds himself enmeshed in such a web of difficulties and unsolvable riddles, of worthless fictions and presumptions, that the only advantage of the appeal to the 'will of statute', its simple obviousness, quickly loses its value. If that will is no longer congruent with what every reasonable human being would take from the wording of the statute, but rather to be ascertained by the use of complicated operations, the question arises what significance is then to be accorded to the wording – and it can by no means be altogether irrelevant. Does it merely represent the boundary within which the decision must move? Is it the firm ground around an inland lake on which interpretation sails? Or is it merely the point of embarkation, the island in the sea, whose infinite spaces are open to the interpreter? Or does one have to think of it as two peninsulas that must, like the sides of an angle, be extended, so that the task of interpretation is merely to stay within the space measured by the extension of the peninsulas? All these are important and obvious questions, and the phrase 'will of statute' does not provide us with any indication, however weak, as to how they might be answered. And further: what point in time is determinative for ascertaining the will? The 'objective thought-content' that the statute had in the eighteenth century, or – if it is still valid after a hundred years – the one it has now? The 'reasonable sense' of many of the provisions of the BGB[ix] is going to be different in twenty years from what it is today. Where is the stable content under which it is going to be subsumed? What is the significance of the oft-mentioned 'historical environment'[39] in which the statute originated – 'the homeland [34] of

(?) meaning of legal enactments and institutions only if one looks to the condition from which they emerged. Legal history, accordingly, is a suitable means to understand what was really intended by some piece of posited law.' On ibid., pp. 313–314, the application of the correct law in practice is explicitly made dependent on whether 'the real will of the *enacted* law imposes this obligation on him (the judge) ... and it may very well be the case that doubts and disputes arise, in the context of some particular question, as to whether this conforms to the true intention of a specific statute', etc. A similar view appears in *Theorie der Rechtswissenschaft* (see n. 14), pp. 340–341, pp. 358–359.

[39] GEORG FRIEDRICH PUCHTA, *Pandekten*, 7th edition (Leipzig: J. A. Barth, 1853), p. 27 (who takes this to pertain to 'logical interpretation'). ADOLF FRIEDRICH STÖLZEL, *Staatliches und staatloses Ausland im preussisch-deutschen Strafrecht. Ein Beitrag zur Gesetzgebungsgeschichte und zur Lehre von der Gesetzesinterpretation* (Berlin: F. Vahlen, 1910) offers a detailed interpretation of § 4 StrGB [*Strafgesetzbuch*, Code of Criminal Law] on the basis of the history of its genesis and then goes on to say, ibid., pp. 64–65, note

the legislator's thought' (IHERING)? How shall one derive answers to all that from the 'will of statute'? It is often said that this is just the advantage of our theory: that it does justice to the progress of time – that the 'will' grows and develops, like the law, which, after all, is also a living organism. Very well. One only has to remain aware that it is impossible to subsume under a 'living organism', that there is no clear understanding of the relation and connection between the different expressions of the supposed will of a statute to its manifest content, that the contradiction remains unsolved – the will that the application of law pretends to fulfil is its own secretion – and, finally, that the word 'organism' does not clarify anything.[40/x] [35]

1: 'Hopefully, due cognizance of the history of the genesis of the provision will ground the general conviction that any other interpretation is scientifically indefensible.' Without thereby intending to cast doubt on the correctness of STÖLZEL's result, it must nevertheless be remarked, against a sentence thus formulated, that the relevance of a proof must be established before one begins with the taking of evidence. – A summary of the different elements in JOSEF KOHLER, 'Die deutsche Rechtswissenschaft und das deutsche bürgerliche Gesetzbuch', in *Grünhut's Zeitschrift für das Privat- und Öffentliche Recht der Gegenwart* 23 (1896), pp. 217–228, at p. 224: only the literal wording of the statute is determinative; the latter, however, is to be interpreted in accordance with the train of thought, the time of enactment, and in the context and in line with the spirit of the modern age; 'statutory-political' considerations are likewise admissible as means of interpretation. Compare also RGZ, vol. 54, p. 382 and RUDOLPH V. IHERING, *Geist des römischen Rechts auf den verschiedenen Stufen seiner Entwicklung*, 5th edition, vol. II.2 (Leipzig: Breitkopf und Härtel, 1898), pp. 463–464.

40 This expression, understandably, still enjoys considerable popularity, although complaints about its indeterminacy have been put forward for a long time. (Against SAVIGNY's and IHERING's use of the word, compare LEIST, *Über die dogmatische Analyse* [see n. 22], p. 123; EMIL PFERSCHE, *Methodik der Privatrechtswissenschaft* [Graz: Leuschner & Lubensky, 1881], pp. 39–40; JUNG, 'Von der "logischen Geschlossenheit" des Rechts' [see n. 9], p. 140, note 1. On the psychology of its employment in the social sciences, see in particular SCHÄFFLE, 'Anatole Leroy-Beaulieu', in *Revue des deux mondes*, 1888, p. 920, as well as the vehement words of LUDWIG GUMPLOWICZ, *Grundriß der Soziologie*, 2nd edition [Vienna: Manz, 1905], p. 23.) Admittedly, no presentation is possible without images. A 'symbolic-naturalistic' point of view (says JOHANNES EMIL KUNTZE, *Der Wendepunkt in der Rechtswissenschaft. Ein Beitrag zur Orientierung über den gegenwärtigen Stand- und Zielpunkt derselben* [Leipzig: Hinrichs, 1856], pp. 66–67) may thus be useful and helpful. But to point to an imprecise and blurry analogy, at the decisive point, is to confuse the question rather than to solve it. SCHÄFFLE has shown for sociology how little real progress can be made in this way. It is hard to see how a critical objectivity will still be possible once other powerful phrases of the philosophical doctrine of organism will have been 'made fertile' for jurisprudence, such as the 'autoplasticity of the law', the 'autotelic character of the law', its 'entelechy', etc., or once someone has come to regard it as a scientific deed to make use of the theory of psycho-physical parallelism, and of what the philosophers have had to say about it, for understanding the development of the law and its relation to the development of society.

The aim of the preceding discussion was to point out how unsuitable a criterion of the correctness of a decision the 'will of statute' is. But the valid legal order (that is, the legal order that ought to be valid) did not stand opposed to the empirical. The discussion did not play out what ought to be statute against what actually counts as statute in practice. Rather, it was to be shown: the legal material that is used to decide concrete cases and the rules that govern how it is to be used are not identical; in order to properly account for practice, other validities must be taken into consideration. (That one has to distinguish sharply between practice and legal doctrine in doing this will become clear.) It might not matter for the *theoretical* investigation of the scope and content of a valid norm, and of its place in a doctrinal system, that the statute itself gains its content only as a result of the investigation. The legislator who has been found in this way can, although he is the creation of interpretation, still be its judge, since juristic interpretation, like any other scientific activity, contains its own unprovable presuppositions within itself and continuously returns to them. VAIHINGER's aforementioned discussions of the significance and justifiability of as-if contemplation likewise become significant here once more, since they take the ground from under the charge that the result of interpretation is not the real will of the legislator, but only regarded as if it were that will. (This objection, to note, has not been made here; rather, it has been shown only that this fiction is devoid of value.) For the method of practice, however, the problem takes on a different complexion. For that method, the fact that it creates what one can refer to as its 'legislator' in the first place must, at least, have the methodological consequence that practice can no longer [36] appeal to that legislator as something that is alien to it – *something that is imposed on it from the outside* and independent of it – not to mention the defectiveness and insufficiency of this construction itself, by means of which one 'constructs' the 'legislator' like the man in the moon: out of words and phrases, out of a 'purpose' (that is itself constructed without any clarity), out of the 'historical environment' and out of the 'spirit of the present'. The only thing that is achieved thereby is that practice is better able to adapt to the demands of legal intercourse. But this advantage is not even intended by the theory of the 'will of statute'. That theory wanted to bind the judge – to refer him to a content that had been fixed in statutes. By contrast, it has been shown that such a bond, if it is not merely used to determine the judge's position in state law, but rather employed as a criterion of the substantive correctness of a decision, is logically impossible, to say nothing of its incompatibility with the facts that characterize the life of the law.[41]

The contemporary methods of interpretation have developed, in the course of centuries, independently of the goal of finding a correct judicial decision, from a throwing together of theological, philological, and historical methods of exegesis,[42] in connection with conclusions [37] drawn from the position of the judge as a civil servant – that is, out of completely heterogeneous elements. These do not amount to a system (which is hardly possible given such ancestry), but rather to usages on whose observation one can practically count with a certain degree of probability. The theory of a decision's 'conformity to statute' adopted this doctrine of interpretation in order to uphold the criterion of 'conformity to statute'. The criterion of 'conformity to statute' itself, however, amounts to the view that a decision is correct if it can be subsumed under a (relatively) stable content of norms. The subsumable decision is the correct one; subsumability (pardon) is the criterion. Alas, it was at length impossible to refuse to take account of the practical difficulties that resulted from the effectiveness of the feeling of justice, from the need for smooth legal intercourse, etc. Admittedly, one did gainsay them and BRINZ[43] gave the following thoughtful formulation of that denial: 'The thirst for further sources of law is unjustified *a priori* ... the *horror vacui*

---

[41] LEIST, *Über die dogmatische Analyse* (see n. 22), p. 28, applies an ingenious idea of LICHTENBERG's very nicely to jurisprudence: 'If our species was eliminated from the face of the earth, and a new species was to take its place, and if the only remnant of this whole earlier period that was to fall into its hands was a female dress, what conception of the female human body would this new species come to form? We laugh and take ourselves to have understanding, since we would never think of trying to study the covered body by drawing inferences from the wide and loosely-fitting covering. But is this not how we proceed in our own study of the law?' LEIST, however, speaks of empirical law, in contrast to valid law – that is, he is engaged in legal sociology.

[42] On the historical connection of theological and juristic interpretation: RODERICH STINTZING, *Geschichte der deutschen Rechtswissenschaft*, vol. I (Munich and Leipzig: Oldenbourg, 1880), p. 88 sqq. Compare also KARL LAMPRECHT, 'Der intellektualistische und ästhetische Charakter des individualistischen Zeitalters der deutschen Geschichte' (16.–18. Jhd.), in *Annalen der Naturphilosophie*, ed. Wilhelm Ostwald, vol. I (Leipzig: Veit 1902), pp. 438–469, at p. 444.

[43] ALOIS BRINZ, 'Review of: Franz Adickes, *Zur Lehre von den Rechtsquellen*', in *Kritische Vierteljahresschrift für Gesetzgebung und Rechtswissenschaft* 15 (1873), pp. 162–165. Compare ERNST ZITELMANN's insightful discussion in his *Lücken im Recht. Rede gehalten bei Antritt des Rektorats der Rheinischen Friedrich-Wilhelms-Universität zu Bonn* (Leipzig: Duncker & Humblot, 1903). The author who is discussed in the quotation from BRINZ is FRANZ ADICKES, *Zur Lehre von den Rechtsquellen, insbesondere über die Vernunft und die Natur der Sache als Rechtsquellen und über das Gewohnheitsrecht* (Kassel and Göttingen: G. H. Wiegand, 1872).

['fear of empty space'] that afflicts the draftsman first afflicted the law itself; there is no lawless space in law.' But BRINZ himself openly remarks in a subsequent passage: 'That is, admittedly, thesis against thesis. But what help could our Bible give us against the unbelievers?' It really does not offer any help. The problem is there; it is not solved by its denial. One can solve it even less by declaring cases in which practice departs from valid law or goes beyond it to be exceptional.[44] One must give a frank answer to the question: [38] are such exceptional cases correct decisions or are they wrongly decided, because they do not conform to statute, and does the judge make himself liable for them, although he is backed up by practice as a whole and to enforce his liability is practically infeasible? To this clear question, one typically answers as follows: 'In principle, such decisions are unstatutory, but … ' – and what most often follows is a disquisition on the power of facts, and that means we give up on conformity to statute as a criterion of correctness.

Given the excessive power that the notion of a decision's 'conformity to statute' has exercised upon legal minds for centuries, it seemed natural to adopt a wider conception of 'statute' so as to save subsumability. It seems to be self-evident: if subsumption under a statute does not lead to a correct result, then the fault must lie with the statute and the latter is to be altered in such a way that it will lead to the correct result. *That is the guiding idea of the free law movement.* Although it supplements the 'positive' law with a 'meta-positive' law drawn from moral value judgments or 'cultural norms' and thus adopts a wider understanding of a decision's lawfulness than the received method, it formally maintains the criterion of norm-conformity and thus moves along the same path as the traditional doctrine of interpretation. The latter likewise strove to extend the content of statute and simply did not have the desired success in doing so. But, with such an extension of the content of the concept of 'statute' and thus of one's notion of 'conformity to statute', one robs the criterion of correct decision that is contained in that notion, subsumability under statute, of all value. The

---

[44] SIEGMUND SCHLOßMANN, *Der Vertrag* (Leipzig: Breitkopf und Härtel, 1876), p. 180: 'A single case of conscious and accepted disregard of statute already suffices to overturn the prevailing doctrine of the sources of law, since a scientific dogma *simul cum in aliquo vitiatum est, perdit officium suum*' [a scientific dogma, 'if it is violated in one instance, loses its justification']. RUDOLF V. IHERING, *Scherz und Ernst in der Jurisprudenz. Eine Weihnachtsgabe für das juristische Publikum*, 10th edition (Leipzig: Breitkopf und Härtel, 1909), p. 325, mocks this and claims that it would be impossible for a single judge who is forgetful of his duty to undermine the law – a typical case of the confusion of the valid with the effective norm, a confusion of which even SCHLOßMANN is not altogether free.

Reichsgericht[45/xi] wants to 'apply statute notwithstanding its deficiencies', but wishes, at the same time, to adapt it, wherever possible, 'to the requirements with which the legal intercourse between citizens confronts statutory law'. This aspiration contains two different criteria of the correctness of a judgment: 'conformity to statute', and [39] appropriateness to the needs of intercourse, whose heterogeneity is recognized in the *Reichsgericht*'s very words. If 'conformity to statute' is then nevertheless portrayed as the sole criterion of correctness, the phrase 'conformity to statute' turns into an empty tautology – into a summary reference to all criteria that are in fact effective – and its *justifiability* is that on which everything turns. The effort to construct norms out of the idea of law, the derivation of such norms from a 'cultural ideal', the reference to the 'nature of the thing' (which, however, is no longer very popular today) or the needs of intercourse:[46] all that is always oriented towards the goal of delivering a norm under which it is possible to subsume, to provide a determinate norm with a (relatively) firm content[47] by appeal to which a judge can legitimate his decision.[48] To be sure, whenever the correctness of the decision is in question, one is engaged in a normative inquiry. But it does not follow from this that one must put the legal consequence and the matter of fact abstractly on one side and the concrete decision on the other, so as to measure the latter by the former. It is unnecessary for there to be such a – so to speak – static relationship. [40] In its further course, this investigation will arrive at the criterion that a

---

[45] RGZ, vol. 20, p. 325.

[46] Others appeal to healthy juristic tactfulness and healthy common sense, and then, if one humbly asks them to establish their standing and to substantiate their case, turn the matter of dispute on its head, by making it clear to those who raise the question that 'external' rules are of use only for blockheads, 'so as to relieve them of the need to think for themselves, but they would do better not to interpret at all.' (GEORG FRIEDRICH PUCHTA, *Vorlesungen über das heutige römische Recht*, 5th edition, ed. Adolf August Friedrich Rudorff [Leipzig: Bernhard Tauchnitz, 1862], p. 40) – as though one could prove one's strength of spirit by appealing to one's unarticulated feelings.

[47] That is, the content that is decisive for the judge and for the concrete decision is a firm one. That this content may change in the course of time – that there can be no natural law with a firm content – is thus not contested. The matter at hand does not concern the development of the law and of its content; rather, what is in question here is merely the moment at which the judge will take his decision. And it is the content that is offered to him for this purpose that is a firm and relatively determinate one.

[48] NEUKAMP, 'Der gegenwärtige Stand der Freirechtsbewegung' (see n. 7), cols. 44–45, likewise sees the fundamental problem that the free law movement aims to answer in 'the method of filling the gaps in the law'. See further STERNBERG, *Einführung in die Rechtswissenschaft* (see n. 12), vol. I, p. 135.

decision is correct if it must be assumed that another judge (as an empirical type) would have issued it in just the same way. This is also a normative conception, but it does not put a 'statute' to one side and a concrete decision to the other, so as to test correctness by subsumability. The theories that appeal to a decision's conformity to statute still live wholly under the spell of the old method of interpretation even if they now reject some of its specific techniques. It is for this reason that they consider interpreting – that is, the determination of the content of a law and the subsumption under that content – as the only possible juristic method, as well as the only possible method of normative inquiry. It would suffice for the proponents of these theories to keep in mind that other forms of normative inquiry (for instance those of ethics) have not developed the method of interpretation in the same way as jurisprudence without thereby ceasing to be normative. If an opportunity presents itself to find a criterion of the correctness of decisions other than 'conformity to statute', which, as things now stand, lacks any clear content and 'resembles all that one wants to see in it', then there is no reason to reject this novel criterion by appeal to the normative character of juristic reasoning – at least not if it fulfils its task better than the criterion of 'conformity to statute'. It would be a banal misunderstanding to fear that the judge would now be able to do whatever he wants if he were no longer bound to decide in accordance with statute. The statute remains a yardstick for the judge; the individual judge may not put himself above it. But the concept of 'conformity to statute' is insufficient to deliver the criterion of correctness that is specific to legal practice and which applies to decisions taken in that practice, as has been sufficiently established. A different criterion is therefore to be sought.

An impenetrable twine of unproven assumptions, presumptions and fictions hides under the phrase of the 'conformity to statute' of a judicial decision. These undoubtedly had the practical value that [41] they made possible an adjudication more appropriate to the requirements of intercourse. Legal practice belongs to the things that 'never succeed without a touch of madness'.[xii] But a scientific doctrine of method must become aware of its fictions and must test them for their usefulness. If it turns out that they veil the true relation of the application of law to statute and do nothing more than to put a misunderstood postulate (that the judge is bound to statute) into a false context, then they are to be rejected. Whoever has to apply a statute only to find in it a decision that does not accord with him (and all others) and hence constructs until he finds a more convenient decision in the statute will call that the 'true will' of the statute. Legal practice would be in a sad shape if it were to proceed in any other way. One only has to remain aware of the fact that the 'true will' is nothing more than the content of the fiction: we regard our construction and its result as if it were the will of the statute. And this is not how one intends the phrase to be understood today. Rather, one takes the phrase 'true will' to mean: correct in a higher sense than the decision that would have been read out of the statute by someone who is beholden to a timid faith in the literal. But now the sophism is perfectly obvious. One now argues as follows: a decision is to be regarded as correct if it conforms to the will of statute. It turns out, however, that there are many decisions that one cannot possibly regard as correct, since they evidently do not conform to the manifest content of statute. Solution: that is only appearance, since the decisions in question conform to the true will of statute. – Such an argument confounds three things that are altogether different, methodologically and in content, even though they are referred to with the same phrase. (The will of statute is identified with (1) a command to the judge; (2) the objective thought-content of the statute; and (3) the content of a correct statute, which is referred to as the 'true' one.) With regard to its logical dignity and its cognitive value, the argument thus stands on a par with the inference: one always returns to one's first love. If one returns to one's third love, the third one must therefore have been the first. – Recently, one hears more and more often that a judge is to decide in the way in which the legislator would have decided. That [42] is a practically valuable heuristic fiction. But it is impossible to overlook that it veils the fact that one has given up 'conformity to statute' as the criterion of the correctness of a decision. The way in which the legislator *would* have decided, of course, is not the way in which he *did*, in fact, decide.

The judge is not to become *legibus solutus* ['unbound from the laws'], but a criterion more useful than 'conformity to statute' is to be sought. The criterion of correctness that is specific to legal practice can be identified only by way of an investigation of legal practice itself.[49] It

---

[49] Let it be repeated once more: the question is not how legal practice participates in the creation of law; it is a fact that practice helps to create law. It is also a fact that the practical application of a determinate legal norm as such has a special psychological significance: a point to which we will have to return a number of times in the further course of our discussion, just as we will have to return to the 'psychological phenomenon that a human being who thinks normally will arrive at the view that some legal order is valid whenever he observes the factual effectiveness of that order for a longer time and expects that this

will become clear that the worry that such a methodological autonomy of legal practice will give rise to a general legal uncertainty is unfounded. That the dominant notion of 'conformity to statute' is not capable of achieving even a shadow of legal determinacy [43] was shown long ago.[50] But, happily, the method of practice is better than what practice takes to be its method.

factual effectiveness is going to continue for some time to come' (ERNST ZITELMANN, 'Gewohnheitsrecht und Irrtum', in *Archiv für die civilistische Praxis* 66 [1883], pp. 323–468, at p. 459). It is easy to see that the psychological and sociological laws that govern the genesis of law continue to influence the application of law. For an investigation of legal practice directed towards these phenomena, such theories therefore come to be important. (Compare the interesting book by ROBERT LAZARSFELD, *Das Problem der Jurisprudenz* [Vienna: Manz, 1908] that is taking its cues from GUMPLOWICZ's sociological ideas, and which sharply and pointedly expresses a number of fitting thoughts: for instance that it belongs to the nature of a real legal dispute that one cannot find a decision for it in statute.) – The sentence according to which the judgment derives from social power or from justice, but not from statute, contains a sociological theory and concerns the causal explanation of the genesis of the judgment, not its juristic correctness. The argument against the will theory in customary law presented by ZITELMANN, op. cit., p. 373, is noteworthy in this context: 'What is more, the legislative power undoubtedly comes to be established in a different way, often enough, for example, through unlawful usurpation on the part of a powerful personality.'

[50] ERNST STAMPE, *Unsere Rechts- und Begriffsbildung* (Greifswald: J. Abel, 1907), p. 37, even says: 'If the supplementation of law is done by such means, no one can be in secure possession of his rights.' That would be correct if there were no other criterion of the correctness of a decision than 'conformity to statute'. – ERNST RABEL, in *Rheinische Zeitschrift für Zivil- und Prozeßrecht des In- und Auslandes* 3 (1911), p. 468, remarks on the view on impossibility of performance expressed in DÜRINGER–HACHENBURG's commentary [Düringer and Hachenburg (1908)]: 'Is this supposed to be free law? It would almost be the law of outlaws.' (This is merely to give an example of how 'conformity to statute' and legal determinacy are taken to be one and the same thing, and how different they are in fact.)

Chapter III

The Postulate of Legal Determinacy[51]

In the last few years, it has often been pointed out that the provisions of a statute usually do not bring anything new in terms of content. The statute leans against existing orders of life and habits of intercourse; it makes use of the moral [45] opinions of the time and of the people, of cultural ideas. In brief, the legislative authority has, as far as concerns the content of its

---

[51] To make the transition from the previous to the following chapters, the following extremely important sentences from JUNG's well-known essay *'Positives' Recht* (see n. 9), p. 45, note i, which have received little attention so far, are to be cited: '[E]ven for statutory law, it is rather doubtful whether one can say that compliance with it is commanded, the judge is not bound to instructions, etc. The obligation thus rests on the fact that a departure from the behaviour that the other party can expect, because the social community in question has hitherto observed it or because the social community has, in general, spoken in favour of observance, is experienced as an injury done to the other party. And thereby positive law has the most significant ground of validity which it could have, that is, the same as the "correct law" or the law as such.' – I do not know whether JUNG will assent to the further results of this work, but its guiding point of view is expressed in these sentences with encouraging clarity. – THEODOR STERNBERG, *Einführung in die Rechtswissenschaft* (see n. 12), the new edition of the *Allgemeine Rechtslehre* (see n. 27), also deserves special mention here. This new edition came out after the present work had already been fully completed. Since occasional references to STERNBERG's book in the notes would not do justice to its importance, the following is also to be emphasized: STERNBERG draws an important distinction between scientific law and unscientific, subaltern law (ibid., § 12). In particular, the legal provisions that will, in the course of the following discussion in the text (which will make this note fully understandable), be introduced as typical examples of norms that are characterized by a relative indifference of content are taken to belong to subaltern law. The difference is that the present work does not regard these provisions (and in particular those concerning time limits and numbers) as something that would have to be opposed to a scientific or otherwise more important law; rather, according to the view developed here, the element of abstract regulation, which is indifferent to the content of the regulation, simply stands out with particular clarity in these examples, but it is, for this treatise, an essential component of any legal determination. (The same holds for KOHLER's 'instructional' law.)

activity, more of an ordering and collecting than a productive character. There is a *'rapport, que les loix ont avec les principes qui forment l'esprit général, les moeurs et les manières d'une nation'* ['The laws stand in relation to the principles that form the general spirit, the habits and the manners of a nation'].[52]

Considerations of this kind, insofar as they specifically concern juris-prudence, have a double sense. For one, it is possible to derive from them statutory-technical and statutory-political propositions: *'c'est au législateur à suivre l'esprit de la nation, lorsqu'il n'est pas contraire aux principes du gouvernement'* ['It is for the legislator to follow the spirit of the nation, as long as it is not contrary to the principles of govern-ment'].[53] What is more, they are often linked to the interpretation of statutes and it seems it is here that we find the point at which the traditional doctrine of exegesis might connect with the aspirations of the free law movement. If the 'will of statute' is to be ascertained, facts such as these appear to be of the utmost importance. Where the statute was understood to derive its content from the value judgments of the people, or from considerations of expediency in intercourse, these factors were, so to speak, mingled into the will of statute and became measure-giving with it. Presumptions to the effect that statute, in cases of doubt, should be regarded to want that which is expedient for intercourse, or that which is just (in the sense of being in conformity with the socially dominant value judgments), and so on, were the result.

However, these remarks – to maintain the focus on the genesis of the content of statutes for a while – apply only to some and not to all statutes, and even for a single statute, they hold only of a part. As far as concerns the other part, there is a lack of any determinacy of content, be it for the reason that the matter at hand is alien to such extra-statutory elements (such as the statute of limitation), or be it for the reason that the indeterminacy of these extra-statutory elements prevents an answer to the particular query (as in the case of statutory regulations concerning the magnitude of the punish-ment for specific delicts). These cases draw attention to an important phenomenon of the life of the law: that what matters is often not the kind and manner of regulation, but rather [46] that there is some regulation at all. Apart from very rare exceptions, every statute contains such a moment of

---

[52] CHARLES-LOUIS DE SECONDAT, BARON DE LA BRÈDE ET DE MONTESQUIEU, *De l'esprit des loix*, vol. II (Amsterdam: La Compagnie, 1758), book XIX, chapter heading.

[53] MONTESQUIEU, *De l'esprit des loix* (see n. 52), art. V, vol. III. In book 29, art. XV, MONTESQUIEU warns against *'de choquer la nature des choses'* ['to shock the nature of things'].

indifference, which a civil lawyer might refer to as aleatory. Up to a certain degree, it is always more necessary that there be a statute at all than that the statute have a particular content. A police ordinance that determines that coaches must steer to the right represents the purest type of a provision that is 'aleatory' with respect to its content. It is indeed indifferent whether one evades to the right or to the left; what is important is only that one knows what direction to evade towards and that one can be assured that others will, in general, evade to the right. It is possible or even likely that the police ordinance merely sanctions already existing customary rules of traffic. But the custom itself does not rest, as far as its content is concerned, on the conviction that it is more useful, more moral or more just to evade to the right; rather, it rests exclusively on the fact that it is necessary to give some decision or other with regard to the matter. Thus there are many rules, including many legal determinations, the nature of which is characterized, as *Savigny*[54] expresses the point, by a 'relative indifference' – that is, the content of which is altogether unaffected by considerations of legal appropriateness or distributive justice and the choice for which was perhaps left to some random mechanism, in the sense that knowledge of the connections between the effective conditions of the choice, a causal explanation, is impossible. Such a moment of arbitrariness with regard to content is contained in all law and one can imagine a line that leads from the aforementioned police ordinance concerning evasion, via the formal determinations of the civil and particularly the many formal determinations of the law of procedure, to penal statutes that, in full conformity with moral opinion, impose a heavy penalty on some offence. [47] But even in the latter example, the moment of arbitrariness makes itself felt in the fixation of the penal framework: it will hardly be easy to give a substantive justification for the fact that the maximum punishment for some crime is set at five years of imprisonment. A rule that prescribes the death penalty for murder could be seen as the extreme opposite of a mere conventional relation of offence and punishment, since this absolute punishment expresses the sense of justice of

---

[54] FRIEDRICH CARL VON SAVIGNY, *System des heutigen Römischen Rechts*, vol. I (Berlin: Veit, 1840), p. 36, where he also lists a number of examples, in particular of legal norms that contain numerical determinations. Compare also THÖL, *Einleitung in das deutsche Privatrecht* (see n. 11), p. 137, as well as HEINRICH THÖL, *Das Handelsrecht*, 5th edition, vol. I (Leipzig: Fues's Verlag [R. Reisland], 1841), p. 46, and RUDOLPH V. IHERING, *Geist des römischen Rechts*, 5th edition, vol. I (Leipzig: Breitkopf und Härtel, 1891), p. 51 sqq.; ZITELMANN, *Lücken im Recht* (see n. 43), p. 29; PAUL OERTMANN, *Gesetzeszwang und Richterfreiheit. Rede beim Antritt des Prorektorats der Königlich Bayerischen Friedrich-Alexanders-Universität Erlangen am 4. November 1908 gehalten* (Erlangen: Junge & Sohn, 1909), p. 19.

at least a part of the members of a legal community in such a determinate way that the abstract significance of the *decision as such*, if put in contrast to its substantive determinacy, appears altogether inconsiderable. But even this is not the final point of our line; the abstract significance of the fact that a decision has been made (which is, naturally, to be distinguished from the legal sanction of a norm) continues to exist even here.

If one sets out from this significance of the mere fact of fixation, from the significance of the fact that a decision has been made, one's attention will be drawn to a function of the legal order that, as far as I can see, has been deemed worthy of special consideration, in its relation to judicial decision-taking, only by HEGEL:[55] **[48]** one can take the view that the law's significance lies in the fact that it ensures that there is some regulation at all. The written, positive statute that is promulgated in a determinate way is, from this point of view, the ideal of a legal norm and the extent to which this point of view is felt to be decisive, in the life of the law, is shown by the fact that nowadays such a statute is, for all practical intents and purposes, regarded to be the legal norm per se. The moment of abstract regulation that was called 'aleatory', in relation to the content of the regulation that derives from certain 'sources', is what gives the written statute a great factual preponderance, although one cannot fail to recognize that a legal norm that conforms to the sense of justice of a people is much more likely to result from the customary

---

[55] HEGEL, *Grundlinien der Philosophie des Rechts* (see n. 17), § 214: 'It is impossible to determine by *reason*, or to decide by applying a determination derived from the concept, whether the just penalty for an offence is a corporal punishment of forty lashes or thirty-nine, a fine of five dollars as distinct from four dollars and twenty-three groschen or less ... . And yet an injustice is done if there is even one lash too many, or one dollar or groschen, one week or one day in prison too many or too few. – It is reason itself which recognizes that contingency, contradiction, and semblance have their (*albeit limited*) sphere and right, and it does not attempt to reduce such contradictions to a just equivalence; here, the only interest present is that of actualization, the interest that some kind of determination and decision should be reached, no matter how this is done (within given limits). This decision belongs to formal self-certainty, to abstract subjectivity, which may rely either on its ability – *within the given limits* – to stop short and settle the matter simply in order that a settlement may be reached, or on such grounds for determination as the choice of a *round* number, or of the number forty minus one.' [Hegel (1991), 245–246, orthography modified to fit with Schmitt's emphases above.] The fundamental difference between the view presented in this text and these sentences of HEGEL is that the former does not regard 'formal self-certainty' (which HEGEL, naturally, does not confuse with the legal sanction or the legal force of a decision) as a kind of ballast of the legal norm or of the decision – as something that stands in some 'non reasonable' connection with the law and that exists within its own limits, to be conceived of in spatial terms. Rather, our view takes 'formal self-certainty' to be an element and ingredient of all legal phenomena: one that may be isolated in a conceptual investigation and used as a point of departure for a methodological investigation.

formation of law. One even regards the advantage in legal determinacy that characterizes statutory law in comparison to customary law as the main reason to make the transition from the latter to the former.[56] Thus justice is not immediately decisive for the judge;[57] what he has to work with is, in every case, a form of second-hand justice – something that has been transformed – whether he [49] simply performs a smooth subsumption under the statute or, taking his cues from § 826 BGB, grants a suit for cessation that has developed only in practice. A third power always steps between the judge and justice: a power that transforms the material of justice into a different aggregate condition, so as to put a compact mass in the judge's hand. Naturally, it is the aspiration both of the legislator as well as of the judge to be 'just'. But the requirement of legal determinacy, which is essential to legal order, steps into the gap between substantive justice (particularly of the concrete case) and its realization in daily life, and it proves its superiority by way of appealing to the very ideal of justice, since one can, after all, portray the postulate of legal determinacy as a demand of justice.[58] Given this state of affairs, it is understandable that the judge, be his sense of justice ever so lively, will not easily elevate himself above the wording of a clear statute. There will

[56] LOTHAR SEUFFERT, *Über richterliches Ermessen. Akademische Festrede gehalten zur Feier des Stiftungsfestes des Großherzoglich Hessischen Ludwigs-Universität am 1. Juli 1880* (Gießen: Brühl, 1880), p. 9. ('The liberty of judicial discretion that dwells within customary law'); BÜLOW, *Gesetz und Richteramt* (see n. 6), p. 18; EHRLICH, 'Über Lücken im Rechte' (see n. 4), p. 449; SCHLOßMANN, *Der Irrtum* (see n. 5), p. 38. [Ibid.,] p. 40 contains an important remark: the reader is reminded that the *praetor*, too, was originally free, but then bound himself by the publication of the *lex annua*, which finally became a permanent statute under Hadrian. Compare also STERNBERG, *Allgemeine Rechtslehre* (see n. 27), p. 139, note.

[57] To clarify this point, one might draw a parallel between the relation of justice to the positive law and the relation of the determination of time by the position of the sun to, for instance, middle-European time.

[58] See, for instance, BRINZ, in his review of ADICKES' *Lehre von den Rechtsquellen* (see n. 43), p. 162, in which he agrees with ADICKES' claim that 'the subjection to prior decisions may be presented as a postulate of justice: so that all are, if possible, measured by the same standard'. ADICKES had said, op. cit., pp. 54–55 that it belongs to the justice of a judicial judgment that 'the judgment on points already decided upon in the past once more contains the same decision'. Like THÖL, *Einleitung in das deutsche Privatrecht* (see n. 11), § 54, he then refers to the significance of precedents as reasons of decision. – RUDOLF SOHM, *Kirchenrecht, vol. I: Die geschichtlichen Grundlagen* (Leipzig: Duncker & Humblot, 1892), pp. 1–2: 'The law essentially depends on form (*summum jus, summa injuria*), and it must, at first, depend on form, since this is the only way in which it can arrive at a decision that stands above the parties.' Or HANS REICHEL, 'Ergänzungen zum Referat Brie', in *Archiv für Rechts- und Wirtschaftsphilosophie* 3 (1909/1910), pp. 534–535, at p. 535: 'The supreme measure of law' is justice, 'but its proximate goal is order' (from which claim REICHEL, however, draws conclusions altogether different from those presented here).

always be room for the consideration that such disregard for a clear statute is liable to raise dangers to legal intercourse, even if the statute itself is felt to be a hindrance to the same. Legal intercourse will sooner adapt to an inconvenient statute than suffer the damages that would result from the fact that one can no longer count on a clear statute. All of these considerations take their start from the thought [50] that the statute, first and foremost, wants to assure us that things are determined at all. *How* and *what* it determines is the second question. Thus an element is put into the foreground that seemingly shunts aside the 'content' of legal order, but which, in truth, belongs to the content of that order.[59] The special importance [51] this moment has for

---

[59]   In this context, mention must at least be made of a theory of customary law that strikes many defenders of the sense of justice as incomprehensible. This theory does not find the criterion of customary law in the inner conviction of the lawfulness of usage, or in this conviction in combination with a habit, but merely in continuous usage itself. Such usage, after all, contains an unambiguous regulation and suffices to satisfy the need for legal determinacy. – A treatise on customary law cannot be offered in this note, of course. An indication of the connection with the discussion in the text must suffice. The content of phrases such as 'external and fixed order', 'component of the existing order', etc. (REGELSBERGER, 'Das Subjekt der Rechtsbildung', in *Kritische Vierteljahresschrift für Gesetzgebung und Rechtswissenschaft* 4 [1862], pp. 321–348, at p. 345; FRIEDRICH JULIUS STAHL, *Die Philosophie des Rechts*, vol. II.1 [Heidelberg: J. C. B. Mohr, 1845], pp. 187–188), or of views such as 'usage is promulgation' (KARL ADOLPH VON VANGEROW, *Lehrbuch der Pandekten*, 7th edition [Marburg and Leipzig: Elwert, 1863], § 14, notes 2, 3), is intimately connected with considerations of legal determinacy. – ZITELMANN, 'Gewohnheitsrecht und Irrtum' (see n. 49), p. 461, declares the question to be, in the end, psychological: the factual usage of a norm as a legal norm generates the notion of its continuous validity. In this way, ZITELMANN grounds the juristic validity of customary law in psychological processes, just as he disposes of the will theory in customary law by pointing out that, from a psychological point of view, there is no common will endowed with a separate existence (ibid., p. 370). The psychological significance of legal determinacy, however, has a different relevance for the present investigation than it has in ZITELMANN's discussion – if only because the problem of the *creation of law*, as already noted, is to be distinguished from that of finding a criterion of legal correctness. ZITELMANN, moreover, says, on p. 419, that 'the grand speculative constructions' of the philosophers do not pertain to the doctrine of the genesis of law. He would likewise exclude them (and justifiably so) from the method of the application of law. He continues to claim that 'only the most sober reflection is within its rights here'. Certainly. But must this reflection be psychological? ZITELMANN aptly refuted SAVIGNY's and PUCHTA's theories of customary law by showing that the latter confused 'formal-juristic with material-philosophical reflection' (ibid., p. 428). To appeal to psychology instead of philosophy, however, contains the same confusion. – The contrary view found its classical expression in PUCHTA's great work on customary law (vol. II). AUGUST STURM's writings on customary law likewise belong there, because they place especially strong emphasis on the importance of the content of legal norms – an emphasis that one also finds, although in misleading phrasing, in the proverb that 'a hundred years of injustice cannot make for an hour of law'.

jurisprudence may have been the reason why many serious men with a strong sense of justice have experienced legal science as a whole to be something dissatisfactory and superficial. But the charges they level against legal science are really charges against the law itself, as was already pointed out by STAHL[60] against V. KIRCHMANN. [52] The fight against what is often misleadingly called 'formalism',[61] as well, is at times directed against nothing

[60] FRIEDRICH JULIUS VON STAHL, *Rechtswissenschaft oder Volksbewußtsein? Eine Beleuchtung des von Herrn Staatsanwalt v. Kirchmann gehaltenen Vortrags: 'Die Werthlosigkeit der Jurisprudenz als Wissenschaft'* (Berlin: A. Förstner, 1848). It may not be amiss to mention, on this occasion, that the negative evaluation this talk –which, by the way, was given in 1847, and not in the 'crazy year 1848', as RUMPF thinks (see MAX RUMPF, *Volk und Recht* [Oldenburg: G. Stalling, 1910], and compare LANDSBERG, *Geschichte der deutschen Rechtswissenschaft* [see n. 16], p. 317) – has sometimes received in times past (for instance in ERNST NEUKAMP, who, in his *Einleitung in eine Entwicklungsgeschichte des Rechts* [Berlin: C. Heymann, 1895], p. 144, speaks of its 'bombastic phraseology', or in ARTHUR NUßBAUM, 'Über Aufgabe und Wesen der Jurisprudenz', in *Wolfs Zeitschrift für Sozialwissenschaft* 9 [1906], pp. 1–17, at p. 3) has now, in all likelihood, been put to rest by THEODOR STERNBERG's book *J. H. v. Kirchmann und seine Kritik der Rechswissenschaft. Zugleich ein Beitrag zur Geschichte des realpolitischen Liberalismus* (Berlin: W. Rothschild, 1908). – An anonymous critique of V. KIRCHMANN's talk about jurisprudence 'by a teacher of this science' (RUDORFF) [compare Note III in the appendix], which is lauded by NEUKAMP, and an 'apology' for jurisprudence by RETSLAG [see n. 103], likewise an answer to V. KIRCHMANN's talk, are cited elsewhere out of historical interest, which is not meant to suggest that they are of special importance. NUßBAUM's judgment that STAHL's reply was 'excellent and unjustly forgotten' also seems to contain an exaggeration. The great historical significance of the talk is made clear by an interesting remark by KUNTZE in *Der Wendepunkt der Rechtswissenschaft* (see n. 40), who said, as late as 1856, that it hardly seemed 'as though the deep and general impression that had been left by the attack was overcome by the quickness of the resistance that was put up against it'. – The present investigation does not concern itself with a discussion of the question whether jurisprudence is a 'science'; given its principled separation of legal doctrine and legal practice, it would, at any rate, have to pose a twofold question. The position of juristic practice in the theory of science is an important and unresolved problem. The many quarrels over terminology, however, offer very little preliminary work of value, since they are teeming with absurd misunderstandings. NUßBAUM, op. cit., p. 10, for example, rejects the classification of jurisprudence as an 'art' by pointing out that jurisprudence does not aim to bring about aesthetic effects. It is not to be assumed that this is what ZITELMANN, for instance, understands by 'art' when he uses the word in the present context. When ALOIS BRINZ (*Rechtswissenschaft und Rechtsgesetzgebung. Rede gehalten zur Feier des Stiftungsfestes der Universität München am 26. Juni 1877* [Augsburg: J. G. Cotta, 1877], p. 4) or SCHLOßMANN (*Der Vertrag* [see n. 44], pp. 189–190) call jurisprudence as a *practice* an art, such a misunderstanding should, one would think, hardly be possible.

[61] In this expression, form is used as the opposite of a particular content (in this case, a content implied by substantial justice). But what one calls the form is itself a content and something substantial. Thus one might regard legal norms as vessels of justice and proclaim the sentence: the form perishes, while the matter remains. – This view of form, however, is in no way similar to STAMMLER's explanation of the law as a form of economic life (which has been criticized by MAX WEBER, 'R. Stammler's "Überwindung" der materialistischen Geschichtsauffassung', in *Archiv für Sozialwissenschaft und Sozialpolitik* 24 [1907], pp. 94–151, at p. 142, with the

[53] other than this specific characteristic of legal *order*, which ought rather to be taken as the starting point in every methodological inquiry into legal practice. This does not mean, naturally, that judges ought to become 'formalists' (which designation, in this context, refers more to a character-ological than to a juristic category). Rather, it is to be denied that one could gain the criterion of the correct judicial decision from some substantial ideal of justice or of material purposiveness.

When it is said here that the *content* of a statutory regulation is, up to a certain degree, indifferent, this is, at the same time, a statement about the content of the regulation – one that concerns its purpose. For the question concerning the correctness of a decision, the investigation was supposed to take a postulate that is factually effective as its point of departure. It is necessary, therefore, to engage in discussions of the significance of legal determinacy for the life of the law in general. These, however, are not to be understood in the following sense: the legislator may, under certain cir-cumstances, be wholly indifferent to the content of a statute and intend no

argument that a legal rule cannot be a form of social life, purely because it is conceived as something that *ought to be* valid and thus cannot be a form of what is, whereas an empirical rule of law is a component of what is and not its form). FRITZ BEROLZHEIMER, 'Eine Rechtswissenschaft der Theorie. Stammlers *Theorie der Rechtswissenschaft*', in *Archiv für Rechts- und Wirtschaftsphilosophie* 5 (1911/1912), pp. 311–320, at p. 319, objects to STAMMLER's statements in his *Theorie der Rechtswissenschaft* (see n. 14), p. 7 sqq., that matter and form are one, and that one cannot separate the form from its matter. But this objection does not hold with respect to theoretical reflection. According to STAMMLER, who (op. cit., p. 7 sqq.) protests vehemently against understanding the distinction of form and matter as a temporal or spatial one, form is to be understood as the method of cognition; the forms, to him, are the forms of juristic thought, not spatial parts of some juristic matter (op. cit., p. 182 sqq.). It is also possible that BEROLZHEIMER understands by matter precisely what STAMMLER refers to as content. If so, his objection would cease to apply, since STAMMLER emphasizes precisely the impossibility to oppose form and content to one another. – It is difficult to offer precise objections to STAMMLER, because it is impossible to pin down his fundamental concept, that of 'volition', without ambiguity. Although STAMMLER, in other respects, insistently aims to achieve clarity, he leaves this hopelessly equivocal word that is so liable to be misunderstood without a sufficient explanation. What, for instance, is supposed to be the meaning of the following sentence? 'The constructive judgment of the legal scholar can therefore never with justification arrive at any other material result than at the particular legal volition, which it formally considers with reference to the impossibility of a unified understanding' (op. cit., p. 358). If the content of volition is here to be identified with the notional content in the mind of an empirical subject, then the impossibility of a divergence between this content and the constructions of the legal scholar will remain incomprehensible, at least without mystical connections. If, on the other hand, the volition is itself a construction, and one that has been undertaken in accordance with the same method that is employed to arrive at the above-mentioned 'constructive judgment', then it is unnecessary to make a big fuss about the identity of the results. We might as well be astonished that all products arrived at by multiplication with a certain number are dividable by that number.

The latter also subsumes, because to extend the content of a statute by way of exegesis means nothing other than to increase the range of factual situations that are subsumable under the statute. Accordingly, one can declare the 'principle of subsumption' to be the essence of a just regula- tion as such; one can speak of a 'logicism of justice'.[69] The activity of subsumption that the theoretician engages in is nevertheless different from that of the practitioner. The practitioner operates with legal con- cepts; as a result, his activity, like any form of thinking, subsumes under concepts. [59] The activity of legal doctrine, by contrast, aims to deter- mine the content of a statute, and what is contained in it by way of subsumption points in the direction of legislative subsumption: legal doctrine conceives of cases as *possible*, and if it offers examples from real life, then it offers these precisely as examples – in much the same way in which concrete cases 'are on the mind of the legislator' while he is drafting a statute. The legislator proceeds from a large number of actual cases so as to arrive at a statute under which he then subsumes innumer- able cases that are conceived to be possible. The judge, by contrast, must always deal with one concrete case.[70] Even if one were to say, therefore, that the judge ought to do nothing more than to try to find out whether the case with which he is faced is one of those that the legislator conceived as possible, one would have to find for his activity a method altogether different, since it is not the same as that of scientific exegesis. The latter lists the cases that are conceived to be possible,[71] and increases or decreases their number, while the judge is to determine that one such

---

[69] THEODOR STERNBERG, in *Archiv für Rechts- und Wirtschaftsphilosophie* 2 (1908/1909), p. 297, in a review of Karl GAREIS, *Vom Begriff Gerechtigkeit* (Gießen: A. Töpelmann, 1907), emphasizes GAREIS's sentence: 'A regulation based on justice differs from a lower one based on mere opportunism (principle of utility) as well as from a higher one based on the principle of love for one's neighbour, by virtue of its immediate connection with the law of thought, the principle of subsumption.' The text explains further why an affirmation of these sentences, which are directed towards a criterion of *justice*, does not stand in contradiction with the struggle against the view that the 'subsumability' of a decision under statute is the criterion of the *correctness of the decision*.

[70] ADOLF FRIEDRICH STÖLZEL, 'Review of: J. Maaßen, *Die Auslegung der Gesetze aus den sogenannten Materialen, dargestellt an der Vormundschaft über Geisteskranke und Verschwender*', in *Gruchots Beiträge zur Erläuterung des deutschen Rechts* 22 (1878), pp. 280–288, at p. 286: 'The intellectual activity of the one who has to formulate a new legal thought, from the point of view of the legislator', is 'squarely opposed to the intellectual activity of the one who, from the point of view of the judge or advocate, has to subsume a question that confronts him in real life under that legal thought.' – At any rate, the two activities are so different that their methods cannot be the same.

[71] STAMMLER, *Theorie der Rechtswissenschaft* (see n. 14), p. 578: the analysis of positive law amounts 'to deciding possible future cases in legal norms that already exist'.

case is present *in concreto*. Even if it were demanded of every decision that it be 'source-based', it would nevertheless be impermissible to hold the method of practice to be identical with that of legal doctrine, for the reason that it is always only a matter of fact that is subsumable under a statute, not a decision. This already constitutes proof that 'subsumability' cannot be regarded as a criterion of the correctness of a decision; at best, one might say that a decision is correct if it subsumes correctly. But this is to recognize that the problem concerns the *correctness* of subsumption and one cannot determine the correctness of a subsumption by engaging in further subsumption. This was our reason, after all, for rejecting 'conformity to statute' or – what [60] likely amounts to the same thing – 'subsumability' as the criterion of the correctness of decision and looking out for a less objectionable one. The discussion of legal determinacy was undertaken in the service of this latter purpose. To understand legal determinacy as a postulate provides us with a normative point of view. The remarks concerning the factual significance of the demand for legal determinacy were meant to further delimit the topic. The aim is to find the sense of contemporary legal practice and to identify its specific criterion of correctness. The choice of this particular postulate (and not, say, of that of 'justice') is justified by the fact that it is capable of answering the question of correctness for every decision. Criteria that refer to substantial justice or some other content cannot do that in all those cases in which it is more important to decide at all than to decide in a particular way.

Now, there have been many attempts to give an explanation of the rich significance of the mere fact of regulation as such. One has pointed to the elementary significance of legal certainty for legal life as a whole. But it would be a misunderstanding to confuse the point of departure and the arguments of BENTHAM,[72] for instance, with those that have been presented here. BENTHAM points out that, without legal certainty,

---

[72] JEREMY BENTHAM, *Principles of the Civil Code*, in *The Works of Jeremy Bentham*, ed. John Bowring, vol. I (Edinburgh: William Tait, 1843), pp. 299–364, especially at p. 307 and p. 311 sqq., and compare the quote further below [see n. 74]. The French edition of the *Principles of the Civil Code*, which appeared in 1820 and is typically cited was, by chance, unavailable to me while I wrote this work.

It would serve no purpose to try to collect the countless occasional utterances of as many different authors as possible. Such utterances are usually made casually and always without the intention to gain thereby a methodological principle for the evaluation of legal practice. What is more, one usually intends to give support to the principle of 'conformity to statute' and to prove its significance for the national economy, which is also what BENTHAM intends to do.

everything would dissolve into war and strife, no one would be able to enjoy the fruits of their labour, industriousness and entrepreneurialism would therewith disappear, and a society based on a division of labour would become impossible. Psychologically, he claims, this is grounded in the fact that **[61]** every citizen expects life to continue to progress along the accustomed path and assumes that changes will take place so gradually as not to give rise to any disorder. This assumption, the 'exspectation' [English, misspelt, in the original], is said to be the foundation of all legal certainty. The legislator, accordingly, is said to have a duty to formulate his statutes in such a way, with such clarity, that every reasonable human being is able to understand them at first glance and capable of becoming acquainted with them. Judicial exegesis, furthermore, will accordingly have to understand the statute in its literal sense – in the way it is understood, without further ado, by every ordinary citizen. Any exegesis that goes beyond the clear literal meaning is to be regarded as a sin against legal certainty: the 'inestimable good' [English in the original] that ought to take precedence, in cases of conflict, even to justice itself.

What is most interesting about BENTHAM is how he takes it for granted that one can draw conclusions for the application of law from the general significance of law in social life as well as from the duties of the legislator, and how he emphasizes the connection between the 'addressee' of the statute – whom he identifies, without further question, with the people[73] – and practical interpretation. The activity of the judge is evaluated in accordance with the (state-political) activity of the legislator. For BENTHAM, this does not mean what it means today when someone declares the 'will of the legislator' to be decisive. It means only that **[62]** one and the same criterion of correctness is held to apply to the

---

[73] HEGEL, *Grundlinien der Philosophie des Rechts* (see n. 17), § 215: 'To hang the laws at such height that no citizen could read them, as Dionysius the Tyrant did, is an injustice of exactly the same kind as to bury them in an extensive apparatus of learned books and collections of verdicts based on divergent judgments, opinions, practices, etc., all expressed in a foreign language, so that knowledge of the laws currently in force is accessible only to those who have made them an object of scholarly study' [Hegel (1991), 246–247]. – Compare ERNST ZITELMANN, *Die Kunst der Gesetzgebung* (Dresden: Zahn und Jaensch, 1904), p. 15, who poses the alternatives: popularity or logical sophistication? What is relevant here are not the different views on statutory technique, but only the fact that there is a connection between one's understanding of the 'norm addressees' and the rules of interpretation, as is clearly outlined in MAX ERNST MAYER's book *Rechtsnormen und Kulturnormen* (Breslau: Schletter, 1903), p. 26 sqq., whose specific views on the norm addressee and on the factors of interpretation are not, however, to be accepted.

activity of both the legislator and the judge: they are both supposed to conform to the general anticipation, to the 'exspectation' [English, mis-spelt, in the original]; their activity is supposed to be calculable. As a result, BENTHAM arrives at conclusions for the position of the judge that are starkly opposed to opinions, as are often voiced today, that attribute to the judge a 'quasi-legislative' activity and demand of him that he think of himself as a legislator, in cases of doubt, and that he decide as the latter would have decided had he been faced with the same concrete case. BENTHAM would have regarded a judicial position as free as this as something impossible and morally objectionable. For him, the question whether a judge ought to create new law, or perhaps only to 'promote' it, cannot even appear. Every departure from the clear and intelligible wording of the statute, every interpretation other than the grammatical, any form of 'construction', every analogical transfer of the rules applic-able to one kind of factual situation to another, appears to him as an unspeakable crime for which he finds the most vigorous words of con-demnation.[74] [63]

---

[74] The passage is worthy of being cited in full. It is also directed against many of those who take themselves to be free of a 'rigid faith in the literal wording' or who want to apply statute in its 'free spirit', but who object to the abandonment of 'conformity to statute' as the criterion of decision by suddenly appealing to 'legal certainty', even though 'conform-ity to statute' is nothing more than a phrase. – BENTHAM says, in *Principles of the Civil Code* (see n. 72), p. 325: 'To interpret has signified entirely different things in the mouth of a lawyer and in the mouth of another person: to interpret a passage of an author, is to show the meaning which he had in his mind; to interpret a law in the sense of a Roman lawyer is to neglect the clearly expressed intention in order to substitute some other by presuming that this new sense was the actual intention of the legislator. – With this manner of proceeding there is no security. When the law is difficult, obscure, incoherent, the citizen has always a chance of knowing it: it gives a blind warning, less efficacious than it might be, but always useful: the limits of the evil which may be suffered are at least perceived. But when the judge dares to arrogate to himself the power of interpreting the laws, that is to say, of substituting his will for that of the legislator, every thing is arbitrary – no one can foresee the course which his caprice may take. It is not enough to regard this evil in itself alone: how great soever it may be, it is a trifle in comparison to the weight of its consequences. The serpent, it is said, can cause its whole body to enter at the opening through which its head will pass: with regard to legal tyranny, it is against this subtle head that we should guard, for fear of shortly seeing displayed in its train all its tortuous folds ... All usurpation of a power superior to the law, though useful in its immediate effects, ought to be an object of dread for the future. There are limits, and narrow limits, to the good which may result from this arbitrary power: there are none to the evil, there are none to the alarm, which may arise from it ... He (the judge) is always sure to save himself, either by the literal or by the interpretative sense ...' [The German text contains the original English version of this quote, which is then followed by Schmitt's own transla-tion. The latter is omitted here.]

BENTHAM, however, practises legal politics and social science, not jurisprudence. If the moment of abstract determination is emphasized here, then this stands in no more than an external connection to legal certainty as BENTHAM understands it. Because, here, it is not its macroeconomic or social-psychological significance that is of interest,[75] **[64]** but rather the fact that the moment of substantive indifference that is contained in any legal norm makes it impossible to portray criteria that make reference to a content, such as that of justice (in the sense of the dominant value judgments of the people), as generally sufficient. If, now, attention is drawn to the empirical significance of legal determinacy (the word 'legal certainty' points too much in the direction of the psychological process of the 'exspectation' [English, misspelt, in the original]), this is not intended to prove the correctness of the criterion and much less to posit a rule of interpretation. It is meant only to show that this methodological principle is not alien to modern practice – that it is not imposed on it from the outside. Practice itself is governed by the aspiration to provide *calculable* decisions. The pursuit of a logically compelling line of proof, of a construction that satisfies the understanding, is nothing more than a misunderstood method of reaching this goal; the very acumen the respect for which seems to have all but disappeared today[76] was meant to help to bring forth legal determinacy. It will therefore have to be regarded as permissible to pursue the problem of the correct decision from this side, for once, instead of searching, as one has always done thus far, for the contents that legitimate the content of the decision. To reject this approach, it already suffices to point out

---

[75] BENTHAM, at any rate, does not intend to provide a method for the application of law. His starting point, the egoism of human beings, can be a justified fiction (compare VAIHINGER [see n. 15], pp. 354–357). But it concerns his theory of the state and of society. He does not perceive the application of law to be problematic in any way.

[76] At any rate, the ability to orient oneself within a large number of complicated statutes and to perform fitting subsumptions under them is not, in itself, a proof of high intellectual culture: the most primitive peoples accomplish astonishing feats of this kind. HENRI ALEXANDRE JUNOD, *Les Ba-Rongas. Étude ethnographique sur les indigènes de la baie de Delagoa* (Neuchâtel: Attinger, 1898) reports, for instance, that the Ba-Ronga (a tribe of negroes in Africa with fetish cults) move within the complicated prescriptions of their religion and law with surprising ingenuity and a great deal of 'logic', and MARY HENRIETTA KINGSLEY, *West African Studies* (London: Macmillan, 1899) says the same about West Africans. (Both cited in EDVARD LEHMAN, 'Die Anfänge der Religion und die Religion der primitiven Völker', in *Die Kultur der Gegenwart*, ed. Paul Hinneberg, vol. 1, part III [Berlin and Leipzig: B. G. Teubner, 1906], pp. 1–29, at p. 10). Happily, this Ba-Ronga ingenuity does not, with us today, seem to hold any longer as an ideal.

that the judicial decision can also be indifferent to such contents, since there are judicial decisions that are driven more by the need to decide at all than by the need to decide in a particular way – [65] just as the statute can behave indifferently towards an extra-statutory content.[77]

The judgment of the judge nevertheless stands in a relation to its justification that differs from the relation of a statute to its 'motives'. In this context, there can be no question whatsoever of any form of equality of position. That one has frequently, in recent times, compared the judge's activity with that of the legislator does not in any way change the fact that the two activities are different in principle. That such comparisons are drawn is only an example of how similarities in the content of activities and in their accompanying psychological processes suffice, for many, to let any difference in method disappear. The complete independence of the statute from its materials manifests itself externally in the manner and form of publication; one has also made appeal to considerations of legal certainty to account for that independence.[78] But such considerations, which lead to a strict separation of the

[77] How difficult it is to maintain methodological clarity in dealing with the question of legal determinacy may be illustrated with the following example. ANTONIO PAGANO, in *Rivista italiana per le scienze giuridiche* 49 (1911), pp. 70–71, contests the claims of HENRI ROLIN, *Prolégomènes à la science du droit. Esquisse d'une sociologie juridique* (Bruxelles: E. Bruylant, 1911), who had said that if one were to imagine that article 544 of the *Code Civil*, with its definition of property (*la propriété est le droit de jouir et de disposer des choses de la manière la plus absolue*) did not exist, the fact of property would nevertheless continue to persist. PAGANO, who declares the law to be a '*scienza deduttiva di principi razionali*' ['science deduced from rational principles'], says that this is no longer jurisprudence. ROLIN, PAGANO claims, overlooks '*la delimitazione e la garantia, che costituiscono l'oggetto proprio ed immediato della norma giuridica*' ['the delimitation and the guarantee that constitute the proper and immediate object of the legal norm'] – as if this delimitation were not already a piece of social science and as if it still had anything to do with the deduction from '*principi razionali*' ['rational principles'].

[78] KRAUS aptly pointed out that the insignificance of the materials of a statute results sufficiently from the need for legal certainty alone (KRAUS, 'Die leitenden Grundsätze' [see n. 34], p. 613 sqq.). He consequently had to arrive at BENTHAM's results, but in the second part of his essay, he focuses exclusively on 'justice', from which perspective the abstract element of determination does not come into view. – It should also be mentioned here that FELIX DAHN, 'Die Lehre von den Rechtsquellen, insbesondere vom Gewohnheitsrecht', in *Behrends Zeitschrift für die deutsche Gesetzgebung und für einheitliches deutsches Recht* 6 (1872), pp. 553–583, at p. 562, says of the law that it is 'not an arbitrary but a reasonable legal order' and that 'a hundred years of injustice do not amount to law for a single year'. To this, he adds the following interesting remark: '[S]poken truthfully: "justice" has a lot less to do with jurisprudence than laypersons and some sympathetic jurists tend to assume.'

statute and the statutory materials, and which imply the irrelevance of the latter for the interpretation [66] of the statute, speak in favour of the demand that a judicial decision be given a justification. There is no judgment without justification; the justification belongs to the decision. Not merely because it helps to make the tenor of the judgment comprehensible and thus, together with the relevant facts, helps to individualize it, but above all because the question of the correctness of the statute contains a problem altogether different from the problem that is contained in the question of the correctness of a decision. The latter always arises within the frame of an existing legal order. The correctness of a decision is therefore dependent on positive statutory norms. From this, one has drawn the conclusion, rather too quickly, that the correct decision must be logically derivable from statute, while one has overlooked that the problem lies in how to determine this *dependence*, in its ground and its scope. The decision must be justified – that is, it must explain why it is correct – given the specific legal situation in which it is issued. Considerations of this sort are, naturally, beside the point in case of a statute.

For the observation of the content of a legal norm in relation to a 'pre-juristic complex of norms',[79] one can draw a line from the point at which these pre-juristic contents uniquely determine the content of the statute to the opposing point at which the content is indifferent and at which fixation alone is what is essential. For the relation of a judicial decision to the contents that play a role in its justification, one can think of a similar line. As far as the exegesis of the legal norm is concerned, legal norms are capable of supporting an exegesis other than the literal the less or more they approximate the point of material indifference; the significance of literal exegesis thus stands in a functional relation to the significance of the moment of abstract fixation. One can see an interesting historical confirmation for this in the fact that literal exegesis is exclusively predominant wherever the statute is considered to be the arbitrary act of an individual (in particular of a God). [67] It remains for the following chapter to show how important it is for a judicial decision to determine the point at which it is located in relation to the contents that figure in its justification. That such a relation of indifference is possible, however, suffices to prove how far criteria that refer to 'pre-juristic' contents are from being capable of explaining all phenomena of

---

[79] Max Ernst Mayer's expression in 'Glossen zur Schuldlehre', in *Zeitschrift für die gesamte Strafrechtswissenschaft* 32 (1911), pp. 492–514, at p. 496.

legal practice. Neither the notion of 'conformity to statute' – that is, of a decision's groundedness in sources – nor that of its justice, or its conformity to culture, or its reasonableness, therefore, can provide practice with its criterion. In the following chapter, it shall be explained why the idea of legal determinacy is capable of doing so.

Chapter IV

The Correct Decision

In view of the facts that the criterion of 'conformity to statute' is worthless, that those criteria that refer to 'pre-juristic' complexes of norms must ignore important facts of legal life and, finally, that it is necessary to find a criterion that is autochthonous to legal practice, the following formula will no longer appear to be paradoxical or challenging:

> A judicial decision is correct, today, if it is to be assumed that another judge would have decided in the same way. 'Another judge', in this context, refers to the empirical type of the modern, legally trained jurist.

The close connection of this formula to the postulate of legal determinacy is intuitively clear and will be spelled out, in its specifics, in the following exposition. To start with, the following characteristics of the formula are to be emphasized. *First*: it explains a number of phenomena that are characteristic of modern legal practice and in such a way that these phenomena can be seen to contain an argument for the formula. The principle of collegiality in contemporary legal practice, as well as the phenomenon of 'reasons of decision', are especially noteworthy among these. *Second*: the formula contains a consistent solution for the complications that result from the fact that, on the one hand, the authority of statute must be safeguarded, even while, on the other hand, decisions *praeter* or sometimes even *contra legem* [decisions that 'go beyond' or 'against the law'] – which are regarded to be correct even though they can hardly be called 'source-based', whether they are backed up by constant practice or by precedents set by the highest courts or not – may, at times, have to be issued. That the decision's 'conformity to statute' is no longer identified with its correctness does not entail [**69**] that one must give up on an objective standard and leave everything to be determined by the subjectivity of the judge.[80] – If the formula, moreover, explains the significance of precedent and has the capacity to bring this explanation into full accord with its other explanations, then it will have proved its entitlement to be regarded as the proper guiding principle of contemporary legal practice. –

One will have occasion to continue to dispute the question whether collegial courts are to be preferred to individual judges for a long time to come. The preference for the individual judge, at any rate, is closely connected to certain views concerning the method of practice.[81] The preference for the principle of collegiality is expressed, in the form of legal practice that prevails today, in the fact that the number of judges who are involved in a decision tends to increase with the importance of the case at hand. It is impossible to make sense of this phenomenon by offering the trivial explanation that three human beings see more than one and that seven see more than five. For one, that rather [70] depends, and it is well known, secondly, that the contemporary procedure of collegial courts is such that a rapporteur works through the case and then reports in deliberation, whereby the 'seeing more' of the larger number becomes problematic. The discussions in deliberation turn exclusively on questions of law on which one must reach agreement. The many attacks on this 'system of rapporteurs' derive from a misunderstanding of the true point of the

---

[80] This is actually self-evident – but, as things stand today, such self-evident truths still need to be given emphasis if they are to be noticed.

[81] KANTOROWICZ finds protection against excesses of subjectivity in the majority of a collegium of judges and in the possibility of appeal to a higher instance – even while he otherwise, in his *Kampf um die Rechtswissenschaft* (see n. 12), p. 41, takes everything to depend on the personality of the judge and denies that there are judgments of general validity. But it would be a misunderstanding to take KANTOROWICZ to be committed to this latter view. The determining factor of his approach is expressed in a sentence in *Zur Lehre vom richtigen Recht* (see n. 23), p. 25: the judge must pay heed to a 'sense of justice that expresses itself authoritatively' and must fill out the gaps in the law in accordance with it; the law that is found in this way 'is to be applied by the judge without regard to his own sentiment'. KANTOROWICZ's talk 'Rechtswissenschaft und Soziologie' (see n. 38) in the proceedings of the First Annual German Conference of Sociologists, is likewise concerned with the identification of heteronomous norms (the published talk also contains references to the literature from which one can infer KANTOROWICZ's position on adjudication *contra legem*). – In order to give an example of what is possible in discussions on these questions, it should be mentioned that TEN HOMPEL, 'Rechtsmethodik und Praxis', in *Archiv für Rechts- und Wirtschaftsphilosophie* 3 (1909/1910), pp. 551–572, at p. 562, wants to portray the view that a judge would be justified, under certain circumstances, in deciding arbitrarily, as proposed by KANTOROWICZ in *Der Kampf um die Rechtswissenschaft* (see n. 12), as the product of the enthusiasm of an overman whose thinking has been unbalanced by NIETZSCHE and that TEN HOMPEL thinks thus to have reduced that view *ad absurdum*.

majority rule in adjudication. Decision-taking by majority is meant to even out individual differences in *legal opinion*. The point, then, is to achieve a general legal determinacy, a communicability (that is, an intellectualiza-tion) of the reasons for the decision, whereby the decision is to be made foreseeable and calculable, as well as to be made to fit in with legal practice as a whole. The complaint has been raised that the individual personality of a judge is getting lost in these majority decisions taken by collegium.[82] But originality as such can have little significance for the law as an existing order, and all ideas of the power and dignity of 'personality' move within extra-juristic categories.[83] It is self-evident that the criterion of the correct-ness of a judicial decision in contemporary legal practice (and in every legal practice) cannot refer to individual emotional processes or to the individ-ual's subjective conviction; it must always take the form of a heteronomous evaluation. It would, however, be incorrect to argue as follows:[84] the sense of justice of the community as a whole is the decisive factor for the correctness of the judgment; the larger the number of judges, the higher the likelihood that the decision fits this sense of justice and the larger the approximation [71] to the views of the whole. This view, which would have to assume that a mass vote is the ideal way of taking every single decision, disregards the fact that the question concerns a multitude of *judges* and their deliberation on *reasons of decision*. There can be no doubt that an individual endowed with a strong sense of justice, if the case engages it at all, will find a solution that is conformable to our sense of justice with as much certainty as three or five human beings and that larger masses are thus unnecessary to achieve an approximation to the average. To decide in accordance with our sense of justice, and with juristic tact, remains, in the last analysis, a matter for the individual. Naturally, a collegium is likewise capable of finding a decision that conforms to the sense of justice, or one that 'juristic tact' would have hit upon at first glance – but it does not do so as a collegium. 'Juristic tact' reduces to a capability for intuitive insight. To exercise intuition, however, is a matter for the individual or – one might think of this as another possibility – for a sociological whole. All this entails

---

[82] ADICKES, *Stellung und Tätigkeit des Richters* (see n. 30), p. 9.

[83] It needs to be emphasized here as well that, in saying this, we do not intend to express any derogatory view on the moral justification, the scientific necessity and the practical usefulness of such ideas.

[84] AUGUST STURM, *Die Bedeutung der Mehrheit in der Rechtsgebung und in der Rechtsprechung. Ein wissenschaftlicher Beitrag zur Lösung der Frage nach der Besetzung der Richterstellen und nach der Bedeutung des Anwaltsprozesses* (Halle: Buchandlung des Waisenhauses, 1908) who, incidentally, deserves credit for having reminded us of this connection between the principle of majority and the correctness of decision.

that a collegium of judges, such as the second civil chamber of a
Landgericht,^{xiii} cannot cognize intuitively. A collegium, moreover, does
not in any way intend to do that; it is always concerned with the presentation and the articulate development of *reasons* for decision. What matters
here is not to adapt adjudication to a popular understanding of the law,
that is not the point of the collegial system. The point is, rather, that a
decision whose reasons have been scrutinized by several judges is more
likely to be foreseeable and calculable. It is more likely that other judges
would have decided in the same way. The issue always concerns *judges* and
legal practice. In making decisions calculable, one also simultaneously
conforms to the sense of justice, since the evenness and predictability of
the decision belong, after all, to the most important postulates of justice.
Both aims are, in fact, accomplished by having decisions taken by a
majority of judges and this is also what is to be accomplished by major-
ity-decision, according to the idea. There is no doubt that if all judgments
were issued by seven judges, adjudication would be more uniform, across
the whole country, than if there were only individual judges. [72] A
collegium, even where the attacks against a certain legal approach become
intense and general, will not move away from its 'constant practice' as
easily as a single judge will abandon his convictions.[85] This tendency
towards stability and thus towards legal determinacy, which is immanent
to the idea of adjudication by majority, must be taken note of and be

---

[85] A 'Sociology of the Collegium of Judges' has not yet been written. It would show that it is
no contradiction for the text to first deny the capability of the collegium as such to arrive
at intuitive cognition on the basis of some matter of fact and to claim that it is not a
sociological unity, whereas the collegium now appears as the bearer of a constant practice
with peculiar tendencies and aims. In each case, the purpose that constituted the unity of
the collegium (the deliberation on reasons of decision) excludes any intuitive cognition,
but not, therewith, the conservative tendency that, as experience shows, governs the
adjudication of collegial courts.
   A confusion that is interesting in the context of the presentation in the text underpins
JOHANNES FRIEDRICH KIERULFF's sentence, in *Theorie des Gemeinen Civilrechts*
(Altona: J. F. Hammerich, 1839), p. 41: 'It is the judge's duty, who ought to effectuate
the true law, to put more trust into the objective feeling of a number of learned jurists than
into his own subjective tact.' What is meant by 'objective feeling'? It is not that the feeling
of a number of educated jurists is the determining measure, but rather that the decision is
correct if the 'educated jurist', taken as a type, would have taken it in the same way. The
assent of a number of learned jurists offers a greater guarantee of that. The 'learned jurist'
is the one who is to be convinced (the precedent is a symptom of a conviction) and this
explains KIERULFF's further sentence: 'In this domain, legal usage is never going to
become dispensable, and it is here that it fulfils its peculiar destiny to further the
determinacy of the law.' – It should be noted that KIERULFF was a respected practitioner,
despite his adherence to a 'speculative positivism'.

explained by a methodological investigation of contemporary legal practice. It is to be mentioned, in passing, that the necessity to take note of a
phenomenon like that of the collegiality of adjudication contains an argument for the justification of a method that is specific to practice, as well as
for investigations of that practice. The very thought of a majority, of a
collegium, would be inappropriate for a theoretical reconstruction of the
positive law, for a scientific system.

The opportunity to move through various stages of appeal stands in the
most intimate connection with the significance of the majority decision in
adjudication. [73] The availability of several stages of appeal likewise
points in the direction of objectivity, it contains a proclamation of the
strictest heteronomy and a negation of everything that is subjective. The
stages of appeal therefore have the same enemies as the collegium. Like
the latter, they tend towards legal determinacy, by appeal to which, taken as
a postulate, they might be justified – although the idea of hierarchical
superiority also comes into play here, due to the inevitable precedential
character of decisions taken by highest courts, all of which suggests very
strongly the (methodological) autonomy of practice (as a unified whole)
with regard to the decision on the correctness of a judgment. The proposed
formula, given that it refers to 'another judge', might be seen to find its
refutation precisely in the phenomenon of stages of appeal, insofar as
modification brought about by a higher instance and the possibility that
all three instances might take different decisions might be seen to undermine the practical significance of the formula. But if someone were to
make this objection, they would misunderstand the purpose of a methodological investigation, as well as the point of a formula for the correctness of judicial decision. Such a formula does not presume to change the
face of practice – to bring all decisions that are issued after it becomes
known into a general conformity with legal prescription – or to reduce the
number of legal proceedings, to lower the income of lawyers, to make
higher courts superfluous or at least to disburden them of some of their
workload. It intends all of this no more than a formula of aesthetics intends
to create geniuses or to offer a practical recipe for the production of eternal
values. What it intends to accomplish – and what it ought to be able to
accomplish – is to provide standards for the evaluation of a judgment, to
assess the probative force of the reasons offered for a decision and to show
up the heterogeneity of the arguments employed in an unmethodical
justification. The formula is supposed to establish what considerations
are at all admissible as arguments in legal practice, and thus to help practice
to reflect on its own means and ways. It is only in doing so that it becomes

practically valuable. Even the decisions of the highest court of justice are subject to our formula's criterion and this criterion casts a novel light on the problem of revision (in the event of a 'violation of statute'). [74] Thus that two judges are taking different decisions is no objection. No more is said than that the tendency and the point of their activity – of the justifications they offer for their decisions – is to decide like every other judge, and to present the conviction that their decisions are foreseeable and calculable. As soon as judges become clear about the point of their activity, they will be in a position to judge which considerations are fit to serve as reasons for decision – to assess what might count as a fully valid argument. By pointing to the dissimilarity of judgments and decisions, one intends to object to the hypothetical formulation of the proposed formula. It is argued that it is practically infeasible to ascertain how another judge would have decided, probably because one imagines that it will be necessary to perform psychological analyses of other judges, and perhaps one will be tempted to add the following clever remark: if a judge decides incorrectly, it will have been shown, therewith, that not every other judge would have decided in the same way. – Naturally, the formula does not speak of every individual judge. Its hypothetical formulation (which was chosen consciously) is not meant to point towards something factual that would have happened if it were not for the fact that something else came to pass. It also does not want to investigate the behaviour of other judges, so as to infer a legal norm from it[86] under which the decision that is to be evaluated would then have to be subsumed; it would be a psychological misunderstanding to regard it as a call to engage in mass psychological observation of judges. To take such a perspective is naturally possible and an inquiry in this direction would be valuable, just as it would be possible to adopt that stance with reference to the sentence, 'act only according to the maxim of which you can at the same time will that it become a universal law', [75] without taking away or even touching its normative significance. The proposed formula likewise has nothing to do with a statutory command addressed to the judge; it merely provides the methodological principle of contemporary legal prac-tice. The reference to the 'other judge' as an empirical type is only an expression for the constitutive significance of the postulate of legal deter-minacy for the question of the correctness of a decision. A judge who

---

[86]   BÜLOW, *Gesetz und Richteramt* (see n. 6), p. 45, aptly says that what he refers to as 'judge-made law' does not consist of abstract legal norms, but that 'judge-made law' nonetheless exists and that its denial would be a self-denial. The only way of explaining Bülow's view without contradiction is to see in the 'judge-made law' a recognition of the methodo-logical autonomy of the criterion of legal practice.

wants to decide correctly does not, therefore, have to codify the views of all other judges, so to speak, and then to subsume under that codification. That, needless to say, would be the old error that regards 'conformity to statute' as the criterion of the correctness of a decision. Rather, the judge has to make an effort to make sure that his decision is conformable to actual practice and that, if he departs from a dominant opinion, he does so with arguments that are so compelling that the departure remains within the realm of the foreseeable and calculable. The reasons offered for decision therefore can, under certain circumstances, possess a creative significance, insofar as they go on to determine the activity of other judges and are capable of bringing about a regular practice. In no case, however, is a judge permitted to exercise an absolutely free discretion – to follow his own particular subjectivity or his personal conviction as such; the 'other judge', of course, is the normal, legally trained judge. The word 'normal' is used here in a quantitative sense that refers to the average, not as the designation of an ideal type and not in a qualitative-teleological sense.This empirical type of the normal judge,[87] of which any practice-oriented methodological doctrine must take account, is something [76] wholly other, in its logical structure, than the 'legislator' or the 'will of statute'. These latter are from the beginning ideal constructions, and this excludes, in their case, any possibility of assigning an empirical probability or of drawing any connection therewith. The empirical type of legislator does not concern jurisprudence. The ideal type of 'legislator' is a construction that legal practice has been unable to complete in hundreds of years. Any derivation from an idea of law that claims atemporal validity is either hostile to any content and thus devoid of value

---

[87] This is the point at which the characterological investigations of the jurist that were undertaken by THEODOR STERNBERG (*Charakterologie als Wissenschaft* [Lausanne: E. Frankfurter, 1907]; *J. H. v. Kirchmann und seine Kritik der Rechtswissenschaft* [see n. 60]; *Einführung in the Rechtswissenschaft* [see n. 12], § 14, unfortunately so far without continuing them) connect to the discussion in the text. It is to be noted, though, that the question concerning the correctness of judicial decision is not, therewith, to be turned into a mere empirical investigation. If the formula of the correct decision contains moments that introduce empirical contents, it does not thereby turn into an explicative explanation for empirical processes. The normative perspective has not been abandoned. We do not say: the judicial decision is correct because it is generally held to be so by judges, but rather that it is correct *if* it is held to be so; if it is to be expected of it that another judge would have taken it in the same way and may the content be ever so similar, these are always two different points of view. For the views expressed in the text, the empirical judge is merely an element in the formula; he is not the point of departure. The point of departure remains a postulate: that of legal determinacy.

for practice,[88] or it surrenders itself in order to become useful to practice. [77] Now, it is to be admitted that the standards that VAN CALKER,[89] for instance, derives from his theory of perfection – by using the valid (i.e. those recognized as valid) evaluative judgments of the people so as to provide the concept of law, which is in itself indifferent and devoid of content, with directly applicate contents – often permit of a direct employment in practice. The same is true of the content that can be given to KOHLER's or BEROLZHEIMER's

---

[88] This also accounts for the marginal influence on legal practice, in comparison to the scientific achievement, of STAMMLER's ideas. Even STAMMLER's 'descent to individual questions' does not provide practice with any of that on which it wholly depends. Nothing is gained by making appeal to the principles of 'freedom' and of 'sharing', unless their *boundaries* are indicated, and on this question STAMMLER does not even provide a formal account (GUSTAV RADBRUCH, 'Review of: Alexander Graf zu Dohna, *Die Rechtswidrigkeit als allgemeingültiges Merkmal im Tatbestande strafbarer Handlungen'*, in *Aschaffenburgs Monatsschrift für Kriminalpsychologie und Strafrechtsreform* 1 [1904/ 1905], pp. 599–601, at p. 600; GUSTAV RADBRUCH, 'Die politische Prognose der Strafrechtsreform', in *Aschaffenburgs Monatsschrift für Kriminalpsychologie und Strafrechtsreform* 5 [1908/1909], pp. 1–7, at p. 5; BRÜTT, *Die Kunst der Rechtsanwendung* [see n. 12], § 7; KANTOROWICZ, *Zur Lehre vom richtigen Recht* [see n. 23], pp. 33–34). A formula can have significance for practice only if it takes account of the specific characteristics of practice. – On STAMMLER, compare also: BERGBOHM, *Jurisprudenz und Rechtsphilosophie* (see n. 20) p. 141 sqq., note 15 (against STAMMLER's argument in the essay 'Über die Methode der geschichtlichen Rechtstheorie', in *Festgabe zu Bernhard Windscheids fünfzigjährigem Doktorjubiläum* [Halle: M. Niemeyer, 1888], pp. 1–64). BERGBOHM says that STAMMLER's argument would have to lead to contents and thus to a natural law; he then goes on to explain it psychologically, as an expression of the wish for justice: NEUKAMP, *Einleitung in eine Entwicklungsgeschichte* (see n. 60), pp. 55–56; WALTER STAFFEL, 'Über Stammlers Lehre vom richtigen Recht', in *Ihering's Jahrbücher für die Dogmatik des bürgerlichen Rechts* 50 (1906), pp. 301–322; JULIUSZ MAKAREWICZ, *Juristische Abhandlungen* (Leipzig and Vienna: F. Deuticke, 1907), p. 7 sqq. See, above all others, MAX WEBER's article, which has already been cited, in *Archiv für Sozialwissenschaft und Sozialpolitik* (see n. 61). – When HEGEL, *Grundlinien der Philosophie des Rechts* (see n. 17), p. 7 (§ 3), opposes the 'philosophical' law to the 'practical' and strictly rejects any derivation of the one from the other, he probably simply means to refer to the contrast between 'theoretical' and 'practical' legal theory, which is also emphasized by STAMMLER.

[89] *Politik als Wissenschaft* (Leipzig, 1899) [see the comment in n. 13]; *Ethische Werte im Strafrecht* (see n. 13); 'Gesetzgebungspolitik und Rechtsvergleichung', in *Festschrift Paul Laband gewidmet von der rechts- und staatswissenschaftlichen Fakultät der Kaiser-Wilhelms-Universität Straßburg* (Tübingen: Mohr Siebeck, 1908), pp. 97–118. What is important here is the distinction between legislative policy and legal policy. The former is the doctrine of the means (which require special investigation) by which the demands that are correctly discovered by legal policy are to be implemented. Compare VAN CALKER's article '*Rechtspolitik*', in *Handbuch der Politik*, ed. Paul Laband et al., 2nd edition, vol. I (Berlin and Leipzig: W. Rothschild, 1914), pp. 11–14, as well as 'Gesetzgebungspolitik', in *Deutsche Juristen-Zeitung* 17 (1912), cols. 177–183, at col. 181.

'cultural ideal' or to M. E. MAYER's 'cultural norms'. It would be an inappropriate objection to point out how difficult it is to clearly determine such value judgments in more complicated cases. The employment of such notions has a purpose wholly other than that of enabling a comfortable and secure decision of every concrete case. VAN CALKER's idea of perfection, for example, has an immediate significance for legal policy, insofar as it offers standards for the evaluation of old and for the identification of new law; it has further immediate significance for the scientific reconstruction of the positive law, insofar as even an interpretation of the positive law, as appears to be generally recognized now, cannot make do without a highest principle of evaluation.[90] The present investigation, however, opposes the method of practice to that of legal science. The immediate validity of the principle of perfection is negated, because the latter can come into consideration only so as to evaluate, in its turn, the principle that is to be regarded as the basis of practice – [78] that is, so as to determine whether the criterion that has been found in practice is itself to be regarded as correct, and whether the decision that must be regarded as correct today can be considered to be true and just from a higher vantage point. It has already been emphasized that the introduction of moments of substantial justice, as it is implied by the employment of ethical value judgments, is incapable of giving an answer to numerous questions that are specific to practice (especially in cases in which, in the face of material indifference, the only thing that matters is that there be some decision at all and also as regards the question of precedent). The value judgments of the people have the following mediate (but therefore practically no less important) influence: insofar as they are generally effective in practice, they are a moment that may ground the assumption that the decision would, in general, have occurred in the same way. If a criterion specific to practice is to be sought, the introduction of the 'other judge', as an empirical type, offers the only possible way of forging a connection between a postulate and *contemporary* practice. –The justification belongs to the decision. It would be naive to want to see the significance of the reasons of decision exhausted by the fact that they compel the judge to exercise

---

[90] 'If one is to proceed to such an evaluation from a point of view that is elevated above mere subjective opinion, then one must identify, as the measure of evaluation, a universally valid and supreme end of human striving': VAN CALKER, in *Vergleichende Darstellung des Deutschen und Ausländischen Strafrechts: Vorarbeiten zur deutschen Strafrechtsreform. Allgemeiner Teil*, ed. Karl Birkmeyer et al., vol. III (Berlin: O. Liebmann, 1908), p. 185.

self-control.[91] This can, naturally, be a desirable incidental effect. It might be the case that the drafters of the civil and criminal codes of procedure were conscious, for the most part, of this purpose alone. This does not change the fact that an evaluation of the correctness of a decision that is not accompanied by reasons would be possible only in the sense that one could say that the result is consistent with that of a correct judicial decision. If the reasons of decision (in the technical procedural sense of the term) may be omitted in default judgments, in cases in which the complaint is upheld (§ 313 par. 3 ZPO), this is not to be regarded as a renunciation of the need for justification, but rather as a pointer [79] towards a justification that is so well known that it does not stand in need of being spelled out. If the 'reasons of decision' really did nothing more than encourage self-control on the part of the judge, one would do better to deny them to the public and to oblige the judge to submit them in writing to the relevant supervisory authority. No one will want to seriously claim or argue for something like this. The reasons of decision are an essential component of every decision (in the criminal trial, they are, for special reasons, made known, in their main content, with the publication of the judgment); they are not merely important in assessing the scope of a judgment's legal force. They do not merely want to individualize the decision; they want to convince. In a methodological inquiry, it is this fact alone that deserves attention.

Two questions result therefrom: of what do the reasons of decision want to convince? And: whom do they want to convince? Both questions are closely related and it is difficult to decide to what extent the answer to the one must precede the answer to the other. First, some remarks will be made on the latter.

From a purely psychological point of view, it would be of the greatest interest to investigate the judge's views as to whom he would like to convince with his reasons of decision. Apart from the fact that these may, in some circumstances, amount to no more than a monologue that the judge holds with himself or his conscience and apart from the fact that the judge may pursue special aims, such as to draw attention to himself by issuing a splendidly argued judgment, the

---

[91] In place of many, we mention only B. P. J. PLANTENGA, 'Motiveering van strafvonnissen', in *Rechtsgeleerd Magazijn* 30 (1911), pp. 318–390, at p. 318: 'eene grondige motiveering van zijne beslissing noodzakt den rechter zich stap voor stap rekenschap te geven van de wijze, waarop hij tot de beslissing komt' ['a thorough motivation of his judgment requires the judge to account, step by step, for the way in which he arrives at the decision'].

reasons of decision could, in principle, be directed at a wide variety of different addressees. The judge, whether in a civil or a criminal trial, will think of the party only in the fewest cases. The party itself (as opposed to its attorney) can safely be excluded from the start – lest we think, for example, of a decision in a trial for someone's legal incapacitation. Things are different with respect to the judge's position towards the court of appeal. (We are still engaged in the contemplation of psychological processes within the judge's soul.) To convince the latter is without a doubt, in numerous cases, the conscious or unconscious desire of the deciding judge in the [80] preparation of the reasons. The precedents set by the relevant court of appeal will then acquire a heightened and special importance. But even this does not yet exhaust the series of addressees of the reasons of decision. Whenever a further legal remedy is no longer available against a decision, as in all decisions taken by the *Reichsgericht*, which provide the most interesting and important material not merely for such a psychological investigation but also in other cases, the addressee with whom one has to imagine the judge to be in a conversation will not be any individual and concrete personality or court, but rather something impersonal that exists only in thought: an average phenomenon, or a circle of human beings, perhaps of jurists or educated laypersons. It is (to continue to speak psychologically-empirically) hardly to be assumed that any other conception of the addressee of the reasons for the decision would have been effective, in the drafting of a decision of the *Reichsgericht*, than this notion of a collegium of jurists to whom the court's juristic argumentations are to be presented and which is to be convinced. This collegium, however, seems at times (particularly in the last few years) to have changed and to have come to include laypersons as well.[92] The educated layperson is the one who appears to be apostrophized by the general references to the needs of intercourse, the duties towards his family, etc., although the fact that decisions are now also addressed to laypersons has, so far, been unable to alter their learned character. It goes without saying that the notion of the addressee does not always, in the preparation of every judgment, appear with the clarity and distinctness with which it had to be analysed here. In many judgments, the justification that a judge offers

---

[92] In some north American states, the view that the judge ought to convince the people has, incidentally, led to a political movement that aims to give the people the right to decide on the retention or dismissal of the judge (the recall ['recall' is English in the original]) by way of a vote.

for his decision will fail to exhibit any conscious conception of the addressee at all. In others, different addressees may be spoken to one after another, or else indistinctly: a circumstance that will, in general, make the arguments [81] addressed to each of the several audiences less convincing. The learned jurist, such as he is today, considers the accompanying reference to some part of a statutory provision to be an important argument, while this makes no impression at all on the layperson; a reference to the needs of intercourse may, on the other hand, elicit no more than a shrug from the jurist, and it will, at any rate, easily give rise to the suspicion that the deciding judge considered the juristic force of his own arguments to be insufficient to amount to proof and therefore attempted, by way of addition, to throw the 'sense of justice' into the balance as well. As a result, the reasons of decision indeed often acquire the character of a vacillating ambivalence that does not satisfy anyone. The methodical instinct, after all, is still stronger with most human beings than their interest in methodological investigations. But all of this diversity in concrete life does not hinder the construction of an average type of the person whom the judge wishes to convince by offering his reasons: that of a learned jurist, who, of course, also possesses an understanding of the practical questions of life. Certain historical problems are loosely connected to this approach. For instance, one might attribute a one-sidedly conceptual and dogmatic argumentation in the reasons for a decision to the fact that its author's conception of the addressee of the reasons of decision is that of a learned jurist who lives only in the world of his constructions. The 'modernist' movement in legal science, in its turn, can be traced back to a change in the conception of the proper addressee. It demands that, henceforth, the educated layperson, or any human being endowed with healthy common sense, is to be convinced as well, so that the difference between 'human' and 'juristic' conviction will be eliminated. But this latter difference, as will be confirmed by any practising judge, is still psychologically effective and by no means as *a priori* damnable as is typically claimed today. It rests on a continuing dualism in the conception of the addressee of the reasons of decision.

The question of this book is: when is the judicial decision correct? In the following sense: when is it [82] to be regarded as correct today? This question entails that it is necessary to pay attention to modern legal life and its practice – but not as though the goal were to develop a typical picture of the normal processes in the soul of the deciding judge, by engaging in experimental-psychological research; rather, in such a way that the answer to the question of what makes the decision correct will likewise determine the proper addressee of the reasons of decision. According to the formula for the correctness of decision that is proposed here, the correct addressee is the 'judge' in practice (as a type), and this does, as a matter of fact, seem to comport with the character and the forms of argumentation one finds in modern judgments. That, moreover, of which the addressee is to be convinced, according to the formula, is this: that this addressee would have decided in the same way, that the decision was therefore foreseeable and calculable, and that it is thus one that fits in with a uniform practice. Legal practice, in other words, justifies itself through itself. Correctness, thus determined, is not to be understood as absolute correctness, but as the correctness of modern practice. The latter is not what is, on average, held to be correct by judges, but what is in fact to be regarded as such, after methodological contemplation. The answer results from the postulate of legal determinacy, in connection with the fact that the law is applied, nowadays, by learned professional judges.[93]

The reasons of decision, correctly understood, therefore want to convince the addressee that the decision, if considered from a point of view in advance of the decision, was foreseeable and calculable, and that it is 'explicable' if considered after it has been taken – [83] not psychologically, but in the sense of being conformable to juristic practice (i.e. they want to convince that another judge would have decided in the same way). The reasons of the decision do not want to convince the addressee that the decision is nothing but an individual instance of a legislative will, or that it conforms to some ideal of justice. If both of these considerations play a role in the reasons of decision, they do so only as parts of a wider argumentation: because the derivability from statute is here so clear, or because the sense of justice makes itself felt so insistently and irrefutably, that it would have led another judge to the same conclusion. The positive law, in this way, is assigned an unambiguous position. A decision that

---

[93] The question concerning the correctness of a judgment by jury is, of course, to be excluded here. These are not decisions of which one could say that they were taken within legal practice. They do not stand in need of justification nor do they intend to be capable of it, unless one were to offer a justification that makes use of unarticulated feelings. These remarks are not intended as a condemnation of judgments taken by jury; they are merely meant to explain why a methodological investigation of current judicial practice does not have to consider them. That judgments by jury do not stand in need of justification is no proof of the irrelevance of the justification. The sole reason why such judgments do not stand in need of justification is that (according to the idea) they resonate with the people – that they are automatically carried by a general conviction.

results from the application of the clear and evident content of a statute is always correct for the reason that the smooth subsumption under a statute is the most secure means of grounding the certainty that another judge would have decided in the same way.[94]

With this solution to the problem, all of the 'factors of interpretation' that have been discussed hitherto acquire a completely novel significance for practice. 'Cultural norms' – that is, norms of intercourse and legal life that result from consideration of our contemporary level of culture – have, for instance, been referred to (by M. E. MAYER) as factors of interpretation. Or one has said (and has repeated until the point became trivial) that arguments drawn from a sense of justice or from our understanding of correct law may serve to fill the gaps of statute. To call these considerations [84] factors of interpretation is to make it understood, through this word, that one wants to extend or modify the content of a statute. The argument exclusively refers to a statute under which the case at hand is to be subsumed and it continues to consider itself the servant of that statute. That it does not, in truth, serve the statute but rather stands alongside it results from its power to change the content of statute, as well as to introduce new contents. The proposed formula avoids such incorrectness. It leaves it undecided, in itself, which of the relevant factors – content of statute, sense of justice, weighing of interests or however it is called – is decisive in the individual case. It does not seek to give the deceptive impression that all adjudication is mere subsumption under positive statute. It also avoids the related notion that the judgment as such is nothing more, according to its essence, than a subsumption either under positive or under free law norms and that the criterion of its correctness ought to be determined accordingly. For us, the positive statute, the cultural norms, the moral opinions of the people are no longer determinate and fixed rubrics under which a complex of events is to be classified – under which the case is to be subsumed – before one

[94] It is the fact that the positive statute is the most secure means of gaining legal determinacy and thus arriving at the correct decision, insofar as the decision is clearly derivable from it, that explains and also justifies the interest that the judiciary has in making decisions that exhibit 'conformity to statute', as well as its rejection of all criteria based on mere feeling. However, to continue to hold that the traditional doctrine of exegesis, with its method of analogy, is the right way towards a decision that convincingly conforms to statute is a misunderstanding that is unjustified and that is explicable only on psychological grounds. Compare (JASTROW's) headnotes, accepted by the II. German Day of Judges in Dresden 1911, according to which judges must always apply statute, interpret it and, in cases of doubt, construct an analogy, but never, in the event that the meaning of a statute is in doubt, exercise free discretion.

can conclude that the decision is correct. They are no longer the vessels into which the judge can pour the facts of the case. They step out of their tranquillity and stability. They become the means of grounding an expectation (that this is how the case would, in general, have been decided); they become mobile and acquire a new function. Their static character is replaced by a new dynamism.

The positive law retains one peculiarity: it tends to help to realize the postulate of legal determinacy to such a degree that a departure from it must therefore render the decision incorrect unless it is the case that considerations of legal determinacy themselves, *despite* the availability of a regulation by positive statute, speak for a departure from the latter. One can therefore say, in general, that an evidently statutory decision is a correct decision. It is from this proposition that the misunderstanding which postulates that 'conformity to statute' is the criterion of correctness took its start and it thus [85] committed the well-known logical error of drawing an inference from the equality of the predicates to the equality of the subjects. The inference that statutory decisions are correct and correct decisions must therefore be statutory decisions is on a par with the following: all Caucasians are humans; if Eskimos are to be humans, they must therefore be Caucasians. While the actual task, correctly understood, was to seek the explanation for *why* statutory decisions are correct (which explanation would then have been able to determine the *limits* of their correctness), one instead identified both, conformity to statute and correctness, and attempted to prove that all decisions which one held to be correct were conformable to statute. The difficulty, however, that arises when a clear subsumption under a positive statute is not possible does not consist in showing that the decision, as taken, is nevertheless in conformity to statute. It consists, rather, in the following: the less evident the connection with the positive statute, the greater the influence of a sense of justice that has not yet become customary law, or which remains unarticulated, and the more difficult it will be to answer the question as to how another judge would have decided. The more necessary, therefore, will it become to invoke other reasons for decision and to pile up arguments for the purpose of arriving at the crucial assurance that another judge would have decided in the same way. Arguments of this sort consequently do not aim to prove, in any real sense, that a subsumption under the positive statute, despite all improbabilities, can nevertheless be accomplished, or that it becomes possible given certain interpretive extensions of the statute, with the help of 'free' legal norms, or else by recourse to the norms of some heteronomous morality. What such arguments do want to establish, rather, is that the considerations that are presented in the reasons of decision are actually effective today, in the sense that they ground a legal determinacy, and that they would, in general, have been employed in practice as they were here. In this context, one must keep in mind that inferences from the reasonable interconnectedness of the provisions of a statutory codification are precisely what suggests such an understanding: one that is directed towards practice as a whole. [86]

The formulation that refers to the 'other judge' is merely a circumlocution for the postulate of legal determinacy, which can be regarded as the basis of every evaluation of judicial behaviour. It is precisely for this reason that the judgment of the medieval juror, who was certain that his decision would find the agreement of all his legal associates and all the fellow members of his estate, did not stand in need of an explicit justification. Such an affective, almost somnambulate, legal certainty no longer suffices for the complicated circumstances of modern life. It vanishes as soon as frequently changing and ambivalent relations take the place of firm and univocal social bonds. It is then no longer possible, as a result, to justify the view that judges are strictly bound to statute, or the degradation of the judge to the 'mouth that speaks the words of the statute', by appeal to the postulate of legal certainty (as BENTHAM did), although this had arguably been the purpose of the judge's 'subjection to statute'. The desire to create a purely logical jurisprudence, and to form incontestable and clear concepts that allow for a quick and secure subsumption of every concrete case, all originated from this postulate. The fearfulness with which the oldest jurisprudence clung to the literal wording of the statute, so that it would rather engage in the most frivolous sophistries than to infringe that literal wording, sprang from the instinct of legal determinacy, which was believed to have found a ground, in the (heteronomous) language of statute, that was governed by objectivity and determinacy, and which it was therefore impermissible to abandon. The so-called logical method of interpretation, in as much as it aims to serve practice, is driven, in effect, by the same intuition.[95] The following point,

---

[95] ADOLF FRIEDRICH STÖLZEL, *Rechtslehre und Rechtsprechung. Ein Vortrag gehalten in der juristischen Gesellschaft zu Wien am 7. Dezember 1898* (Berlin: F. Vahlen, 1899), pp. 57–58, mentions a sentence with which BETHMANN-HOLLWEG, as a young professor, used to introduce his lectures on civil procedure: 'We jurists should never forget that the main end of our efforts is a practical one: *theory* is developed, in the first place, in order to have a law in practice that is simple, *certain*, and corresponds to social needs.' – That 'logical' interpretation must really be a form of teleological reasoning if it is at all to arrive at practically useful results has already been said. Here, we wish to remind the reader in particular of the concept of the legally protected interest in criminal law: a concept that

especially important to practice, **[87]** is to be added: once a particular method of 'interpreting' has come to rule, this will satisfy, in large part, the requirements of legal determinacy and the reasons of decision that follow such interpretations will then ground correct decisions. The fact that the method in question rules will justify the assumption that another judge would have decided in the same way, so that the decision will become foreseeable and calculable. Such dominance of a method of interpretation is a real power: it creates conceptions of law that are as effective as the contents of formal statutes. The connection between interpretation and statutory technique thus becomes manifest. The modern doctrine of statutory technique is a doctrine of interpretation that is applied to the drafting of statutes; it is interpretation from the other side; it considers the relationship from the point of view of a legislator who anticipates the employment of the ruling method of interpretation. The dominance of the latter reaches its point of culmination once it is taken into account in the drafting of statutes, when, for instance, something that interpretation will certainly ascertain to be the content of the statute is not included in the statute because it is 'self-evident'. As soon as the legislative authority, which likewise sets out from the postulate of legal determinacy, knows that statutes will be professionally applied by determinate persons among whom certain rules of exegesis have become firmly established, it will satisfy the requirement of legal determinacy most easily by taking these methods into consideration from the beginning. It would be a great error to see in this a legal sanction of the current method of exegesis and of all of its results. The way in which the legislative authority (more precisely, those who draft the statute) proceeds is nothing more than an expression of the practical aspiration to bring about a regular and determinate practice. **[88]** A formulation of statute that consistently takes the ruling methods of exegesis into account serves that aspiration best. For this reason, statutes, nowadays, are usually revised by jurists and are fully understandable only to jurists, whereas it was something altogether self-evident to, for instance, MONTESQUIEU or BENTHAM that every reasonable human being ought to be able to understand all of the content of every statute: '*Les loix ne doivent point être subtiles: elles sont faites pour des gens de médiocre entendement* (naturally, these cannot be the jurists); *elles ne sont point un art de logique, mais la*

establishes most clearly how intimately 'juristic' construction, purposive considerations and constructions of the 'legislator' or of his 'will' are related to one another. Compare the introductory chapters of FRIEDRICH EISLER's book *Rechtsgut und Erfolg bei Beleidigung und Kreditgefährdung* (Breslau: Schletter, 1911).

raison simple d'un père de familles' ['The laws must not be subtle: they are made for people of mediocre understanding, they are not an art of logic, but the simple reason of a family father'].[96] The advantage that is gained by the opposite, modern method is that the desired results will be reached, through exegetical practice, with a high degree of probability and that the practical harmfulness of a method of exegesis that may be incorrect is paralysed. That may be a factual success and perhaps even the conscious purpose of the drafters of a statute, **[89]** but the actual recognition of some method of exegesis or of some method of practice on the part of those who draft statutes does not have any methodological significance for establishing its correctness. A well-versed drafter of a statute simply accepts the ruling methods of exegesis as a fact and he will direct his activity accordingly, even if he is personally convinced of the incorrectness of those methods. Perhaps he does believe in their correctness. At any rate, they are of interest to him only as means for the implementation of his ideas and he will begin to criticize them only once he is in danger of seeing them thwart his intentions. Whoever composes songs for piano has an interest that there be good singers and good pianos, but he does not begin his activity with a reformation of these two necessary means of his effectiveness. The formation and technique of the latter is a problem of its own. It is for this reason that

---

[96] *De l'esprit des loix* (see n. 52), vol. III, book 29, art. XIV, in which the 12 tables are praised as a *'modèle de precision'* ['a model of precision']. Compare also the passage in HEGEL, *Grundlinien der Philosophie des Rechts* (see n. 17), § 125, which was cited above [see n. 73]. –GEBHARD's saying, made during the deliberations [in the preparation of the BGB] on mental illness as a ground for divorce, as reported by ENDEMANN, 'Der zehnte Jahrestag des neuen bürgerlichen Rechtes', in *Deutsche Juristen-Zeitung* 15 (1910), cols. 18–24, at col. 22, is very interesting: 'Here, as elsewhere, we were well aware that we didn't know what exegesis would make of our prescriptions one of these days.' – STAMPE, in particular, vehemently objected to the drafting of statutes by jurists (*Unsere Rechts- und Begriffsbildung* [see n. 50], pp. 33–34): 'Now, since this will of the legislator, for the most part, has committed conceptual jurists for its authors, even in our recent legislation, and in particular in the BGB, one can imagine that the new source has brought only very small gains in socially useful elements.' This is to be compared with, for instance, the following remark of SCHEIN (*Unsere Rechtsphilosophie und Jurisprudenz* [see n. 12], p. 141): 'We do not, incidentally, regard this way and means of codification (that is, that statutes are drafted by jurists) as mistaken, but think, to the contrary, that it is an advantage insofar as the presupposed matter of fact and that which has been defined will, given sufficient attention and correct assessment, coincide, so that to diagnose mechanically will no longer give rise to mischief.' Or ibid., p. 213: legislation 'was forced to produce statutes as accurate and precise as possible, which, as far as this is possible, exclude any doubt'. – Since the question of who is more suitable to sit in legislative committees, jurists or laypersons, is, of course, a political and not a juristic question, it is excluded from the present inquiry.

the drafter of a statute accommodates himself to the terminology of those who are likely to interpret his products. He may, perhaps, design a system of civil law, in a statutory codification of civil law, by following a scientific theory and by using 'technical' expressions. But all this has no significance whatsoever for the juristic legitimation of a method of interpretation, just as it has no significance for a methodological analysis of practice. Such a legitimation would, after all, have to be based on the idea of the individual historical legislator – on the error that the 'legislator' is a concrete person and that it is the task of interpretation to ascertain the content of a real, psychological will. As paradoxical as it may still sound (strangely enough): the legislator cannot think and deliberate; only those who draft a statute and those who interpret it can do that, above all those who have to apply the statute in practice on a daily basis. It would appear that it is a view generally held today (at least theoretically, if one understands the opposition of theory and practice as that between word and work) that the drafters of the BGB are not the ones whose will is what matters. But they are the ones who created its 'clean technique', its uniform juristic terminology, this 'well-known sharpness with which the technique of statutory language is employed in the code of civil law [90] and in the statutes that accompany it'.[97] It is therefore in vain to ask what significance it may have for the interpretation of the BGB that its authors were cautious and precise people. That this is what they were is nothing more, initially, than the private knowledge of the interpreter. For the exegesis of the BGB, it must first be ascertained, by way of scientific analysis, that the BGB does have a firm terminology; only at that point may legal doctrine attend to that fact. A uniform terminology influences practice, in turn, by helping the latter to attain legal determinacy via the shortest route. The certainty of the language of a statute is, in essence, nothing but legal certainty.

This postulate of legal determinacy appears everywhere as an effective force and, in order to achieve completeness of exposition, we are yet to mention proposals that wish to see juristic controversies decided

---

[97] So RGZ, vol. 72, p. 332. STAMMLER's sentence in *Die Lehre vom richtigen Rechte* (see n. 38), p. 259, is not fully clear from a methodological point of view: 'It will be possible, in many cases, to achieve a higher degree of security if the legislator provides his own formulation of the real content of his will.' – There are, naturally, exceptions from a 'solid' terminology. A particularly noticeable example is the use of the word 'permission' in § 415, which received a legal definition in § 184 and is nevertheless understood, in § 415, as 'consent': RGZ, vol. 60, pp. 495–496.

authoritatively, through a kind of resurrection of the *jus respondendi*[xiv] (KUNTZE), or by a court of law with the relevant competences (of late ZEILER).[98] The adumbrative presentation of the effectiveness of the postulate taken as a starting point does not intend to claim that the postulate's factual validity is a proof of its correctness; it is meant to show only that the postulate serves to explain many phenomena of legal life and thus to establish its suitability as a methodological starting point for the identification of the criterion of modern practice. Previous discussions have held that the means of achieving legal determinacy (whether it be 'logic', or 'construction', [91] or the 'free law norm') are ends in themselves, and have failed to think of the possibility of understanding those means in light of their mediating position and to evaluate them from the point of view of a methodological investigation of practice. This misapprehension of the true relationship also forms the basis of the aspiration to find a positive statutory provision, for every legal case, if at all possible in the written law, even where the facts that are to be evaluated are in no way foreseen in statute,[99] of the view, that is, according to which the judge is a function of statute, so that the latter assumes sole responsibility for the decision – an opinion that has been rejected and derided in due measure.[100] The factual success of this misunderstanding was the total annulment of all calculability of the decision, wherein there lies a remarkable irony. Since one disregarded the sense that a statute has for legal practice, while one left the unchangeable determinacy of the statute seemingly intact, a complete arbitrariness and a desultory lack of method came to replace calculability and determinacy, in the 'exegesis' of the statute as much as in determinations of fact. This problem cannot be remedied by pointing to the factor that is decisive in psychological reality – that is,

---

[98] ALOIS ZEILER, *Ein Gerichtshof für bindende Gesetzesauslegung* (Munich: Schweitzer, 1911); JOHANNES EMIL KUNTZE, *Über das jus respondendi in unserer Zeit* (Leipzig: J. C. Hinrichs, 1858).

[99] The psychological significance of the attempt to shift one's own responsibility onto the statute that is implicit in this view has been expressed in the following way in REINHOLD KÖSTLIN's statement (*System des deutschen Strafrechts* [Tübingen: Laupp'sche Buchhandlung, 1855], p. 102, note 5), rightly emphasized by KURT HILLER (*Das Recht über sich selbst* [Heidelberg: C. Winter, 1908], p. 29) that most find it very convenient 'to withdraw behind the ramparts of the positive law, in order not to have to express an opinion of their own'.

[100] So as not to give the impression of striking out once more against an opinion that has already been overcome, we will mention only the discussion in IHERING, *Scherz und Ernst in der Jurisprudenz* (see n. 44) – in particular, p. 63 sqq.

to the judge's subjective sense of justice. It has already been said that a psychological ascertainment of the latter decides nothing for the correctness of the decision. The 'sense of justice' gains a decisive influence on that evaluation only once the notions that are summarized by this phrase are of such general effectiveness amongst judges that they come to ground legal determinacy. The true reason for the decision may then be concealed underneath 'juristic' argumentations: [92] perhaps it will also be mentioned in passing, at the end of the presentation of the 'reasons of decision', that the result that has 'thus been found' also conforms to the 'sense of justice', so that this 'sense of justice' is sometimes given the function to decide on the correctness and choice of a juristic construction, although juristic constructions are wholly heterogeneous to it, an altogether alien language. In such cases, the 'sense of justice' is indeed what grounds the correctness of the decision. Not, however, because it is the real (psychological) cause of the decision, but rather because it makes it the case that the decision would, in general, have been taken in this way. It is often claimed: if several different decisions are derivable from a statute (that is, almost always, in difficult cases), the judge is to choose between them on the basis of his sense of justice. This proposition is correct, but in an altogether different sense than that in which it is usually intended. The form in which the claim is typically put forward does nothing to explain why the sense of justice, the 'needs of intercourse', or precedent (RUMPF, *Gesetz und Richter*, p. 132) are suddenly supposed to be relevant. Either one must be serious about the view that the judge is exclusively 'bound to statute', as well as about the demand that all decisions are to be justified by appeal to statute – and then there will be no place left anywhere for the 'sense of justice' – or one must admit that there are factors other than statute that play a decisive role in practice. It will otherwise remain inexplicable whence the 'sense of justice' is to draw its legitimation to provide the measure, the decisive determination, where there is a contradiction or ambiguity. This dilemma does not arise for the formula of the correctness of decision that is proposed here. The 'sense of justice' has value as a means to achieve legal determinacy and therein lie, simultaneously, the limits of its significance for practice. From the perspective of practice, correctness derives exclusively from the law that is employed within practice. A decision is correct – to make use of a phrase formulated by ZITELMANN (*Archiv für die civilistische Praxis* 66, p. 449) in a discussion of the question of the creation of law – only if one may, with reason, presume [93] that practice is uniformly guided by the decisive reasons of the decision. The sense of justice has significance for practice only in the function of a collaborator in the task of achieving general legal determinacy. In this endeavour, it takes second place to positive law only as far as the *scope* of its effectiveness is concerned, not with respect to the *way* in which it functions in the constitution of correctness. The same applies to other 'transpositive' or free law norms, to the moral value judgments of the time and the people, to cultural norms or to the norms that one wants to derive from the 'needs of intercourse': they are capable of grounding the correctness of the decision if their power suffices to give rise to the certainty that they will generally be effective in like cases.

The difference between our view and other theories that point to norm-contents that flow into the law from the outside is therefore the following: the latter take their norms to be significant prior to the decision (temporally and logically); the judge is to set out from those norms so as to subsume under them, so that the decision remains one that exhibits conformity to a norm and so that some form of norm-conformity remains the criterion of correctness. According to the view put forward here, however, the significance of those external contents is to be sought in an altogether different sphere. The judge, in offering his reasons for decision, aims to create a general decision for the concrete case in the first place; his reasons for decision are to lead towards a general conviction that is yet to form. He does not subsume under norms as though subsumption were the final end of his activity. The subsumption under a norm (no matter which) is no longer the conclusion and the goal of the reasons of decision, but the means for the achievement of legal determinacy. That by appeal to which the decision legitimates itself is not *prior* to it (like a positive statute, a cultural norm or a free law norm), but rather to be brought about to begin with (*with the aid* of positive statute, of cultural norms or of the norm of the free law). The correctness of the decision is not constituted by the fact that the judge acts in accordance with some command, but rather by the fact that it satisfies the postulate of legal determinacy. One is not to assume that [94] the judge is looking backwards towards a will or a command; rather, he is using a norm (that is, its effectiveness) as a means, in order to calculate what would today, given these positive statutes and given this influence of extra-positive norms, as well as such and such precedents, in general be regarded as correct by legal practice.

In order to calculate: this means that the activity in question is essentially an activity of the understanding – an intellectual process – no matter how deeply the judge's sense of justice may be involved with the result.[101] The judge does not evaluate for himself as a participant; he investigates relations of value in their actual vitality. It is, of course, a psychological fact that no one can develop relations of value – that no one can fully understand them in their validity and significance – unless he has himself experienced the evaluations in question. The 'personality' of the judge, which has always been highlighted with special emphasis, becomes significant to that extent. Without a knowledge and experience of life, without familiarity with practice, the judge will, of course, remain ignorant of the evaluations that he is to employ. But it would be a misunderstanding – one that arises from a confusion of 'personal' evaluations with the employment and presentation of accepted values – to go further, so as to attribute to the judge an activity directed towards the enactment of his own, subjective evaluations, or to emphasize 'voluntarist' moments in the justification of the judgment and to infer therefrom the need for a judge to be a significant judicial personality. The unarticulated interjections of a sense of justice are not what makes for a successful justification; a judge cannot just appeal to his intuitive 'sense of the matter'. Every psychological activity, of course, itself rests on a voluntaristic process; every decision [95] is based on a valuing and a willing. That has been emphasized and repeated thousands of times in recent years. But what, if anything, does that decide for the question of the correctness of the decision? Which psychological factors are effective within the judge is a problem that concerns the psychologist, but no psychological analysis is capable of providing a criterion of correctness. – Perhaps this error finds its (psychological) explanation in the following: one had identified 'intellectual activity', all too readily, with 'subsuming under positive statute'. (A clear example of such a confusion can be found in O. BÜLOW.[102]) When one became aware of the fact that the judge is doing something wholly other than merely to subsume under statute, one fell

---

[101] 'The judge who decides in a certain way on the basis of his legal instinct, or the legal associate who believes that he must act towards another in a certain way, do, after all, make judgments, even if the *ratio sufficiens cognoscendi* ['the reason that is sufficient for understanding'] is not drawn from concepts with a fixed cognitive content': JUNG, *'Positives' Recht* (see n. 9), p. 12, note 1. – Compare, for the following, MAX WEBER, 'Kritische Studien auf dem Gebiet der kulturwissenschaftlichen Logik', in *Archiv für Sozialwissenschaft und Sozialpolitik* 22 (1906), pp. 143–207, at p. 181.

[102] *Gesetz und Richteramt* (see n. 6), p. 6: the judge's verdict is 'more than mere intellectual activity, more than mere subsumption'; it 'contains and signifies' a legal directive. (Compare RUMPF, *Volk und Recht* [see n. 60], p. 22: 'The judge does not merely subsume, he also renders value judgments.') It is to be noted against BÜLOW that the

victim to the venerable juxtaposition of intellect and will; one created a 'voluntarist' method and considered a pronounced subjectivism to be the only tenable approach. As a result, [96] one did not know any way of reassuring oneself other than to demand that a judge ought to be a 'personality of character'. Once the error that adjudication is nothing but a 'subsumption under statute' is abandoned, this confusion likewise disappears. The criterion of the correctness of the decision does not lie in the subjectivity of the judge; it is altogether independent of him as an individual. It is practice that decides whether the decision is correct. Practice has its own specific criterion. To this corresponds the formula: a judicial decision is correct in the event that another judge would have decided in the same way.

Neither the individual judge nor the judiciary as a whole are thereby elevated into a legislator, not even when a case is decided that is not covered by any positive statute. If a judge is told, in the event that there are doubts about the content of or gaps in a statute, that he ought to imagine himself to be a legislator and to decide in the way he would decide if he were the legislator, that usage of the word 'legislator' has significance only as a heuristic principle. The question of the correctness of the decision has nothing to do with an appraisal, in state law, of a judge's constitutional position. The judge is neither a legislator nor the mouth of the statute. The truth of the matter, what is more, is not to be found in the ever-popular 'mean between two extremes', which, naturally, cannot exist here. That the

fact of the legal force of a judicial verdict, or the possibility that it will acquire such force, to which BÜLOW constantly refers is altogether irrelevant for the *logical* significance and qualification of judicial activity (likewise its place 'amidst the bustle of the market': RUMPF, op. cit., p. 94). Neither the logical dignity of the judgment nor a methodological investigation of the practice of law is affected by the fact that the positive law connects legal consequences to the fact that the judgment has been rendered. That the judge is aware of such consequences may have psychological significance, but that does not belong here. – It is noteworthy that BÜLOW (op. cit., pp. 23–24), who, notwithstanding his emphasis on the law-making power of the judiciary, strictly holds to the view that the judge is subject to statute, argues against a judge's independence from statute by claiming that to deny such independence is necessary so as to avoid all arbitrariness. To limit arbitrariness is, of course, necessary, but if the criterion of correctness is therefore to consist in 'conformity to statute', one must either accept BENTHAM's point of view and demand the strictest subjection to the literal wording, or else admit that what is to be understood by 'subjection to statute' or 'conformity to statute' no longer guarantees strict determinacy and the exclusion of all arbitrariness. – H. REICHEL, 'Zur Freirechtsbewegung', in *Deutsche Richterzeitung* 2 (1910), p. 465, distinguishes a quietist (historical), positivist, formalist and an intellectualist current in jurisprudence, and says of the intellectualist that it considers the judge to be a mere 'subsumption-automaton'.

legislator and the judge are frequently and repeatedly put alongside one another offers a striking example of how the correct has become intermingled with the incorrect as a result of a lack of methodological clarity.[103] **[98]**

---

[103] One has always attributed a 'legislative' activity to the judge, even before Bülow's book on *Gesetz und Richteramt* (see n. 6). Compare, for example, Jordan, 'Bemerkungen über den Gerichtsgebrauch' (see n. 16), p. 191 sqq. – an essay that contains many noteworthy opinions that were presented as novelties just a few years ago (for instance p. 208, p. 195) – or Carl Retslag, *Apologie der Jurisprudenz. Eine Erwiderung auf den vom Herrn Staatsanwalt von Kirchmann in der juristischen Gesellschaft zu Berlin gehaltenen Vortrag* (Berlin: Braune, 1848), p. 25 (the judge is a legislator in individual cases; he continues the legislator's work), or Adickes, *Zur Lehre von den Rechtsquellen* (see n. 43), p. 11 ('the judge, therefore, has legislative competences'). Kraus, 'Die leitenden Grundsätze' (see n. 34), p. 629, cited Aristotle's phrase, 'ὅ κἂν ὁ νομοθέτης αὐτὸς ἂν εἶπεν ἐκεῖ παρών, καὶ εἰ ἤδει, ἐνομοθέτησεν ἄν' ('To say what the legislator himself would have said had he been present, and would have put into his law if he had known') [Aristotle, *Nicomachean Ethics*, Book V.10, 1137b. Aristotle (1995), 1796]. – Of late, the 'legislator' is employed in Börngen, *Internationale Wochenschrift für Wissenschaft, Kunst und Technik* 5 (1911), p. 874, and in Löffler, who, in *Österreichische Zeitschrift für Strafrecht* 2 (1911), pp. 522–525, at p. 524, in a review of Kantorowicz's talk 'Rechtswissenschaft und Soziologie' (see n. 38), cites the following sentence from the commentary to the Austrian BGB [ABGB or *Allgemeines Bürgerliches Gesetzbuch*, the civil code of Austria, 1811], vol. I, p. 37 [Löffler cites Von Zeiller (1811), 71]: 'The judge, in such cases, is to decide as the consistent legislator would have decided if he had thought of the case.' – A derivation of the judge's 'legislative' position from the practical insufficiency of the positive law can be found, for example, in Géza Kiss, 'Billigkeit und Recht mit besonderer Berücksichtigung der Freirechtsbewegung', in *Archiv für Rechts- und Wirtschaftsphilosophie* 3 (1909/1910), pp. 536–550, at p. 547, to whose references to the literature we can refer here. Kiss also speaks of a 'law-making judicature' and of 'judge-made law'. The reverse inference – the judge is not a legislator; he is therefore permitted to consider only the positive statute – can be found (apart from the *Reichsgericht*'s many remarks to this effect, compare Note IV at the end of this book), for instance, in Pachmann, *Über die gegenwärtige Bewegung* (see n. 65), p. 64. – The confusion of an investigation of the creation of law with an investigation that aims to identify the method and criterion specific to legal practice becomes palpably clear in Fridolin Eisele's remarks ('Unverbindlicher Gesetzeshinhalt', in *Archiv für die civilistische Praxis* 69 [1886], pp. 275–330, at p. 289, note 15) on O. Bülow's book: 'We can be sure that no one will deny that the judicial office has been importantly involved in the formation of law in all peoples. What is open to question is whether we are faced with a source of law that is *sui generis*. Now, it should be clear – although attention is not always paid to this point – that what one understands by "law", in speaking of a "source of law", is *the* law *in abstracto*, not the law that is realized in the concrete case. Judicial verdicts produce such abstract law only by way of constant repetition, and they thus place themselves under the *genus* of legal custom [...] I am unable to understand why this approach is supposed to fail to recognize the significance of judicial production of law' (Bülow, pp. 19, 44). What is insufficiently recognized here is neither the opposition of valid and factual law nor the (historical, psychological, sociological) significance of legal practice for the creation of new law, but rather the significance that is to be attributed to the fact that, for practice, there is only the law that is 'realized in the concrete case' and that the question of the

One wanted to give the permission to consider factors not contained in positive statute only to the 'legislator', and if the judge, who is supposedly 'bound to statute', was unable to circumvent their use, one preferred to bring them into the 'positive statute', rather than to drive the judge into the arms of his own 'arbitrary will'. The judge was not supposed to engage in 'legal-political' deliberations, or to be influenced by them; he is to be on guard against them as an *occasio proxima* ['proximate occasion'],[xv] since everything is determined for him, even if only after interpretation. Once one had gained insight into the actual difficulties and had come to see that this view stands in open contradiction with legal practice (not merely because we are faced with the contrast between is and ought, but also because law and practice are two altogether different forms of content), one came, adapting the antithesis legislator-judge, to express oneself in the following way: the judge has certain legislative functions; his activity is a 'quasi-legislative' one. But nothing is explained with this. One simply wanted to point out that one cannot get along, in practice, with the content of the 'positive law' alone. In truth, this means that 'conformity to statute' is

correctness of a decision taken within practice might be what is at issue (although this is not how BÜLOW intended to be understood). The methodological investigation of practice must pay attention to the fact that the judge, vis-à-vis the positive statute, is necessarily productive. But since one regarded this productivity, without further ado, as a production of new law (which is something wholly other), the discussion did not arrive at any sharp separation of the two issues and scholars constantly talked past one another. The antithesis put forward in KONRAD HELLWIG, *Lehrbuch des deutschen Zivilprozeßrechts*, vol. II (Leipzig: A. Deichert, 1907), p. 163 sqq., that the judge is creative, but not a creator of law, is also not to be confused with the view presented here, because of the way in which HELLWIG argues for it, because he appeals to the procedural fact that the judgment enjoys legal force (compare BÜLOW, op. cit., p. 7). –

Of the countless discussions of the topic 'legislator – judge' that are not otherwise cited in this book, the following deserve to be mentioned: DANZ, *Die Auslegung der Rechtsgeschäfte* (see n. 37); see also ERICH DANZ, 'Rückständigkeit der Rechtswissenschaft. Richterrecht und Gesetzesrecht. Neue Rechtsprechung', in *Deutsche Juristen-Zeitung* 16 (1911), cols. 565–567, which offers a cogent presentation of the fact that most decisions are not taken in accordance with statute, and OSKAR BÜLOW's essay 'Über das Verhältnis der Rechtsprechung zum Gesetzesrecht', in *Das Recht* 10 (1906), pp. 769–780, at pp. 770–771. See also PERITSCH's sentence ('Der Einfluß des deutschen BGB auf die französischen Juristen', in *Deutsche Juristen-Zeitung* 15 [1910], cols. 30–35, at col. 34): 'To redact a statutory codification in such a way that it leaves sufficient latitude to the judge to move freely enough between the texts to be capable, in applying the principles of that statutory codification, to follow the changes and shifting circumstances of his people's legal life amounts, evidently, to endorsing the principle that the regulation of relationships in private law does not exclusively belong to the competence of the legislator – that is, to the competence of people who, in their legislative work, necessarily proceed in accordance with reason – and that this regulation, in the first instance, is the result of a slow evolution among the mass of the people.'

no longer the criterion of the correctness of a decision. Under the compulsion of the traditional antithesis legislator-judge, which is a half-truth at best, one came, 'as a result', to call the judge a legislator. Or, the other way around: **[99]** one tried to prove that the judge was allowed, therefore, to consider only the positive law and nothing else, for the reason that he was not, after all, a legislator. The one reasoning is as skewed as the other. The juxtaposition of the legislator and the judge intersects with that of substantial and formal justice, and, moreover, with that of sociology and conceptual jurisprudence. Methodological clarity will be gained in this question only once legal practice receives its own criterion of correctness – one that is independent, in particular, from legal doctrine and its method. The judge is not a legislator. But from this it does not follow that there is nothing for him to consider other than the content of statute, as it results from the use of a certain method of interpretation. What follows, rather, is simply that the correctness of his decision is determined by criteria that are situated outside of his own subjectivity and are objective. Neither, conversely, does it follow from the fact that contents other than those contained in the positive law are of actual significance for the judge that he is to be regarded as a legislator. The judge does not create any law but appeals to it.[104] He remains subject to the principle of legal determinacy. Even though he helps, with his decision, to ground legal determinacy in the first place (if several decisions can be justified equally well), he does not do so as a legislator or an autonomous authority, but rather as an individual who collaborates in a larger work – one whose progression and force are independent of himself.

Cases of this kind are perfectly conceivable. There is a line – as in the case of the explanation and interpretation of the content of a statute in relation to its 'source', so also for the judicial decision – whose extreme point, on the one side, is a case in which all that matters is to give some decision or other, whatever it may be, while the other consists in a case in which the clear wording of statute or an established practice that conforms to the sense of justice **[100]** uniquely determines the content of the decision. The largest number of examples of a relative indifference of the content of the decision, in relation to the importance of the decision itself, is found in so-called formal statutes.[xvi] It is only if things are seen from this point of view that it seems justified for the *Reichsgericht* to draw a distinction – one that would otherwise

---

[104] 'Individual knowledge and volition is not law', says KIERULFF, *Theorie des Gemeinen Civilrechts* (see n. 85), p. 44, note. (As a reason, he offers the following: the 'particularity' of the individual is 'insignificant compared to the state'.)

remain altogether inexplicable – between its view of a judge's liability for his interpretation of the BGB, on the one hand, and his interpretation of the GBO,[xvii] on the other. In applying the BGB, the judge may give consideration to practice and to the literature;[105] his decisional latitude is far greater than in the application of the GBO, where doubts are declared to be unjustified whenever the *Reichsgericht* (or, for Prussia, the *Kammergericht*[xviii]) has already decided a question.[106] To offer a further example relating to questions of material law: if an essential component of a bill of exchange has been modified – if, for instance, the sum of the bill is changed from 3,000 Mark to 30,000 Mark and the 'three' is turned into a 'thirty' in the text – the question may arise whether he who signed the bill before it was changed is still liable for the sum of 3,000 Mark or (because of the modification) no longer has any obligation at all. The *Reichsoberhandelsgericht*[xix] answered this question in the following way: the bill is now a bill for 30,000 Mark; the original bill for 3,000 Mark does not exist anymore. If the individual determinacy of a purely formal obligation, such as that arising from a bill of exchange, requires a determinate sum as its content, then an obligation for 30,000 Mark is different from one for 3,000 Mark, even though the latter sum is contained in the former. The *expression* 3,000 is no longer present, even though 3,000 is arithmetically enclosed in 30,000. Whether 3,000 is struck through and overwritten with 30,000, or whether a zero is added can make no difference; the previous [101] signatory is no longer obligated as a result. Outstanding practitioners, such as STAUB, STRANZ and BERNSTEIN, voiced their support for this view. The *Reichsgericht*, however (in vol. 8, p. 42, and vol. 54, p. 386, of its decisions), with the assent of a man of such high practical insight as DERNBURG, rejected this as an excessively formal view and decided instead that the original text remains unaffected if it is possible, either in thought or in fact, to remove the addition – in this case, the zero and the syllable 'ßig' in 'dreißig' [*drei* is German for 'three' and *dreißig* for 'thirty'], and thereby to restore the bill to its previous condition. If, on the other hand, a digit is changed – if, for example, a '3' is transformed into an '8' – the previous content can 'not come to life again' and the original obligation is extinguished. – No one will call this line of proof and this distinction compelling. If faced with the objection that their view is excessively formal, opponents are likely to point to the decidedly formal character of a bill of exchange; in response to the question as to whether the original text is affected or not, they can be expected to argue that the sum is an essential component of the bill,

---

[105] RGZ, vol. 59, p. 388; *Juristische Wochenschrift* 35 (1906), pp. 53–54.
[106] *Juristische Wochenschrift* 35 (1906), p. 134.

and that it is impossible to decompose it into a valid and an invalid part. To do so would conflict with all of the basic rules of the doctrine of scriptural obligations. (LEHMANN in *Deutsche Juristen-Zeitung* 4, p. 694.) HUGO REHBEIN, finally, therefore rejects the view of the *Reichsgericht* (*Allgemeine Deutsche Wechsel-Ordnung mit Kommentar in Anmerkungen und der Wechselprozeß nach den Reichs-Justizgesetzen*, 8th edition [Berlin: H. W. Müller, 1908], pp. 105–106) and remarks that this approach is '[not] capable of justification'. It is indeed very difficult to see how it might be possible to put forward a compelling reason, or even only decisive considerations of utility and purposiveness, for one or the other opinion. But a decision nevertheless has to be taken and it is more important that one be in a position to know how the question is going to be decided than that it will be decided in one or the other way. It is in such cases that precedent acquires a decisive influence on the evaluation of the judge's decision. Whoever has once had an opportunity to **[102]** observe how experienced and perfectly self-reliant judges are making use, in their deliberations, of such decisions of the *Reichsgericht* will find therein a confirmation of the factual validity of the formula of the correct decision that is proposed here. The casualness with which even the most intelligent judge appeals to precedent here, typically without discussing its reasons, stands in a remarkable contrast to those decisions of the *Reichsgericht* which determined that an agreement between an employer and an employee according to which any salary in excess of 1,500 Mark is to be paid to the employee's wife may not be challenged by creditors who are thereby disadvantaged. In these decisions,[107] revealingly, one finds, next to the purely juristic consideration that, in the event of such an agreement, the salary in excess of 1,500 Mark never becomes the employee's property to begin with, an additional reference to the employee's duties towards his family, which is meant to do more than merely to deny that the agreement is contrary to good morals. – One is accustomed to saying that it is the 'scientific value' of the decisions of higher instances alone that is responsible for their significance – that there are no binding precedents.[108] But this principle is neither

[107] RGZ, vol. 69, pp. 59 sqq. For a summary of these decisions, as well as a presentation of the arguments that can be put forward against the *Reichsgericht*'s point of view, see BECKER's essay 'Rechtsbehelfe des Gläubigers gegen die Vereitelung seiner Rechte durch vertragliche Zuwendung des pfändbaren Gehaltsteils an die Ehefrau eines Angestellten', in *Rheinisches Archiv für Zivil- und Strafrecht* 109 (1913), pp. 105–120.

[108] It is noteworthy that BRINZ, in his review of ADICKES's book on the sources of law (see n. 43), p. 162, sees a sign of ADICKES's 'healthy sense of the significance of positivity in the law' in the fact that he derives the authority of customary law from long usage and 'portrays the submission to precedent as a postulate of justice: so that all are, if possible, measured by the same standard'. ADICKES continued to demand that precedents be

methodologically correct [103] nor factually valid. In all of those cases in which the need to have some decision at all takes priority over the reasons for decision, so that the content is then relatively indifferent, the authority of the *Reichsgericht* provides the measure for an assessment of the decision in direct proportion to the significance of the element of abstract decision. Since every decision contains this moment of abstract determination within itself, we arrive at a theoretically unambiguous evaluation of the problem of precedent: if a question has been answered by a previous decision and if a judge has to decide the same question, then precedent will gain a significance, in the inquiry into how another judge would have decided, that has nothing to do with its 'scientific value'. The precedential force of decisions is to be assessed from the vantage point of legal determinacy and it is a function of the element of substantial indifference in the decision. This solution, to note, concerns only the *correctness* of the decision. To say that precedent is *binding* would suggest the old mistake, as though it were a matter of proving the judge's subjection to statute, its content now determined by precedent, so that 'conformity to statute' once again became the criterion of a decision's correctness and everything came down to a command to the judge. – The strong suggestive force of precedent is likewise not at issue here. The latter concerns the factual, psychological consequences [104] of a precedent and, as such, has nothing to do with the correctness of the decision; rather, the ground and the limits of the significance of precedent follow from the postulate of legal determinacy. Precedent becomes relevant where the contents that are to be taken into consideration in arriving at the decision are incapable of justifying the assumption that another judge would have decided in the same way.

accorded binding force later on, likewise by appeal to the requirement to treat like cases alike (*Stellung und Tätigkeit des Richters* [see n. 30], p. 13). THÖL's view (*Einleitung in das deutsche Privatrecht* [see n. 11], § 54) that there is a law of practice and that a norm that has once been applied becomes law in accordance with the maxim 'what is right for one is just for the other' refers to the creation of law, but may also be consulted for the evaluation of the decision and its criterion.

ALBRECHT MENDELSSOHN-BARTHOLDY's reports in *Rheinische Zeitschrift für Zivil- und Prozeßrecht des In- und Auslandes* 4 (1912), p. 131, are important in this context. These conclude that the system of precedent is coming to be more and more recognized in Germany. The commentary appended by the higher administrations of justice is especially interesting here. It mentions a passage in JÄGER, *Bayrische Zeitschrift* 7, pp. 77–78, that attributes to the Supreme Court of Bavaria the task of 'supervising the adjudication of mid-level courts. On case law ['case law' is English in the original], compare also ERNST NEUKAMP, 'Das Gewohnheitsrecht in Theorie und Praxis des gemeinen Rechts: Referat und Kritik', in *Archiv für bürgerliches Recht* 12 (1897), pp. 89–184, at pp. 162–163. NEUKAMP, however, considers case law to be retrogressive in comparison to rule-based law.

The judicial decisions that particularly deserve to be mentioned, in this context, are those that assign a punishment. These tend to measure the punishment according to certain usages that develop over time and provide a rough measure. From a theoretical perspective, it is not even approximately possible to arrive at an incontestable measure of punishment in the individual case, given that there is no complete clarity on the fundamental problems of the criminal law or on all of the questions linked to that of the essence and purpose of punishment. Even if such clarity were to obtain, the determination of such a measure would be possible only within very wide boundaries. A multitude of heterogeneous considerations play into any determination of a measure of punishment and these would be incapable, even if considered individually, of specifying the proper length of the time of imprisonment down to a day. To refer a judge who wants to know why he is to assign one year of prison, as opposed to one year and a day, to the principles of general and special prevention would be to take him for a fool. Summary solutions of this sort do not explain anything. The truth is that a practice forms over time. (The question of how long the sentence typically tends to be 'in cases such as these' is therefore quite justified.)[109] Naturally, that practice cannot have the same significance as the practice of the *Reichsgericht* in the above example of the obligations of the signatory of a bill of exchange. But it is still more than mere imitation if a judge comes to follow it – more than the result of a conservative instinct or unthinking inertia. The existence of the practice may imply [105] that a punishment that goes beyond the typical measure stands in need of special justification. In these assignments of a measure of punishment, the question, again, is how another judge would decide. Here, as well, the tendency towards legal determinacy shows itself: a tendency that – at least in all cases that, within certain bounds, are governed by the need to take some decision at all – completely silences the aspiration to determine a punishment that is provably just. These questions concerning the due measure of punishment are likewise cases that constitute a parallel to statutory provisions whose content is relatively indifferent. It is a special characteristic of all such cases that the question about the 'other judge', here, does not have the meaning: which considerations would be determinative for him? Rather:

---

[109] KLEE says, of verdicts by jury and of the pecuniary punishments that they may impose, in his talk at the II. German Day of Judges (*Deutsche Richterzeitung* 3 [1911], p. 661): 'These are punishments proportionate to the deed, which take shape within practice'; 'Everyone knows that particular courts will, over time, tend to form a specific scale for a certain kind of delict.'

what is the result (indifferent in content) on which one has come to agree? If a practice has not formed yet, then there is – with respect to the type of a judgment that decides under the circumstance of indifference of content – no incorrect answer at all. It is no objection to this view that such cases, being abstractions, do not arise in practice in typical purity. It should be conceded, moreover, that, under the view presented here, the evaluation of the *Reichsgericht's* judgments can no longer proceed as casually as it used to. It does not suffice to criticize those decisions simply for being 'unjust' or 'out of touch with reality'. Although the evaluation of the *Reichsgericht's* judgments is made more difficult, it is not by any means made impossible. Criticism is made more difficult, by the view presented here, for the reason that the *Reichsgericht's* decisions are recognized to have a special factual significance for legal determinacy and because legal determinacy is employed as a constitutive element of the criterion of correctness. But the abovementioned example of the *Reichsgericht's* judicature on the contestability of contracts of employment made by debtors should suffice to prove that it remains perfectly possible to criticize its judgments.

Just as to precedents, this theory assigns a clearly determined position to the preparatory materials of a statute. As long as the aim is to find some starting point or other, the materials of a statute will suggest themselves particularly strongly and every judge is going to employ them. This psychological probability, **[106]** however, is in itself insignificant. But, in virtue of the fact that it turns into an effective element of a 'practice' and thus comes to stand in relation to the postulate of legal determinacy, it will influence the conclusion that decisions are, in general, taken with reference to the materials and it is thus of importance for the *evaluation* of the judgment. The appeal to the materials can therefore turn out be a probative argument; it does not matter whether it is of 'scientific value' or has the character of a 'work of industrious evaluation and thought'.[110] In this role, the materials are no different from earlier statutes to which a judge will refer if a new statute does not give him clear guidance. Here, as well, the earlier statute is not thereby given statutory force, just as we cannot speak of such force with regard to the materials; its force, to quote RUMPF, is based on a 'tacit consensus in practice'. And the reason for this is that the judgment gains its correctness only in relation to legal practice as a whole.

A judicial decision is correct when it is foreseeable and calculable. This thesis results from the postulate of legal determinacy and our

---

[110] As RUMPF, *Gesetz und Richter* (see n. 23), p. 120, expresses himself.

investigation of legal practice. Our position on the question whether a judge may decide against the literal wording of a statute follows, with all desirable clarity, from the formula that has been proposed here. The psychological fact that every judge will be hesitant to adjudicate *contra legem* and will initially prefer to appeal to the wording of the statute rather than to considerations of equity, however evident and pressing, acquires its methodological significance from the fact that it can be related to the principle of legal determinacy. It is a historical fact, which has been ascertained countless times, that practice occasionally departs from the wording and the literal meaning of a statute, even where it cannot appeal to customary law: a sufficient number of examples of this phenomenon can be found even for the BGB as it is now in force.[111] [**107**] A decision that conflicts with the literal meaning of a statute – that is, a decision *contra legem* (naturally, as soon as reference is made to the 'spirit' of the 'whole' statute, or even of the 'law as a whole', the decision ceases to be scientific) – is correct under the same conditions as any other: namely, when it would have been taken in the same way by another judge (by practice as a whole). It follows that it is precisely the positive law's function to bring about legal determinacy that provides an argument against any unconditional rejection of adjudication *contra legem*. Considerations of legal determinacy necessarily limit the decisiveness of positive law.[112] As long as the positive law [**108**] is

---

[111] It suffices to compare the commentaries to §§ 2039 or 1361 BGB. A beautiful example of how a 'will' of statute that can, according to all the rules of traditional hermeneutics, only be called 'evident' is no longer being respected is provided by RUMPF, *Gesetz und Richter* (see n. 23), pp. 166–167, in the form of the decision of the *Reichsgericht* that is reported in the *Monatsschrift für Aktienrecht*, 1897, p. 24. Compare MAX RUMPF, 'Urteilsbegründung bei freier Rechtsprechung', in *Archiv für Rechts- und Wirtschaftsphilosophie* 2 (1908/1909), pp. 202–211 (on the treatment of § 1910, par. 3 BGB). And what does it mean that the fact that § 1353, par. 2 BGB makes no exception for a spouse who is mentally ill is claimed to be an oversight in redaction, or that it is claimed that such an oversight is to be assumed in § 82 of the statute concerning the GmbH [*Gemeinschaft mit beschränkter Haftung*, a limited liability company] (RGZ, vol. 40, p. 191)? – IHERING, *Geist des Römischen Rechts* (see n. 39), p. 465: 'No statute is able, in the long run, to stand up to the condemnatory judgment of the jurists.'

[112] When KOHLER draws attention, in many passages, to the phenomenon of *duplex interpretatio* ['twofold interpretation'], to the fact that a changed understanding of the law can come to be effective without any modification of the wording of a statute, in playing out the letter of a statute against its sense (as Portia does in the *Merchant of Venice*), one can accept his point insofar as this general and conscious self-deception of practice contains the thought to respect the most important pillar of legal determinacy, the wording of a statute, for as long as possible. But the attempt to maintain the formal authority of statute, which KOHLER (for instance in *Archiv für Rechts- und*

able to guarantee legal determinacy and to call forth a consistent practice, a decision's 'conformity to statute' will be a proof of its correctness. As soon, however, as elements that lie outside of the positive content of statute come to unsettle this practice and are able to modify the statute in its actual validity, even if only by way of 'interpretation', this congruence between 'conformity to statute' and correctness of decision will lapse, and a judgment issued against the meaning of the statute may nevertheless be correct. The great concerns that are invoked against a recognition of adjudication *contra legem* are all based on the mistaken understanding of the problem of adjudication that has been prevalent thus far. They all come down to considerations of 'legal certainty', but precisely these considerations have been employed as our foundation.[113] That the individual judge [109] can

Wirtschaftsphilosophie 3 [1909/1910], p. 581) connects to this point does not belong here anymore. KOHLER claims that if one were to push aside the statute and to adjudicate *contra legem*, this would lead to a 'lack of discipline, to arbitrariness, and to an unparalleled insecurity'. But does the sly kind of interpretation that is offered by Shylock [Schmitt's full German phrase '*mit dem Schein Shylocks*' is hard to translate: it suggests that Shylock's argument is unserious or inauthentic – that it is a play with appearances and offered in bad faith], in the *Merchant of Venice, not* lead to legal insecurity? Is one not faced, in that case, with a sophistry so arbitrary that everyone would be incensed by it if it did not serve a purpose that evokes sympathy? And if the sympathetic purpose were to justify such methods, is it not the case that an uncontrolled jurisprudence of sentiment would thereby once again become decisive? If the avoidance of legal insecurity is what matters, the criterion of correctness can be sought only in the uniformity of legal *practice*, taken as a *whole*. The 'formal authority' of statute and questions pertaining to the creation of law are to be separated from this methodological investigation.

[113] It is always the fear of legal insecurity – of arbitrariness on the part of the judge – that is the decisive argument in any emphatic rejection of adjudication *contra legem*. See, for instance, BRÜTT, *Die Kunst der Rechtsanwendung* (see n. 12), p. 184 sqq.; RUMPF, *Gesetz und Richter* (see n. 23), pp. 77–78 (who says that a disregard of the wording of a statute would lead to legal insecurity, and that there is no secure criterion as to when it might be permissible to decide against statute and that all would come to depend on the 'personality' of the judge); S. BRIE, 'Billigkeit und Recht mit besonderer Berücksichtigung der Freirechtsbewegung', in *Archiv für Rechts- u. Wirtschaftsphilosophie* 3 (1909/1910), pp. 526–534, at p. 532; JOHANN GEORG GMELIN, *Quousque? Beiträge zur soziologischen Rechtsfindung* (Hanover: Helwing, 1910). SCHEIN's sentence, in *Unsere Rechtsphilosophie und Jurisprudenz* (see n. 12), pp. 208–209, is noteworthy here: in the interest of legal security, public servants ought rather to be slaves of statute than agents of the state; 'an exception can be made only for the exceedingly rare cases in which the consequences of the application of the law would be so harmful that they outweigh the interest in legal security, and in which these consequences are so evident that every organ of state would have to acknowledge them, so that considerations of reliability do not come into play'. – The difficulties that result from the introduction of meta-positive norms have an interesting historical parallel in the questions that arise for supporters of natural law with regard to the relation of the law of nature to the positive law. The

take a correct decision *contra legem* is explicitly denied here, even for cases in which such a decision reflects the judge's best conviction. A sense of justice, however strong, is not to be able, by itself, to topple statute as the measure of correctness. What is decisive is always legal practice as a whole, which grounds the predictability and calculability of decision, and thus legal determinacy. To repeat, the question of the creation of positive law by legal practice does not belong here. The present concern is exclusively to gain a criterion of the correctness of decision that is specific to practice. Of course, the factual preponderance of clear positive norms looks so strong, from the point of view of legal determinacy, that imprecise extra-positive norms might appear to be little more than stand-ins. A look at the current practice of the *Reichsgericht* would seem to offer incontrovertible confirmation of that view. But, on closer inspection, one cannot overlook that the appearance of a preponderance of the 'positive' is achieved, in many cases, only by way of a very loose connection to some positive provision or other that is invoked to 'legitimate' the decision. Such an approach does not amount to proof of the claim that it is only the truly statutory decision that is, in fact, recognized as valid today. It is a mere symptom, rather, of the power of the postulate of legal determinacy, which one believes, in this way, to honour, under the impression of the salient law-determining force of positive statute. It has already been pointed out how erroneous a view this is. The norms that are really effective (for instance norms of intercourse, of justice or of equity) are the factors that ground legal determinacy here, which make it the case that another judge would have decided in the same way.[114] **[110]**

---

solution proposed in the text, by contrast, offers a theoretically unambiguous answer, which is at least noteworthy, in the context of discussions of the juristic doctrine of method – though I say it ['though I say it' is English in the original].

[114] Authors who emphasize the independence of the judge from statute most often refer to the individual judge, unless they mean to discuss the power of legal practice to create law. BRUNO SCHMIDT, for one, says, in *Das Gewohnheitsrecht als Form des Gemeinwillens* (Leipzig: Duncker & Humblot, 1899), p. 37, note i, that BÜLOW, in *Gesetz und Richteramt* (see n. 6), failed to draw out the ultimate consequences of his own view – that is, that the judge, 'or spoken more accurately and precisely the authority of the state which is embodied in him, is free from any subjection to statute in a case of emergency'. In order to ward off as far as possible the misunderstanding that is to be expected here, and this is the background on which the discussion in the text is to be understood, we must repeat that: (1) SCHMIDT speaks, in this passage, of the process of the creation of law, and of the doctrine of the legal norm in state law theory; (2) for us, a judge cannot become free of his subjection to statute in a case of emergency. The cases that SCHMIDT has in view will typically be cases in which the decision is correct, notwithstanding the

It suffices to establish the advantageousness of the proposed formula for solving the difficult problem of adjudication *contra legem* to point out that the correctness of a judicial decision is not derived from any will or command contained in statute[115] and that the question [111] of correctness is thus made independent of the quarrel over the nature of the legal norm (whether it is an imperative or a judgment). The vacuous and worthless fictions that are supposed to 'explain' or to 'justify' a factual departure of legal practice from positive statute by reference to a 'tacit' acceptance on the part of the legislator are no longer necessary. One derives the correctness of the decision from the will of statute, for instance, and then responds to the

> fact that it disregards the content of statute. Because he likewise employs 'subjection to statute' as the criterion of correctness, he is bound to find an inexplicable 'exception' here.
>
> [115] BÜLOW, *Gesetz und Richteramt* (see n. 6), p. 40: the judge is authorized by the state 'to also perform such determinations of law as are not laid down in statute, that are willed and chosen by him, and not by statute.' Or SCHMIDT, *Das Gewohnheitsrecht* (see n. 114), p. 39: the state can suspend its law, tacitly or expressly, and the state makes use of 'its jurisdictional organs' to perform a declaration of suspension 'by conclusive action'. (He adds that this is 'better and more dignified' than to play around with the interpretation the statute, which is correct, but does not therefore amount to an argument yet.) – Especially clearly, BÖRNGEN, *Internationale Wochenschrift* 5 (1911), p. 873: the statute is a command; 'Every command has its limits, and it must be left to him who executes the command to find out where these limits are ... If it is [not] possible to request a new command, he who is tasked with implementing the command does not act according to the spirit of the old command. He does not go to work on the old command with the principles of logic, so as to construct for himself a new command. Rather, he puts himself in the position of the commander and asks how the supreme commander would have acted in the novel situation.' Judges, likewise, are supposed to find themselves in this position. – SCHEIN's comparison (*Unsere Rechtsphilosophie und Jurisprudenz* [see n. 12], p. 191) of the 'juristic servant' who receives the command, in the winter, to fire up the stove every day and then continues to do so in the summer is frequently cited. But this example, with its plausible considerations of purpose, misunderstands both the practical and the theoretical difficulties of the doctrine of the legal norm.
>
> ZITELMANN, 'Gewohnheitsrecht und Irrtum' (see n. 49), p. 446 sqq., has driven the question of the state's competence to enact statutes, as well as the question of the competence to create this competence, to the point at which any further derivation becomes impossible. This important and excellent essay has already been mentioned, and it has been explained how its subject differs from that of the present methodological investigation into the criterion of the correctness of a decision. Nevertheless, the following sentence of ZITELMANN must still be cited *in extenso*: 'Apart from this production of statutes with a validity that is derived (from legal norms), there is also another form of the creation of law, which is primary and, so to speak, autochthonous. According to consistent psychological experience, the fact that some norm can be expected to continue to be followed constitutes one of the strongest sources of the motivation to go on to comply with it, and it is precisely because one experiences the effectiveness of a continuous source of motivation that the concept of the factual transforms into that of the lawful.'

STATUTE AND JUDGMENT   139

question as to why one nevertheless occasionally regards a decision contrary to statute as correct: 'That results from a silent change in the legislative will.' In this way, one arrives at a proposition whose scientific value is roughly comparable to those that explain the soporific power of so many books by appeal to their *vis dormitiva* [soporific power]^{xx} and the opposite effect of certain others that address the same topic by appeal to the cessation of that power – or perhaps to those that emphasize that only a good human being can be well, and that conclude, from the fact that someone is doing badly, that they probably are not a good human being anymore. –

It is facile to object to the whole presentation so far, and to its constant reference to the postulate of legal determinacy, that it is possible to derive any number of things from principles and considerations as general as that of legal determinacy. It must therefore be repeated, to summarize, that this objection overlooks that the postulate of legal determinacy, which is undoubtedly recognized in practice, is provided with a secure and determinable content by the reference to the empirical type of the 'other judge'. This content, admittedly, may change as practice develops, but it is not therefore any less clear. Of course, [112] our formula does not contain any moment that would rule out a change in practice: we deliberately avoided talk of the 'stability' of the law.^{116} The answer to the question of how another judge would decide may come to change very quickly, in the event of sudden upheavals in legal life, or in the event of a 'tempestuous development of legal consciousness' (EHRLICH). Even if the proposed formula, due to its receptivity to the changing contents of legal life, does not offer an answer that is ready to hand in the concrete case, it does not thereby become uncertain. In the case of such methodological formulations, the goal can only ever be to attain a theoretical certainty: an unambiguous position on all of the problems that belong to this complex – an open answer to all of the relevant difficulties. It would be wrong to expect the reliability of a logarithmic table or of a train schedule, which is usually postulated as an ideal. The abstractness of the principle of legal determinacy that has been chosen as a point of departure in our methodological inquiry is deliberate. It is to enable us to find a formula that, notwithstanding the polymorphism of practice, does not refuse an answer whereby it sufficiently shows its

---

^{116} ALEX FRANKEN, *Vom Juristenrecht* (Jena: G. Fischer, 1889), p. 6, speaks of the 'instinct of stability'. – That the use of such 'instincts' is excluded in this work results from its approach. The same holds for the 'instinct of order' (RÜMELIN) or of the 'ethical instinct of sociability' (A. STURM).

justification. – The formula itself is likely to draw forth the objection that it does not say anything new (although it will appear to many to be a baseless novelty) – that it sets out from practice only to go back to it and that it never transcends practice. Insofar as this objection is based on the common misunderstanding that a methodological inquiry ought to do more than put practice in order and help it to reflect on itself, it does not stand in need of refutation. Insofar as the objection wishes to claim that the formula does not contribute anything novel and worth knowing, it is unjustified. Practice has been referred to here since its autochthonous principle of correctness was to be found. The expression 'autonomous' has been avoided [113] because it might easily give rise to the error (which, despite all our protestations, is likely to be levelled against this work) that it is claimed that practice creates its own law, that it legislates and that the difference of the solution proposed here to others is to be seen merely in the fact that we put a new species of 'norm', the 'laws of practice', in the place of free law norms, or cultural norms, or other similar norms. It is simply a matter of a principle of methodological investigation that is specific to practice. If a new answer to the question of the correctness of judicial decision is given here, and if this answer contains a novel ordering of the decisive factors that figure in the reasons of decisions, which hitherto stood apart in motionless isolation and in unsatisfactory ambiguity, then the denial of our proposal's scientific right to exist has already been refuted. Whether there is a further criterion of the correctness of the criterion that is to be regarded as valid in practice is a question that was already excluded from the inquiry in the first chapter. This question is mentioned here once more only because these two altogether different problems are identified again and again, which gives rise to confusions and misunderstandings. And actual practice? There is hardly a more convincing proof of the actual validity of the proposed formula than that which is provided by the *Reichsgericht's* judicature on the presuppositions of the judge's liability according to § 839 BGB or in connection with § 12 GBO. If a decision's 'conformity to statute' really were a criterion of its correctness with which one might rest content, there would be no need for further decisions by the *Reichsgericht* on questions relating to § 839 BGB or to § 12 GBO. It is a mere illusion to think that one can successfully uphold conformity to statute as the criterion of correctness by drawing the following distinction: the judicial decision taken in contravention of statutory law is the *objective* fact that triggers the applicability of said statutory provisions; the doubts, by contrast, that give significance to the judicature of the

Reichsgericht relate to the *subjective* fact – to the culpability of the judge. [114] But the one is dependent on the other: the objective fact is the content of the psychological relations that are contained in the concepts of intent and negligence, and without it the subjective fact cannot obtain. Thus the *Reichsgericht* states that the judge is not to be held liable if he has well-known legal scholars on his side.[117] What is decisive, in particular, is whether the *Reichsgericht*, '*as the highest court that gives the measure to practice*', has already decided the question or not.[118] To overlook that an interpretation other than that which was in fact employed might be correct amounts to negligence only if this interpretation *has already been discussed in the literature or been employed in other decisions*.[119] Finally, the case already mentioned: if the *Reichsgericht* or (for Prussia) the *Kammergericht* have decided on an issue in matters of land registry, any doubts a judge might have as to the correctness of the decision are, as a matter of principle, to be deemed irrelevant.[120] – Exactly how the questions of 'free' discretion, of 'important' reasons, of violations of 'good morals' are put into a special sphere by the practice of adjudication itself, in as much as a firm judicature by and by comes to take the place of these factors, requires a further, separate investigation. The latter would have to concern itself with the 'living law' and to take the form of a historical-explicative inquiry into the empirical life of the law. The treatise presented here could be of use as a preliminary methodological investigation of these more specific questions.

---

[117] RGZ, vol. 59, p. 388.

[118] RGZ, vol. 60, p. 395.

[119] *Juristische Wochenschrift* 35 (1906), pp. 53–54 (where the interesting psychological remark is made that whoever has good reasons will often be incapable even to recognize the possibility of taking an opposing view).

[120] *Juristische Wochenschrift* 34 (1905), p. 139, (35) 1906, p. 134, and, with particular determination, the decision reported in *Gruchots Beiträge zur Erläuterung des deutschen Rechts* 50 (1906), pp. 1005–1009, as well as RGZ, vol. 65, p. 98.

Appendix

Note I

Examples of how one can justify the most differing judgments with 'strictly juristic' exegetical arguments have been provided in such number in the last few years (it suffices to remind the reader of those cited by STAMPE und FUCHS) that an attempt to offer as many as possible here could lead only to repetitions. J. H. VON KIRCHMANN already cited a series of apposite examples in his talk 'Über die Werthlosigkeit der Jurisprudenz als Wissenschaft' (which is reported in the *Entscheidungen des Königlichen Geheimen Obertribunals. Neue Folge*, vol. 4 [Berlin: C. Heymann, 1847]), to which we can point here. Let us present *in extenso* ['in detail'] only the following deductions of F. LASSALLE, which should convince even the warmest adherent of traditional hermeneutics of how much one can prove juristically and of how little depends, in fact, on juristic acumen. Lassalle was taken into pretrial detention in 1848. He had been charged with delicts under articles 87 and 91 of the *Code pénal* ['Code of Criminal Law'] (high treason, impermissible arming of the people, etc.).[xxi] In the *Code pénal*, these delicts are expressly designated, by the relevant title headings, as *crimes* in the technical sense. According to article 113 of the *Code d'instruction criminelle* ['Code of Criminal Procedure'], the release from pretrial detention, even on bail, is impermissible in cases of these delicts. After Lassalle's appeals for release had, naturally, been rejected, he argued as follows in submitting a renewed, likewise unsuccessful, appeal:

> Since I permit myself to lodge an appeal for provisional release on bail, though I have been arrested on the basis of articles 87 and 91, and am thus charged with a *crime* [French in the original], I believe I must begin by pointing out that article 113 StrPrO,[xxii] which excludes a release on bail in case one is charged with a *crime*, is not unknown to me. If I nevertheless [116] submit such an appeal, then this happens

142

only because I believe that I am able to prove, in the clearest and most indubitable way, that this excluding provision of article 113 of the Code of criminal procedure was rescinded, with regard to political crimes, by the statute of 15 April 1848. The *Königliche Ratskammer* ['Royal Council Chamber'] will surely not be prevented from doing justice to my argument, assuming I am able to develop weighty reasons supporting my case, by the fact that this seems to have escaped the notice of the public. This view, however, results in a convincing manner from a consideration of the statute of 15 April 1848 as a whole, and subsequently of its individual paragraphs: 'We, Friedrich Wilhelm, etc., by means of § 2 of the ordinance of 6 April, have reinstated the competence of jury courts for political crimes and crimes of the press in the Rhenish province, and have extended the same to political and *press offences*. To secure the implementation of this provision (that is, of the provision in § 2 of the law of 6 April 1848), we decree the following.'

This statement is followed by a number of particular provisions, among which § 12 reads *as follows*: 'In all other respects, in particular as concerns preliminary investigation, *provisional release on bail*, legal remedies against the decisions of the *Strafratskammern*,[xxiii] notification of the content of the files to the defence, the provisions of the Code of criminal procedure that apply to *matters of disciplinary police*[xxiv] apply as well to *political and press offences*.'

A Rhenish judge will, naturally, in line with the French practice and the terminology of the *Code*, be tempted, at first glance, to understand the expression 'political and *press offences*' at the close of § 12 – and in the event of which, as the paragraph makes clear, a provisional release on bail is to be permissible, in analogy with the prescriptions that apply to matters of disciplinary police – as referring to minor offences in the sense of the French law – that is, in the narrower sense of *délits* ['delicts'] as opposed to *crimes*. On closer inspection, however, one will, first of all, [117] arrive at the conviction that the statute of 15 April 1848 does not merely not operate with this distinction – that it does not only apply the word 'offence' in the same way to serious offences (*crimes*) and to actual *délits* – but that it *expressly and positively abolishes* this French legal distinction, with respect to political actions, by means of an express definition. Therefore, if the statute declares the norms concerning provisional release that apply to matters of disciplinary police to be applicable to political and *press offences*, it includes political crimes and crimes of the press under these offences, and thus declares a provisional release to be permissible. One might go so far as to say that this statute had the altogether explicit intention to extend to political *crimes* the more relaxed form of preliminary investigation, including the possibility of release, which the code permits only for *offences*. Political crimes were, in virtue of this statute and *in specie* ['in particular'] in virtue of § 12 of the same, to receive a preferential treatment. Although still materially subject to the penalties fixed in the code, they were to be put on an equal footing with mere offences with regard to the form of investigation, the possibility of release, etc.

To substantiate this interpretation, one would first have to establish that § 12, in declaring the provisions on provisional release that apply to matters of disciplinary police to be applicable as well to political and *press offences*, refers not merely to offences in the narrow sense but, in departure from the usage of the code, also to *crimes*.

This proof will have been provided in the most unassailable manner if it can be shown that the legislator himself *defined* his expression 'political *offences*', in such a way that it is clear that the latter expression *is meant to comprise all political crimes and offences, without consideration for the severity of the sentence, and in deliberate exclusion and abolition of the French legal distinction.* [118] And, indeed, the statute of 15 April provides this definition in explicit words. We read in § 2 of the statute that the offences which are described in book III, title I, chapters 1 and 2 of the *Rheinisches Strafgesetzbuch* ['Rhenish Code of Criminal Law']ˣˣᵛ are to be regarded as 'political offences' in the meaning of § 2 of the ordinance of the sixth of this month. *Code pénal*, book III, title I, chapter 1 and 2, however, encompasses both crimes (*crimes*) and minor offences (*délits*). Chapter 1 (articles 75–108), in particular, contains only and *exclusively* grave *crimes*, including the articles 86–92 under which I have been charged.

And, nonetheless, § 2 explicitly *defines* the crimes of the *Code pénal*, book III, title I, chapter 1, as '*political offences*' – or rather, the other way around, it defines the expression 'political offences' as applicable to all of chapter 1, title I, book III (articles 75–108) of the *Code pénal*. If, therefore, the statute of 15 April 1848, in § 2, explicitly determines that the actions regulated in the *Rheinisches Strafgesetzbuch* book III, title I, chapter 1, and therefore also those regulated in articles 86 and 92 are to be included under 'political *offences*', and if it, moreover, declares the provisional release on bail to be permissible for political *offences*, in analogy to the provisions on matters of disciplinary police, then this implies – the inference is so simple that it is tautological – that a provisional release is permissible, according to the law as it stands, for all actions that are covered in Book III, title 1, chapter 1 of the *Code pénal*.

The statute of 15 April 1848 has thus brought about a complete identification, alien to the *code*, of political crimes and offences, as far as *formal* procedure is concerned.

That this identification of crimes and offences in § 2 of the statute of 15 April 1848 was perfectly deliberate also results from the fact that crimes and offences are explicitly mentioned alongside each other, [119] and are thus treated as quasi-distinct, in the preamble to the statute, which reads: 'We, Friedrich Wilhelm, etc., by means of § 2 of the ordinance of 6 April, have reinstated the competence of jury courts for political crimes and crimes of the press in the Rhenish province, and have extended the same to political and *press offences.' Later*, however, in § 2, where the definition is given, the difference between crimes and offences is explicitly dropped. The interpretation offered here is also further supported by the fact that § 2 of the statute of 15 April 1848, which determines that the actions in question 'are to be regarded as "political offences" in the meaning of § 2 of the ordinance of 6 April', and § 2 of the ordinance of 6 April explicitly mention both crimes as well as offences. It reads as follows: 'In the district of the appellate court of Cologne, the competence of jury courts applies to political crimes and crimes of the press as well as to minor political offences and offences of the press.'

Here, as well, the wording, at least, still distinguishes between crimes and minor offences, and mentions both alongside one another. And § 2 of the statute of 15 April 1848 makes it clear that the meaning of the ordinance of 6 April, which explicitly mentions both crimes and minor offences, extends to all political *offences* in the wider sense of the term.

Finally, this identification did not result from an imprecise use of language – an objection that is ruled out by the explicit definition of § 2 of the statute of 15 April, as well as by the preamble to the statute and by the reference to the ordinance of 6 April – but from a use that is appropriate to the spirit of the statute as a whole and which must evidently have been intended by the legislator. The whole statute of 15 April, after all, has no purpose other than to introduce an identification, with regard to formal procedure, of political crimes and minor offences that is alien to the Rhenish StrPrO, as well as to regulate it in more detail, and in such a way as to accord a preference and a mitigation to this species of offence. If this [120] identification was to take place to such a degree, on a procedural level, that even minor offences, through the employment of the provisions of the Rhenish StrPrO, were supposed to benefit from being adjudicated by jury courts, then it is evidently in the spirit of the statute as a whole for article 113 of the same to accord the benefit of provisional release also to political crimes and thus to drop the formal difference, which it is the whole purpose of the statute to eliminate, in this respect as well.

If there should remain any doubt whatsoever as to the intention of the legislator to permit provisional release for all political offences, irrespective of the severity of the penalty, then the same will stand refuted, in the *most authentic* way, by the *ministry of state's proposal* that occasioned the enactment of the statute of 15 April. In this proposal of the ministry of state, of 14 April 1848 (printed in the *Cölnische Zeitung* of 19 April of the year), we read: 'In virtue of § 2 of the statute of the sixth of this month on some principles of the future constitution, the competence of juries for political crimes and for crimes of the press has been restored, and has been extended to political offences and offences of the press, in the Rhenish province. The ordinance, which we most deferentially attach, contains the further implementation of this provision. It serves to determine (– that is, the ordinance *defines the concept of political offences*, it does not adopt it from Rhenish criminal law, but determines it anew, and by means of the definition in § 2, which, as we have seen, explicitly identifies crimes and offences –) the *concept* of political and press offences (– here, crimes are no longer given special mention –), and *regulates* the procedure concerning these offences in such a way that the *stricter* procedures that are prescribed for the *investigation and prosecution of crimes* are not to be applied unless this is *required* by the fact of the competence of a jury court.' The ministry of state here expresses the intention of the statute in wholly positive and unambiguous words. [121] It is its purpose to regulate the procedure *in politicis* ['in political matters'], so that the stricter forms that are mandated in the prosecution and investigation of crimes do not come into use any further than is necessary as a result of the trial by jury court.

Pretrial detention is not necessitated by the competence of a jury court, as is shown by the provisions of the statute itself. Section 12 of the statute of 15 April of the year has therefore not only actually permitted provisional release in the event of political crimes, insofar as it permits such release for all political *offences*, while § 2 defines actions under articles 75–108 of the *Code pénal* as offences; rather, the paragraph *explicitly intended* to bring about the release of those detained under charges of political crimes.

This cannot be established more irrefutably than by reference to the ministry of state's own words: '[T]he stricter procedures that are prescribed for the investigation and prosecution of *crimes* are not to be applied unless this is required by the competence of a jury court.' How could the ministry of state have spoken about the *cessation of the stricter forms* if it had intended, in § 12, to extend the possibility of provisional release on bail only to *délits*, in the event of which the release *was, at any rate, already permissible beforehand*!

It has thus been established without any doubt that § 12 of the statute of 15 April, in analogy to the provisions applicable to matters of disciplinary police, permitted and *wanted* to permit the *beneficium* ['benefit'] of a provisional release for criminal charges *in politicis*, even though this benefit is otherwise available only in matters of disciplinary police.[xxvi]

Note II

A good summary of the historical conditions of the great impact of the free law movement [122] can be found in BRIE (talk, printed in *Archiv für*

Rechts- und Wirtschaftsphilosophie 3 [1909/1910], p. 31). – A history of the 'struggle for legal science' has not yet been written. In order to show here how incessantly the idea of free law norms has come to expression in the work of real legal academics (and not merely in that of social scientists such as LORENZ V. STEIN), we would like to quote some relevant remarks here. EINERT, for instance, published a book entitled *Das Wechselrecht nach dem Bedürfnis des Wechselgeschäftes im neunzehnten Jahrhundert* (Leipzig: F. C. W. Vogel, 1839), although he apologized for his method in his cautious and humble preface. FICK says of this book, in the Heidelberger *Kritische Zeitschrift für die gesammte Rechtswissenschaft* 1 (1853), p. 479, that it 'brought about a revolution in the doctrine of bills of exchange, of a sort that is not often the work of one individual legal scholar'. EINERT is credited with having 'turned a method of legal-scientific activity that was firmly established almost into its opposite' and 'developed a theory of the law of bills of exchange that became the basis for a law-making deed on the part of the nation the like of which cannot be found in any other sphere of legal life'. J. E. KUNTZE assented to this view (*Der Wendepunkt der Rechtswissenschaft* [see n. 40], p. 15), and in his *Jus respondendi in unserer Zeit* (see n. 98), p. 20, he claims that one must not make it depend on happenstance whether 'the anxiety of the court of law can draw its corrective immediately' from statute. He is fully acquainted with talk of a 'teleological' treatment of the law; he objected to HEINRICH AHRENS (*Juristische Enzyklopädie*, vol. I [Vienna: Gerold & Sohn, 1855]), for instance, that the latter's 'theory of the circumstances of life' was working towards a juristic teleology and thus had nothing new to offer (*Der Wendepunkt* [see n. 40], p. 26, note 2). KIERULFF claimed, at the same time as EINERT, in his *Theorie des Gemeinen Civilrechts* (see n. 85), pp. xxii–xxiii, that the time was ripe for independent creation. And with KUNTZE stood W. LEIST, *Über die dogmatische Analyse* (see n. 22), p. 39: 'It is life – as it surrounds us in its moving fullness and freshness, the life of our present, the life of our nation – that we want to discern.' LEIST emphasized the 'nature of things', and he took [123] the real and empirical life of the law, as opposed to the 'valid' law, to be contained in this expression (just like EHRLICH, later on, in 'Über Lücken im Rechte' [see n. 4], p. 529 sqq.), although he also proved to VANGEROW that the latter had used the expression in seven different meanings (in BURKARD WILHELM LEIST, *Naturalis ratio und Natur der Sache* [Jena: Frommann, 1860], pp. 51 sq.). – All these citations show that the awareness of the contrast between the abstract legal norm and the actual life of the law has always been present. Still, even IHERINGS writings were unable to bring forth the impact that has been achieved by the modern free law movement.

Note III

The striving, born of some conception of science or other, to impose a certain method on jurisprudence (that of the exact natural sciences, for instance) so as to transform it into a 'science', the comparisons with other sciences of all sorts and the inferences to the claim that jurisprudence develops in parallel to these other sciences: all this has taken on an unusual extent, and has often led to precipitate generalizations and demands. One must distinguish, however:

1. Jurisprudence has been compared with other sciences for a long time. The best-known examples, perhaps, are IHERING's comparisons with the natural sciences (*Geist des Römischen Rechts*, 5th edition, vol. II. 2 [see n. 39], pp. 357 sq.), and in particular with chemistry (LEIST, *Über die dogmatische Analyse* [see n. 22], p. 100, offers the same comparison). These comparisons – which, in IHERING, stand in the context of his conception of the reality and 'fertility' of legal concepts – become dangerous once they are used to draw conclusions about method. This is so in particular when authors contrast the inductive and the deductive procedures, and expect to find the salvation of jurisprudence in the former, like NEUKAMP in *Einleitung in eine Entwicklungsgeschichte* (see n. 60), pp. viii–ix – a move that has already been criticized by PACHMANN, *Über die gegenwärtige Bewegung* (see n. 65), pp. 32–33. [124] Insofar as such views are meant to emphasize the procedural importance of the discovery of the facts (compare HANS REICHEL, 'Induktion in der Jurisprudenz', in *Grünhuts Zeitschrift für das Privat- und Öffentliche Recht der Gegenwart* 22 [1905], pp. 99–108, at pp. 104–105), they are unobjectionable. However, if jurisprudence is thereby to be transformed into a natural-scientific discipline, so that it may discover 'laws', by way of a hypothesis that is to be verified inductively, through the observation of empirical facts, one is no longer engaged in jurisprudence, but is doing sociology or psychology or national economics instead. The demands that jurisprudence be turned into a pure 'science of fact' spring from the ideal of 'exact natural science', as well as from the unwillingness to recognize any other method of inquiry than that of inductive inference, as it governs in the natural sciences, as a legitimate way of proceeding. AUGUST FOREL (*Die Zukunft* 11 [1895], p. 11) says, in this vein, that the jurist lacks 'any connection with life; he is devoid of any sense for the scientific use of inference by analogy, for the slowly progressing, ever doubtful, but always improving natural-scientific method of induction'. And ALFRED BOZI, 'Recht und Naturwissenschaft', in *Annalen für Naturphilosophie* 1 (1901/1902), pp. 414–437, at p. 426, goes so far as to say that 'just as zoology distinguishes mammals, birds, amphibia, etc., the law divides into the large

spheres of the civil law, the criminal law, and the law of nations'. ERNST
FUCHS (*Die Gemeinschädlichkeit der konstruktiven*[121/xxvii] *Jurisprudenz* [see
n. 23], p. 175, like EHRLICH before him, with greater caution, in *Die Zukunft*
54 [1906], p. 238) draws the conclusion, from the development of medicine,
which led from a stage of abstract deductions to the use of the inductive
method, that a parallel development will take place in jurisprudence. It is
noteworthy, in this context, how FUCHS's discussion of the decisive significance of the personality of the judge, the *daimonion*[xxviii] ('Die soziologische
Rechtslehre: Eine Erwiderung', in *Deutsche Juristen-Zeitung* 15 [1910], cols.
283–288, at col. 284), stands in tension with the natural-scientific ideal and
with the parallelization of medicine and jurisprudence. The successful out-
come of an operation, after all, can hardly [**125**] be explained by appeal to the
doctor's *daimonion,* whereas there is a relation, of course, between the just
decision and the judge's *daimonion.* With the use of such comparisons, it is
just as easy to combat the free law movement. RUDORFF, for example,
predicted in his response to v. KIRCHMANN's talk on the uselessness of
jurisprudence as a science (*Kritik der Schrift des Staatsanwalts v.
Kirchmann, etc., von einem Lehrer dieser Wissenschaft* [Berlin: Plahn,
1848], p. 21) that 'without a doubt a second Mr v. Kirchmann will soon
advise our doctors to abolish medical science and to appoint shepherds and
wise women to their councils, so as to spread the blessings of free and
unregulated juristic enterprise to the area of the medical sciences'. In a
similar vein, STAHL (*Rechtswissenschaft oder Volksbewußtsein* [see n. 60], p.
24). It would be easy to increase the number of such examples to infinity. A
remark of SCHLOßMANN (in *Grünhuts Zeitschrift für das Privat- und
Öffentliche Recht der Gegenwart* 7 [1880], pp. 544–545; see also *Der Irrtum*
[see n. 5], pp. 2–3) bears a special methodological significance, in that it
makes clear, in response to ERNST ZITELMANN's work *Irrtum und
Rechtsgeschäft: Eine psychologisch-juristische Untersuchung* (Leipzig:
Duncker & Humblot, 1879), that juristic terminology is independent of
psychology. Or compare STAMPE's following sentences, in *Unsere Rechts-
und Begriffsbildung* (see n. 50), p. 42 – the traditional classification of legal
transactions into unilateral and bilateral transactions is far removed from
any classification in terms of purpose or function:

> It takes the aspect of the structure of the fact as its criterion of classifica-
> tion, a criterion that is wholly unsuitable, from a didactic point of view, to
> ground a fundamental classification that is to be presented to the student
> at the outset. This is as though national economy, in talking about goods,
> or pharmacology, in talking about drugs, was to introduce a principal

---

[121] Who would not think here of Nietzsche's antithesis: constructive-explosive?

classification of goods or drugs based exclusively on the differences
between the respective techniques of their production.

[Ibid.,] pp. 79–80:

> How would one evaluate a doctor who unthinkingly prescribed a drug
> that is effective against a certain illness against a novel and altogether
> different malady? In my opinion, there is no more flagrant violation of a
> statute than the use of a legal institution for a purpose other than the one
> that is attributed to it by that statute, and in spite of the awareness [126]
> that this unchanged application of the law for a novel purpose will, *in
> concreto*, lead into a legal-political *cul-de-sac.*

2. The parallel between the free law movement and the free religion movement that Gnaeus Flavius (H. U. KANTOROWICZ) put forward in *Der Kampf
um die Rechtswissenschaft* (see n. 12), pp. 35–38, has been especially conse-
quential. A parallel of this sort is entitled to methodological consideration,
because there is a systematic connection – one that is also historically
demonstrable – between the methods of traditional juristic hermeneutics
and the theological doctrine of interpretation, whereas comparisons to
medicine or to the natural sciences are only ever capable of illustrating
individual claims. It must be conceded, however, that the time of the transition of the natural sciences to their modern method exhibits many parallel
cultural-historical phenomena and it must occasion surprise that these have
not yet been made use of in the discussion of the last few years. (The
following sentences of PARACELSUS [*Werke*, vol. I, ed. Johannes Huser
(Straßburg: Lazarus Zetzner, 1616), p. 608] might be worthy of consideration
here, as expressions of a certain *conviction* – that is, characterologically:
'What are you looking for in logic and in your dialectic, which are repugnant
to the doctor, and which dim the natural light? Do not waste your precious
time with such books.') – As far as theological interpretation is concerned, it
has always been common among jurists to compare their own method to the
theological. Of the newer authors, see, for instance, JORDAN, 'Bemerkungen
über den Gerichtsgebrauch' (see n. 16), p. 231: 'The judge's activity – similar
to that of the theologians, who, in the spirit of its founder, further specify the
Christian doctrine for the circumstances of their time and thus allow it to
continue – is never anything more than an application, not of the letter, to be
sure, but of the spirit of the law to actual cases.' Because there are here a
number of fundamental notions that are shared between theology and jurisprudence, a parallel will, in this context, amount to more than just an
interesting illustration. The discussions in KRAUS ('Die leitenden
Grundsätze' [see n. 34], pp. 616–617), and SCHLOßMANN (*Der Irrtum* [see
n. 5], p. 43, note), are also noteworthy here:

The interesting parallel between [127] a legal science that is not addressing itself to the literal meaning of the words of statutes and a theology that
vindicates for itself the right to free inquiry, and likewise the observation
of the way in which the conflict between the authority of statute and the
free discovery of the law can be resolved in a legal context …

Compare also TH. STERNBERG, *Allgemeine Rechtslehre* (see n. 27), p.
130, note 1.

Note IV

When the *Reichsgericht* expresses its view on its own position towards the
'materials' of a statute, it usually emphasizes that the materials do not have
decisive significance; they may be given only an 'adminicular consideration'
(RGZ,[xxix] vol. 8, p. 84) – they may only 'inspire' (vol. 16, p. 194, whereas the
'purpose of the statute' is inferred, in the same volume, p. 55, from its
motives – vol. 21, p. 357; vol. 62, p. 291 – particularly RGSt,[xxx] vol. 13, p.
171: 'Neither the occasion, nor the purpose, nor the views of the drafters of
the statute, nor the legislator's thoughts concerning the content and scope of
the statute are what determines the true content of a statute, but rather the
will of the legislator that is declared in the statute itself'). The 'materials' are
significant if they emphasize what truly is willed in the statute, but not if
they express a different view (vol. 21, p. 437; vol. 23, p. 41): an approach that
compels the question of why they have significance only if they repeat what
can otherwise be read out of the statute – that is, only if they are superfluous.
Either they have juristic significance, in which case it will be necessary to
give a precise account, or they do not. Whoever wants to ascertain the
Reichsgericht's position on the doctrine of interpretation will find himself
compelled to interpret the *Reichsgericht's* utterances on interpretation,
which is sometimes difficult. This overview is merely to illustrate the extent
to which conscious clarity is still lacking in discussions of this fundamental
question. Although the court denies that the significance of the motives can
ever be decisive, one can find, [128] elsewhere than in the older decisions
(for example RGZ, vol. 7, p. 430 sq.), sentences such as the following: 'As the
materials of the statutes on accident insurance allow us to see on every page,
the legislator (a few lines earlier, there is talk of the factors of legislation)
was well aware that', etc. (vol. 21, p. 54). To identify the 'reason of legislation' (vol. 53, p. 203), the court refers to the motives. Or it is said that a
certain interpretation was 'mandated neither by the wording nor by the
history of the genesis of the statute, and as long as a divergent will of the
legislator is not clearly visible', etc. (vol. 59, p. 148); 'It is not to be doubted

that art. 405 of the (A)HGB[xxxi] was present to the factors of legislation to its full extent during the enactment of the PO,[xxxii] thus this provision (§ 35 PO), which is altogether clear in its wording, must be understood so as to', etc. (vol. 43, p. 100). In vol. 51, p. 274, the motives are regarded as indecisive for the reason that they 'neither have the purpose nor the power, as a private work that cannot be attributed to the factors of legislation, to declare the statute'. Then it says further: '[I]t has surely not been the intention of the authors of the legislative text in its present form …' (vol. 62, p. 86, in which decision we also find a distinction drawn between the 'legislative' motive, the occasion of legislation, the legislative decisions and the legislative goals, and in which the court finally speaks of the aims of legislation). In vol. 69, p. 181, it is said that it is almost unthinkable that the reasons (that is, the motives) for a statute were given without awareness of the way in which the disputes at issue are decided in practice, wherefrom it is concluded that the statute must be understood to intend to continue this practice, unless it explicitly disavows that intention. And what is the point of emphasizing that the report in the protocol does not 'permit the ascertainment of the majority opinion in the commission' (vol. 66, p. 254)? – The *Reichsgericht* expressed its true view of the matter as follows:

> Given this legislative situation, the *Reichsgericht* regards it as appropriate to hold on to the almost 30-year-old practice of the *Obertribunal*,[xxxiii] since the latter mediates between both interests in a way that is suitable both to the statutes and to demands [129] of commercial intercourse. It may well be a part of the task of practice to highlight the deficiencies of a statute, but its most important task nevertheless remains to apply the statute, flawed though it may be, while adapting it, where possible, to the demands that commercial intercourse imposes on it.

From the literature that is chiefly addressed to practice, let us pick out at random the following examples: OTTO FISCHER, *Grundbuchordnung für das deutsche Reicht nebst den preussischen Ausführungsbestimmungen. Text-Ausgabe mit Einleitung, Anmerkungen und Sachregister*, 5th edition (Berlin: J. Guttentag, 1909), note 6 to § 14, who appeals to the 'clear intention of all' who 'participated' in the drafting of the statute; or REINHARD FRANK, *Das Strafgesetzbuch für das Deutsche Reich nebst dem Einführungsgesetze*, 2nd edition (Leipzig: C. L. Hirschfeld, 1901), p. 316, commenting on § 246 StGB,[xxxiv] Nr. II, 4: 'Since the statute expressed itself positively, and since it did so – as is clear from the motives – with full awareness, interpretation is bound to this.' One needs only to open some commentary or other to find further examples.

Altogether, we arrive at the following list of effective factors of interpretation: literal meaning, economic or political purpose, the views voiced in the materials, the historical origin of the statute, and, with subsidiary force, the sense of justice and the needs of intercourse. No further word is needed to show that methodological clarity on these heterogeneous elements (each individual one of which is itself again composed of further elements in the most different ways) is necessary.

Notes

[i]   ZPO = *Zivilprozessordnung*, Code of Civil Procedure.
[ii] GVG = *Gerichtsverfassungsgesetz*, Courts Constitution Act.
[iii] Implicit reference to Montesquieu (1989), 147: 'But the judges of the nation are, as we have said, only the mouth that pronounces the words of the law, inanimate beings who can moderate neither its force nor its rigour.'
[iv] Schmitt transcribed this reference from Hatschek's *Englisches Staatsrecht* (see n. 4). Hatschek, though, seems to have confused Austin's *Province of Jurisprudence* with the *Lectures on Jurisprudence*. The claim that it is a 'childish fiction' to say that judges do not make law is to be found in the *Lectures on Jurisprudence*. See Austin (1911), 634.
[v]   *Gesetzgebende Faktoren*: German juristic term of art that refers to the organs of state involved in the process of legislation. See Giese (1948), 30.
[vi] The *Positiones Iuris* is a list of theses that Goethe submitted for oral defence to the Faculty of Law at the University of Strasbourg to achieve his licentiate after his dissertation had been rejected. See Landau (2007).
[vii] The *Bundesrat*, or Federal Council of the Wilhelmine Empire, was made up of representatives of the governments of the constituent states of the Empire. It had to assent to federal legislation and participated in the exercise of the emperor's executive competences.
[viii] Schmitt here seems to refer to Francis Bacon's *Novum Organum* I.lix-lxi, where Bacon is discussing the idols that beset human minds. Between his discussion of the idols of the market (*idolum fori*) and idols of the theatre (*idolum theatri*), Bacon notes that 'there are also names which lack matter by fantastic supposition' ('*ita sunt & nomina, quae carent rebus, per suppositionem phantasticam*'). See Bacon (2004), 92–95. Schmitt's implication would seem to be that 'the will of the legislator' is a term that lacks matter or a basis in things that are real.
       The implicit reference at the end of n. 36 is to Richard Wagner, *Lohengrin*, act 2, scene 5.
[ix] BGB = *Bürgerliches Gesetzbuch*, Code of Civil Law.
[x]   'Schäffle' in n. 40 likely refers to economist and sociologist Albert Eberhard Friedrich Schäffle (1831–1903).
[xi] The *Reichsgericht* in Leipzig was the Supreme Court of the German *Reich* from 1879 to 1945.
[xii] Implicit reference to Richard Wagner, *Die Meistersinger von Nürnberg*, act 3, scene 1.

xiii   A *Landgericht* is a mid-level court in the German system of courts.

xiv   The *jus respondendi* was the right accorded by Roman emperors to some legal scholars to issue opinions that were legally binding. See Tuori (2004).

xv   In Catholic moral theology, a proximate occasion of sin is a circumstance that is likely to incite a sinful act, so that one has an obligation to avoid it, if possible. See Delany (1911).

xvi   Formal statutes (as opposed to material statutes), in German jurisprudential terminology, are decisions taken by the organs of legislation, by the use of the ordinary procedures of legislation, that lack the character of general legal norms. See Schmitt (1928), 181–196.

xvii   GBO = *Grundbuchordnung*, Land Registry Act.

xviii   The Prussian *Kammergericht* was the highest court of appeal for the Eastern provinces of Prussia.

xix   The *Reichsoberhandelsgericht* – literally, the *Reich*'s Supreme Court of Commercial Law – was the predecessor institution, from 1869 to 1879, of the *Reichsgericht*.

xx   In Molière's play *Le malade imaginaire* ['The imaginary invalid'], a candidate doctor, in an oral examination, answers the question 'Why does opium put people to sleep?' by pointing out that opium has a sleep-inducing power.

xxi   The Rhenish province of Prussia continued to use French law at the time, which had been introduced by Napoleon. See Mieck (1992), 98–100.

xxii   StrPrO = *Strafprozessordnung*, Code of Criminal Procedure.

xxiii   A *Strafratskammer* is a criminal court.

xxiv   *Zuchtpolizeisachen* = lesser crimes or misdemeanours.

xxv   Lassalle appears to use the German '*Rheinisches Strafgesetzbuch*' interchangeably with the French '*Code pénal*'.

xxvi   Schmitt gives no source for this lengthy quotation attributed to Lassalle and we have been unable to identify it among Lassalle's published speeches. It is possible that Schmitt had direct access to the (unpublished) court records relating to Lassalle's trial in 1848–1849, which took place in Düsseldorf. (For biographical information on Lassalle, see Fetscher [1982]). Schmitt wrote *Gesetz und Urteil* while serving as a *Referendar* or trainee lawyer at the *Oberlandesgericht* in Düsseldorf. See Mehring (2009), 37–40.

xxvii   Reference to Nietzsche's contrast between the Apollonian and the Dionysian in *The Birth of Tragedy*. See Kaufmann (2013), 155–160.

xxviii   Socrates, in Plato's *Apology*, 31c, refers to a spirit or inner voice he calls his *daimonion*, which prevents him from doing injustice. See Plato (1997), 29.

xxix   RGZ = *Entscheidungen des Reichsgerichts in Zivilsachen*, Decisions of the *Reichsgericht* in matters of Civil Law.

xxx   RGSt = *Entscheidungen des Reichsgerichts in Strafsachen*, Decisions of the *Reichsgericht* in matters of Criminal Law.

xxxi AHBG = *Allgemeines Handelsgesetzbuch*, General Code of Commercial Law.

xxxii PO = *Postordnung*, statutory regulation of the postal service.

xxxiii High Tribunal, the Supreme Court of Prussia, the competences of which were transferred to the *Reichsgericht* in 1879.

xxxiv StGB = *Strafgesetzbuch*, Code of Criminal Law.

The Value of the State and the Significance of the Individual

A Note on the Text and the Translation

In the aftermath of completing *Gesetz und Urteil,* in a letter sent to his sister Auguste postmarked 4 April 1912, Carl Schmitt wrote that he was 'writing a new book. In one and a half years, I'll be done.'[1] In a diary entry dated Tuesday 5 January 1914, Carl Schmitt observed that he 'Saw my book in the *Frankfurter Zeitung.* Very fine. Ernst Lamberts announced its arrival. I was quite joyous; went to the library, was very lazy and exhausted and didn't arrive at working. Gave my book to the library, wrote suddenly to Gentsch and was eager, but hopeless.'[2]

Dated in press to 1914, Carl Schmitt's *Der Wert des Staates und die Bedeutung des Einzelnen* was published by J. C. B. Mohr in Tübingen and had already landed in the hands of its readers by the last days of the prior calendar year.[3] Following the intervening success of the work in its acceptance as an *Habilitation* at Strasbourg,[4] conferring on Schmitt the right to teach in universities, the book was republished under the same title and with the same pagination by Hellerauer Verlag-Jakob Hegner at Hellerau in 1917.

---

[1] Schmitt (2000), 140–141. Schmitt announced his completion of *Gesetz und Urteil* in a letter to Auguste Schmitt dated 28 November 1911 (ibid., 109).

[2] Schmitt (2005 [2003]), 135: 'Sah in der Frankfurter Zeitung mein Buch. Sehr schön. Ernst Lamberts kündigt seine Ankunft an. Ich war sehr froh; ging zur Bibliothek, war sehr faul und müde und kam nicht zur Arbeit. Schenkte mein Buch der Bibliothek, schrieb plötzlich an Gentsch und war eifrig, aber hoffnungslos.' Reinhard Mehring confirms the anecdote materially with reference to the dedicatory copy of Schmitt's *Der Wert des Staates* in the Stadt- und Landesbibliothek in Düsseldorf, which is dated to '5. Januar 1914'. See Mehring (2009), 605, note 6.

[3] In an entry in his diary dated 11 December 1913, Schmitt notes that 'die Bücher kommen von Mohr' ('the books have arrived from Mohr', the publisher of *Der Wert des Staates*): Schmitt (2005 [2003]), 125. See also Mehring (2009), 65.

[4] Mehring (2009), 89, dates the success of Schmitt's habilitation to the winter semester of 1915/16.

In the early twenty-first century, *The Value of the State* was republished twice by Duncker & Humblot in Berlin, with a new pagination and textual arrangement on the page. The first of these editions, in 2004, was likely based upon a faulty scan of the early twentieth-century editions, generating numerous typographical and orthographic errors. The second of these editions, in 2015, corrected some of these errors and helpfully added Schmitt's own corrections in his personal copy of the book as an appendix. This later edition, checked against the twentieth-century versions of the text, forms the copy text of the present edition and translation. Schmitt's notes to the German original are preserved as footnotes, whilst notes on the edition and translation are presented as endnotes.

In accord with prior translations of Schmitt's work, the present translation aims at terminological accuracy and consistency within the limits of readable English. The translation thus renders *der Mensch* as 'the human' or 'human being' rather than 'man', and aims at retaining Schmitt's distinction between *Recht* and *Gesetz* to the greatest extent possible. Where it was not possible, the German original has been indicated in brackets in the present translation and edition.

The Value of the State and the Significance of the Individual

CARL SCHMITT

Dedicated to Pabla v. Dorotič.

OVERVIEW OF THE CONTENTS

III. Chapter: The Individual   217

The individual in the state. – The empirical individual and the subject of a legislation. – The great personality in the state and its great affairs. – The absolute ruler and the state. – The individual as mere fact and the norm as foundress of all value. – The legal subject. – The theory of contract. – The political question concerning the protection of the individual from the state. – The opposition of law and state as an individual case of a general opposition of immediacy and mediacy.

~

Introduction

[9]
First is the commandment, the humans come later.[i]

Däubler, *Das Nordlicht*, II. p. 542.

The objections that can be raised above all against a book about state and individual, are directed either against the results or the methods of the investigation, and, in accordance with this bipartition, proceed from two different kinds of critics. Whoever expects, in any author, an unbroken harmony with the content of the views that are held to be timely, or whoever faces the empirical manifestations of the law and of the state with concrete purposes and goals, will compare the finished formulations that articulate the conclusions of a book with their own results, which are presupposed as self-evident, and pass judgment accordingly, or perhaps even miss a 'result'. It is not only the human who calls himself modern, the one for whom the temporal succession of the dominant opinions *a priori* founds a criterion of their growing value, who will judge in this way, but also the politician and the party-man, the practitioner in the specific sense of the word. The philosopher of law, by contrast, who is interested in the method alone, is the sole competent judge, needless to say, of a legal-philosophic investigation; yet he, too, may see in his method a self-evident result and then raise objections that, ultimately, are based on a positioning and gestures towards scholarly matters similar to that which, on various grounds, determined the [judgment of the] 'modern' human **[10]** and the practitioner, on a dogmatic disposition that solely collates results. If now a special attempt is undertaken, in the introduction, to clarify the trajectories of thought of this book and to answer objections – and this is what, fundamentally, every advanced development of a theme consists in – then such an effort towards understanding has another sense here than in the finished presentation in [the body of] the treatise. It is thus not unjustified and superfluous; whether it is on point is another question, one that it is best to attempt to lay to rest via the deed itself.

The first kind of critic, who takes note, in any academic book, only of the result, will take the present book to be of interest insofar as it finds the meaning of the state exclusively in the task of realizing law in the world, whereby the state becomes the midpoint of the sequence 'law, state and individual'. The law, as pure, evaluating norm, which cannot be justified by appeal to facts, logically represents the first member of this sequence; the state brings about the connection of this thought-world with the world of real empirical manifestations and represents the only subject of the ethos of law; the individual, however, as a singular empirical essence, disappears, in order to be grasped by the law and the state, qua the task of realizing law, and in order to receive its own meaning from that task and its own value from this closed world, in accordance with its own norms. Other modes of judgment may yield another value for the individual, or perceive in it an autonomous instance for legislation; for a legal-scientific inquiry, however, the strictest heteronomy of all legal norms is the only thing that decides in this matter, not in order to annihilate the individual, [11] but rather to make it into something that it is possible, in the first place, to evaluate from a legal perspective. This is the sense of the equality of all before the law, if indeed it ought to know no distinction between persons. –

The impression of such propositions upon the merely modern human allows itself to be lightly reckoned. The modern human, in his normal empirical type, is of the view that his time is a 'free', sceptical, authority-inimical[ii] and thoroughly individualistic time, that it is the first to have actually discovered and to have honoured the individual, and to have overcome antiquated traditions and authorities. In view of these achievements, these 'results' [might appear to] contain an inexplicable atavism, a relapse into a barbaric and anti-cultural enmity towards life. If in truth this were so, then the critique of the modern human could signify an objection. No author, who seriously concerns himself with questions that arise from the law, the state and the individual, may lightly ignore that which, with any justification whatsoever, can be labelled as the spirit of the times. In this there would lie a frivolous arrogance, the just punishment of which would be impressively executed by enduring ineffectiveness and sterility. But the spirit of the times is to be distinguished from that which individual spirits think and write about their times, and, to the objection of the modern human, one ought to reply – after a due reminder has been given, in parentheses, of the numerous points of contact of this 'inimicality to culture' with Plato's theory of the state –, that the impression, which determines the objection of untimeliness, is based on an errant, or at the least uncritical, presupposition about the actual character of our time. A time that presents itself as sceptical and exact cannot call itself individualistic in the same breath; [12] neither scepticism nor the exact natural sciences are capable of grounding an individuality; they can no more rest with the singular individual, as a final fact, not to be clarified or to be doubted any further, than with a personal God. If individuality can be spoken of at all, then such talk already contains the definition of the object of which individuality is predicated as a point of imputation for evaluations according to norms. Perhaps the modern human does not understand this argument. Perhaps what our time understands by individuality relates to what the great thinkers of about a hundred years ago understood by it in the same way that modern internationalism relates to their cosmopolitanism. Only thus is it possible to grasp why an age is called individualistic, although numerous symptoms, recognizable at first glance, protest loudly against the assumption that the freedom of the individual is indeed regarded, today, as the peak and the measure of all aspirations. The age of the machine, of organization, the mechanistic age, as Walther Rathenau called it in his *Critique of the Times*[iii] – in a book which is so timely that the age could be named accordingly as that of the *Critique of the Times* – the age that shows, in the objects of its yearning and swooning, what it lacks, whose culture, as it rules in fact, culminates in the notion of the 'business', which expands even into the domains of spiritual life, of art and science, the age of the money economy, of technology, of the art of directing, of absolute mediacy and of the most general calculability, which extends itself even into literary productions – if [this age] is at all to be called an individualistic one, then only *per antiphrasin*,[iv] as should be clear from the inexhaustible words and discourses [13] that are made about it. No other time has had such a need for codifications and subsumptions. No spirit inimical to authority can be said to rule, no matter how much critiquing is taking place, but rather the entire submissiveness of good taste, where there are, so as to mention only the most delicate blossom, rake's manuals and digests of good taste under whose provisions a great part of cultivated humanity subsumes as hastily as Don Quixote subsumes his experiences under the matters of fact of the knight's tales that he holds to be exemplary. This phenomenon finds its polar supplementation, important for the judgment [of our times], in the fact that, today, many humans are held to be individualities because they are no longer ashamed of their meanness and their bad manners. It is true that good taste can be formed wealth,[v] but it can also be the product of a lack, of a spiritual poverty not to be confused with the poverty in spirit.[vi] I do not wish to decide to which type [*Art*] the good taste that is so enormously common today pertains; the number of learned persons who have accomplished nothing more than to acquire this good taste is, at any rate, very large and determines the overall picture.

Our age is not an individualistic one, it need not therefore be a small one. There have been great times that were emphatically anti-individualistic. To point out the error of many contemporaries about the individualism of the present time, thus, contains no judgment of disvalue about it. Precisely today, rather, a new grandeur appears to loom, in numerous currents of the times that abstract from any empirical happenstance and already find an expression in art and in aesthetics, to the extent that the latter turn away from the exemplary images of the Renaissance and towards another comprehension of the world. To mention two additional symptoms of greater probative [14] force: first, sociology, as the new science of the factual relations without which the individual human cannot be conceived and in which he fully disappears, is a specifically modern science; the contemporary theory of knowledge, moreover, seeks the epistemological subject, which can only be located in a supra-individual consciousness, by addressing itself to a problem that has never been formulated as precisely before.[vii] Thus, before the apparently anti-individualistic results of the book can be repudiated *a limine*[viii] in view of their [supposed] untimeliness, the critic's own results, which unwaveringly appear in the role of the judges, even though they are appointed only by [the critic's] thoughtlessness, would themselves have to be legitimated. In the course of this, it will turn out that the value affirmation that is contained in the proclamation of individuality as a recognized requirement of the times necessarily leads back to the critique of the method with which it was attained. No evaluation can rest content to point to individuality as a mere empirical characteristic of individual humans, of everyone who bears a human face. It is compelled to go beyond this, perhaps to destroy [this mere empirical individuality] and rip it apart, in order to attain a newly grounded unity. The unity, which lies in individuality and makes up its value, can only ever be a spiritual bond, one that is gained by way of normative observation. Whoever recognizes this will cease to confront results without retracing the trajectory of the argumentation. Whoever does not recognize this should feel free to regard this book as a symptom of an unedifying disposition and he may lay it aside or refute it: he is then in the happy position, as a merely and in and for himself 'modern' human, that he cannot be refuted himself. What is empty of content cannot be refuted, what is stuck wholly in the absurd cannot be led *ad absurdum*. One must consign it to the time to which it appeals. – [15]

To the human of practical life, however, who rightly points out that no practice is possible at all unless we hold some things to be self-evident and who regards the results on which he bases his judgment as indispensable instances of the self-evident, this book can justify itself only by appealing to the fact that it wants to recognize the state in its rationality, but not to put forward political demands. If the result of the book is something positive, in the highest sense, for the state, this has to do neither with a 'government' nor with some party program, and the politician who supposes something of the kind ought to keep in mind that the political construct the design of which he strives to realize must also be a state. The state to be reformed as well as the reformed state are both states, and a scholarly investigation is interested in the commonality [of both], but not the technical means and the concrete content of the reform, which precisely concerns the politician, to whom, by contrast, any commonality is, for the moment, irrelevant. The interests are different, not only in their distance to contemporary events and in their perspective, but rather in their method and thus in their object. Should the legal-philosophic inquiry find a specific definition of the state, then this is a result, in any case, for scientific inquiry, even if the definition of law remains restricted, for the time being, to a few necessary [but] negative claims; if numerous phenomena of legal life turn out to be explicable, in consistent interpretation, by appeal to the position that the state is allotted by the definition, and if, in particular, the important proposition that the law precedes the state results [from the definition], then something will therewith already have been accomplished. Admittedly, for whomever is fixated on the 'abundant proposition' [*erklecklichen Satz*],[ix] the concept, essence, modality, value and nature of 'abundance' [*Erklecklichkeit*] will have to be quarrelled about beforehand, [16] but that would already no longer be a quarrel about results but rather about methods.

Nothing is gained by putting significant accentuation on the 'polymorphism of life' or even on the 'living facts of the case' and by emphasizing other similar things that, as far as they are rightly observed, could indeed be an inducement to occupy oneself with the theory of practice, but which do not constitute the end or even the core of a theory. As soon as one enters into theoretical inquiry, the specific differences show themselves, even in cases where the object of inquiry is a practice. The methods and interest of a philosophy of the state thus are incompatible with the methods and the interests of this or that practitioner of political life. No one will refuse to give his admiration to the great politician, but the qualities that found his greatness as a politician lie in a domain into which no legal philosophy can penetrate. The significant politician cannot be refuted by a theory, no more than the great effect of his politics is capable of refuting a theory. It is to be emphasized that only arguments, but not aims, tendencies, currents of the times are capable of a refutation. Science, according to its concept, stands in fundamental opposition to active life. 'Living is essentially non-philosophizing, philosophizing is essentially non-living', said Fichte (in a fragment from the year 1799), who was not only a great philosopher, but also a truly capable human.[x] Any philosophic investigation, which is worthy of the name, will be able to be useful to politics only mediately. Still the result of this book, that the state has a grounded value, expresses a self-confidence, one that signifies the point at which theory and practice touch, because the theory of practice turns [17] into the practice of theory. There is no theory[xi] without the presupposition of a consequence and its possibility; one[xii] may call it optimism, or even arrogance, that a truth is sought at all and a duty to it is felt; one can also, with appeal to many historical events, put forward the proposition that no good theory of the state has remained without far-reaching real consequences and that there is at least a finite mutual relation between both. Nonetheless, this must not lead one to fail to recognize the distinctions and to undertake the disastrous attempt to 'conform' heterogeneous things to one another, to bring two irreconcilable methods into 'interplay' with one another. Whoever wishes, from the beginning, to hold both in view will accomplish nothing, but rather at most arrive at a dissembling and cross-eyed eclecticism that is particularly repulsive in philosophic matters. The trust in an ultimate harmony and in a final effect, which is to establish the liaison of theory and practice in philosophic things, is no longer a scientific matter. It is necessary and useful; but the harmony must result from the fact that each of the participants does their duty; it cannot be brought about by violence or mutual concessions. –

The opposition between life and science is particularly sharply articulated in contemporary legal philosophy. The thought, that the law qua norm cannot be derived from facts, is familiar to many. What stands at the centre of the discussion today is the question concerning the law, as the norm that is indifferent to facts, not the question concerning the state as a reality. In contrast with this, this book is interested in the question concerning the state, while the discussion of the law is limited to what leads to a legal-philosophic definition [18] of the state. Therein appears to lie the distinction between a predominantly juristic interest and a purely philosophic interest, a distinction that emerges particularly clearly in a consequence that this book, like others, has been unable to avoid: that the law becomes independent in relation to ethics, that it receives its dignity ἐξ αὐτοῦ,[xiii] and not from a μετουσίᾳ[xiv] with ethics, and that no relation between external conditions and inner freedom, no gradual transition from one into the other, is to be recognized. The consequence that the law cannot be derived from ethics, which puts Feuerbach[xv] in opposition to Kant – which opposition is frequently blurred, not by Feuerbach, who clearly articulates the separation, but by Kant, who does not represent the unity clearly enough – is contested precisely by those legal philosophers least inclined to derive the law from facts. But the contradiction has its ground in a neglect of the inquiry into the state and of the consequences that result, from the essence of the state, for the legal-philosophic construction of individuality. The demand for a separation is in no way a mere individual opinion that emerges only in philosophizing jurists. It dominated the views of many centuries and it ought to be easy enough to infer it from the distinction between external and internal freedom, as well as from the impossibility of subsuming the visible and the invisible, the temporal and the eternal under a single concept. Neither the state nor the law end in the individual: they are not acquainted with perfection in an individual; they are not acquainted with the saint. The construction of a type, as it is undertaken in the immortal *bonus pater familias*,[xvi] could not proceed in any autonomous ethics. In the desert, there is a saint, but no just men. If, according to Luther's word, **[19]** the jurists ought not 'to mingle in the realm of Christ', then the pure ethicists, likewise, should at least concede the validity of the methodical autochthony of the realm of the world.

For many, admittedly, all the questions that can arise here have long since been laid to rest; many will regard our hesitation to address a larger range of problems as a deficiency. The newly awakened interest in legal-philosophic questions had the courage to attempt a comprehensive solution *in complexu*,[xvii] with the principled generality that marks the beginning of every new spiritual movement. In the works of *Stammler* and *Cohen*, that interest has already borne the fruit of finished systems, which might easily give the impression of being the final culmination of centuries of philosophic thought-work, as they link up with a world of thought that is closed, at least with regard to the terminology in which the essential problems are expressed. In truth, however, these systems merely announce the beginning of a new life for legal science, which articulates itself most clearly in the aspiration to achieve clarity about questions of general legal theory, as well as in the discussions about the relations between legal norm and legal life and about the differences between theory and practice. It is necessary first to treat questions of general legal theory and the relation of individual legal concepts to one another, before the Kantian or Copernican question concerning the possibility of legal science qua science or the problem of its categories is posed and solved. Cohen, in his *Ethics of the Pure Will [»Ethik des reinen Willens«]*, wanted to see in jurisprudence the science that has a significance for the solution of the problem of ethics analogous to that of mathematics for the theory of natural scientific knowledge; in making this assumption, he presupposed that jurisprudence, beyond any doubt, can claim to be a science, [20] and he thus had to put up with the perhaps peremptory objection that the question whether jurisprudence was a science had barely even been raised, and that Cohen's premise is liable to appear to the jurist, in particular, to be an instance of involuntary irony. By ignoring the greatest difficulties, a highly unclear domain of knowledge is brought into parallel with mathematics and the system of law is derived, with careless certitude, from the juristic concept of action, for which there are, as yet, only a few works that have not led to recognized results. These are indeed valuable, but they merely serve to highlight the general perplexity. Thus, however infinitely many striking and clever thoughts have thereby come to light, as far as the result is concerned, it is apt, unfortunately, for[xviii] Kantorowicz to claim (*Archiv für Sozialwissenschaften Neue Folge* vol. 13. pp. 602/4) that such attempts bring legal philosophy into discredit with jurists. If the jurists, for their part, were to draw the conclusion of the worthlessness of legal philosophy, they would, admittedly, also be guilty of a mistake,[xix] but nothing is saved by this insight. I am persuaded that Cohen, in recognizing the concept of action as the central concept of legal science, shows himself to have an impressively sharp vision, but a juristic account of this central position, which alone would merit scientific attention, is still lacking. The determination of the juristic categories and of a theory of legal science cannot succeed without a legal science that is free of objections, if it takes its purity seriously, it cannot at any point carry out a 'descent into particular questions' of the science of positive law, such a transition and descent would be the most egregious of all gradual-nesses [*Allmählichkeiten*].[xx]

If even an authority like Cohen was unable to avoid overhasty syntheses, then it is not astonishing – given the refinement of language and of the general [21] currency of philosophic turns of phrase; given the abundantly fertile soil [*Nährboden*] represented by the fruitful bathos[xxi] of rich libraries – that the air is everywhere full of pompous phrases and that grand words, such as culture, critique and life, strike one's ears from all sides. But these important things attach to most people much as his honour and force attach to Don Octavio (in Mozart's *Don Juan*[xxii]): one recognizes the honour only from the fact that he constantly swears by it, while the force can be inferred only from the numerous prayers for force, which, given that they proceed from such a decent man, cannot possibly have remained unheard. –[xxiii]

In view of all this, the investigation restricts itself to several definite questions: that concerning the relation between law and state, [as well as] that concerning the definition of the state and of the consequences that result for the individual in the state. The numerous questions, in particular, which are connected to a definition of the law [*Recht*] are discussed only to the extent that this was requisite to laying out the essence of the state in order to find the path through a plethora of problems and to provide the context for a complete legal-philosophic theory of the state.

Chapter 1

Law and Power

If the opinion that all law is only a result of actual power relations and is based in the final instance upon violence were permitted to experience a transposition, by analogy, onto the domain of scientific opinions, then the question concerning the relation between law and power would already have been decided. The number of those who, in plausible discussions and with numerous examples drawn from history and from everyday life, give the law a solely factual ground is so great that they undoubtedly have the preponderance of power – as long, at least, as one considers the factual popularity of their opinions only. However, as soon as the grounds and their correctness are submitted to scrutiny, this actuality no longer comes into consideration and arguments alone decide the matter.

The opposition of both theories, which is referred to by means of the antithesis of law and power, is altogether irreconcilable. If the law is conceived by the power theory as a particular distribution of social forces, and if its concept can be gained for legal philosophy by an explanation of the historical events that gave rise to an assessment connected with the idea of rightfulness, then it does not make any difference for the matter whether the superiority from which the law proceeds is a purely physical or a psychological power. The big fish, which, according to the famous phrase, have the right to devour the little ones,[xxiv] [23] and the ruling social class, which, as a result of the after-effects of a successful subjection centuries ago of the original inhabitants of a land, is enabled to define the content of the statute laws [*Gesetze*], both have legal right only because they have power. However much infinitely fine distinctions may come to the fore within power, these distinctions do not come into question for a philosophic treatment, which is concerned with the distinction in principle. The power of the murderer over his victim and the power of the state over the murderer are not essentially different for the power theory, but rather only in their external manifestation, conditioned by an historical development, and in their scope, their impression upon the human masses. It remains for this view only to investigate, with consideration for such accidents, which likewise belong to reality, how the concept of law may be more narrowly encompassed, and how that which is specific to the power of the state over the murderer is to be determined. As long as the theory lays claim to consistency, this specificity must, in any case, lie exclusively within the domain of purely empirical reality and must not be brought into contact with a 'justification' in the particular sense of the term. It would thus be possible to ground the state's power to punish, in distinction to every other power, upon the general opinion of the members of the state, and to say that the state has the assent of the people on its side when it exercises its power in this way. The assent, however, which gives the state's power its particular imprint, will then be based upon the psychological fact of agreement with the majority. It is the latter that, in this view, stamps factual superiority into authority, power into law. The common opinion conceives of the question concerning the ground of the law in this way. It holds that the regress that arises when we ask, again and again, for the lawfulness of the law[xxv] finally [24] takes its end in a fact. This is thoroughgoingly consistent, at least as soon as we draw upon the consent of the people, or some other factual process, to offer an explanation of the law. Even the elements [of the explanation] that refer to the approbation or disapprobation of the people or of specific social groups are here deployed only as psychological facts, not because they are correct, but because they are there. For the power theoreticians, the law is thus a mere part of being, no further and not otherwise to be explained; not otherwise to be justified than any other being, of particular interest on account of its immediate significance for the people and for their common life, but wholly inserted into the mechanism of factual events, out of which it emerges at no point.

For this theory there is thus no refutation of the justification of a power. Whoever is subordinate to it is not to be helped, he stands there with his arguments like a poor fool, *e vinculis ratiocinatur.*[xxvi] Perhaps this is better concealed in the terminology; perhaps one might claim that a separating juxtaposition in the sense of a primacy of the law must collapse upon the irrefutability of a fact, in virtue of the unavoidable reciprocity with which the power of the law results from the law of power; in a more folkish idiom, it is said that a hand full of violence is more valuable than a sack full of law; in banal discourse one speaks, today, of the logic of the facts. The sense is always the same: every appeal to a law contains the reference to a power, every attempt to help a legal right to achieve recognition signifies a striving for power, the arguments with which a legal right is proven to exist are only sublimated calculations of one's chances of getting one's way, their probative force, it is said, is equal to their attractive force in the given moment. [25]

Should the law be treated simply as something that is there, then it must be subject to the law of causality like everything that is there. Should the law become power, every explanation other than the causal one evaporates into nothing, and every cause, which generates an effect, becomes power, to that extent, and therewith again turns into law. Even if the fact in which the regress that arises in the attempt to account for the ground of the law finally comes to a halt is pushed back as far as one pleases into the past, this train of thought remains wholly within a theory that only describes and explains, but which does not desire to and that cannot justify or ground the law.

In contrast to this a reference to the opinion of the majority of decently and equitably thinking humans signifies a reference, in legal theory, to something that does not hold of its own authority, but rather marks a content that corresponds to what ought to be. A more precise treatment of this reference is particularly instructive in laying out the opposition of both theories. Should the positive statute contain such a reference, then it can come to be contested whether the opinion of decent humans therewith turns into a part of positive statutory law, whether it flows into statute, or whether it is an autonomous complex of norms that is referred to, one that is independent of the law and that remains independent even when statute refers to it. Now, if positive statutory law [Gesetz] is law [Recht] only because it is the ruling view, the one that is able, via the means of particular forms, to give itself validity, then the statute's reference to a ruling view signifies a return to its own origin, to the state of nature; the view of the decently and equitably thinking humans is measure-giving because the decent humans are in the majority and thus get their way with their opinion, which would be valid, because it rules. Its validity would not result from the fact that it is the decent [26] humans that hold it, but rather from the fact that these humans are permitted to call themselves decent, without having to face effective dissent, and from the fact that they have the power to get their opinion recognized. In the strictest opposition to this, however, it is also possible to find the ground of validity in the words 'decent and equitable', so that the views which are referred to attain their own dignity; they are valid, under this view, only insofar as they merit both honorific predicates, and they continue to be valid, consequently, even if most humans are of another opinion and even in case there are no decent humans left. They are not the result of the joint action of humans and of their opinions, they do not result from facts, but rather from arguments. The circumstance that the [statutory] reference is to decently or equitably thinking human beings, and not the decent and the equitable in the abstract, is incapable of altering anything about this – its sole significance would be to make it easier to determine what is decent and equitable. The opinion of humans would not be a ground of validity, but rather an indication of a value.

The question is not whether law or power prevails in the world, but rather whether the law can be derived from facts. Even the recognition of the law by humans is just another fact, and the real question is whether facts are capable of grounding a right. Should the question be negated, then an opposition of two worlds is given. Should the law be autonomous and independent of power, then this entails a dualism that corresponds to the antitheses of ought and is, of the normative and the genetic, of a critical and a natural-scientific inquiry. The sphere of the law cannot, then, be encompassed within the domain of positive, actually valid law; rather, if actual validity is added to the law, in order to [27] constitute its positivity, it is added as something external, as something that is, in this regard, inessential. Whoever puts forth the assertion that all law is necessarily positive, whoever concludes the grounding of the law with the processes that 'generate' the positive law, thereby professes their adherence to the theory of power and negates the irreconcilable opposition between law and fact, as well as the proposition: *non potest detrahi a jure quantitas*.[xxvii] The law, which ought to have nothing to do with any factual explanation, receives an autonomy, in its own world, that is nowhere interrupted. Should the law, however, turn into power, that is, into a mere fact, there is no place in which it can raise itself above mere factuality; in every individual legal implementation it is permissible, then, only to speak about facts, and not about inferences and arguments, and all that has ever been brought forward as 'reasons' for a decision dissolves into a magnificently veiled *argumentum ab utili*.[xxviii] What is more, it will be impermissible to stake out, within the theory of the law as mere power, a domain that remains reserved for a treatment via legal constructions and questions about what would consistently have to follow from them. It is not possible, accordingly, to declare one's agreement with the common method that grounds a complex of norms – norms, which the State, as a particular power, emanates – on the mere factual will of the state, but that, within this complex, works with the means of juristic argumentation and desires to ascertain the reasonable and correct will, although the ground of the validity of the norm is a merely factual one. A fact does not allow itself to be demonstrated away, a will cannot be proven to be present by proving that it is rational and correct. Kant's attacks on the ontological proof of the existence of God are more important for the jurist than for anyone else. [28]

If the law is defined as power, then it is no longer essentially [a] norm, but rather essentially will and purpose. The actually valid law is then a sum of definite prescriptions, which proceed from a purpose-setting position and an evaluation of the law [is] only possible in the way that purposes are measured with reference to one another. It is entirely manifest that the law is in need of no further grounding and is also not capable of it, as soon as it becomes a will, becomes a purpose, of which a reality like the state wills that it should be achieved. Of course, all manner of other purposes may then be compared with this purpose, but if the law, according to its concept, stands in some relation to the purpose-setting reality [the state], then such a comparison and judgment of purposes is legally irrelevant, since the factuality, which is brought into the law via the purpose and the state, cannot be refuted. The living principle in the world of law would not be juristic argumentation in its correctness, but rather the will of the state in its concrete factuality.

Strictly taken – and philosophy can only ever take everything strictly – both worlds, of the law and of power, must stand next to one another in irreconcilable autonomy. The theory that brings the law together with power at any point must consequently renounce any explanation other than a causal one, it must dissolve all law and any legal norm in a game of impelling or restraining forces, so that it would be senseless to evaluate or to exhibit a pathos of approval and disapproval – or not even senseless, in as much as a disapproval would already be contained in this qualification. Now, although it is[xxix] the one who grasps a view in its last consequences who alone rightly understands it[xxx] and although whoever expresses an opinion must not invoke the factual [29] content of his own notions so as to raise the objection of a misunderstanding against an opponent when he himself is not in agreement with a correctly derived conclusion, it is nevertheless useful for the clarification of the question to make reference to certain unspoken but causally effective notional contents. It is indeed possible to hear an evaluation in the definition of law as power, one that appears to attach to the concept of power, in that every power, or at least every relatively enduring and abiding power, is considered not merely to be explicable, but to be justified and grounded. In the trust that indeed there will be good reasons, for the fact that precisely this and no other proposition was able to acquire the power of a legal norm, or precisely this will to attain a position of authority, law and power are often identified, while one silently passes over the sole important question, whether indeed there are any 'good reasons'. Such a trust in the path of things and in the justice of history expresses itself exemplarily in the words of Luther's text *de potestate Papae:*[xxxi] Primum, quod me movet, rhomanum pontificem esse aliis omnibus superiorem, est ipsa voluntas dei, quam in ipso facto videmus. Neque enim sine voluntate dei in hanc monarchiam unquam venire potuisset rhomanus pontifex.[xxxii] In this attribution of a factual power to the will of God there lies the recognition of a justification. The recognition of good reasons likewise contains an assent and an evaluation, just as the accentuation of the non-accidentality of an historical result, which would express a self-evident superfluity if it did not imply an evaluation.

In the word power there lies, to take into account the associations that are bound up with it today, a moment of recognizing respect, through which it becomes possible [**30**] to make the law into a particular kind of power, into a conscious superiority, as it is silently presupposed when the proposition of the big fish, who have the right to devour the small fish, is generally perceived as a paradox. The elevation of power into the domain of purposive human action already implies the conferral of a distinction, since the conscious and purposive human being is a privileged being precisely for the utilitarian – if only because the honouring predicate of purposiveness can be attributed only where there are purposes of which the observer himself has become[xxxiii] conscious. If even the weakest moment of evaluation comes to be contained in the specificity of law, as juxtaposed with power, then the law must appear, from this stand-point, as a privileged power. The law will become qualitatively distinct from power and alter its essence. The predicates, in which the particularity of the law is found, lead in their consequences to a precise inversion of the antithesis: the law is not explained by appeal to power, but power is explained by appeal to the law. The power to which appeal is made in the definition of the law is itself understandable only by reference to the law, it is a lawgiving power only because it exists 'with right [*mit Recht*]'. If it is then said, in view of some event, that whoever has power, also has the right [*das Recht*], that which for a perfect scepticism would signify a negation of the law becomes, in the use of literally the same verbal expression, a profession of the highest trust, one that says that no power gets its way unless that power is justified. Precisely those who compare the relations of states and human classes with those of individual humans in the state of nature, gladly emphasize that it is no accident that particular states or races[xxxiv] are superior, while others [31] sink down into powerlessness and therewith into lawlessness. The only surprise here is that nobody has yet attempted to approach the problem from the other side and, for example, to establish a statistics of the victims of murder. Just as it is not an accident that precisely this or that human is [a] murderer, it also cannot be an accident that precisely this or that other is the murdered.

There are people for whom the general human agreement on important legal judgments appears to signify nothing other than the uniformity with which, for instance, many hundred thousand people, in contemporary Germany, have the need to drink coffee in the afternoon. And yet not one of these utilitarians has been able to determine the historical moment at which the great epiphany illuminated 'egoism', so that the latter raised itself up, of its own force, from the flat earth, in order to levitate in a sphere in which it must recognize the 'equal right' of the egoism of the other and be willing to sacrifice itself. Perhaps this process was possible where intelligent individual humans were in a position to impose their own superior insight upon others – in something like the way in which the great Friedrich convinced the Prussian peasants to potato farming – and to bring about a condition, via their factual superiority, through which it was possible to subject the unenlightened egoism to an enlightened one and to bridle it in such a way that a sufferable order was established. Stahl is right when he (*Philosophie des Rechts* I. p. 240) claims: 'If one were to paint a picture for a human who knew nothing of the state of the stormy movement in innumerable directions of the life of a people, of the constant undulating surge against the state – as all interests of the individual are against the state and its order – he would believe in the possibility of the state even less than most people now believe in the realm of eternity [*das ewige Reich*].' What is said here of the state holds [32] for any reasonableness, enlightenment, correctness or however one likes to call it. In the end, it can only be the better insight that, as such, compels humans not because it is more powerful, but because it is better. This, however, amounts to a grounding from an evaluation that is no longer an empirical one. This evaluation cannot be removed, what is more, by calling only that insight a better one which retains superiority, over the course of time, as the result of a selection in the struggle of opinions. Every evolutionary theory of selection must proceed from values and presuppose values, on account of the fact alone that the assertion of a goalless development involves a *contradictio in adjecto*.[xxxv] The goal that is necessary, in each case, to speak of a development cannot result from the consciousness of that which develops itself, or from the mere succession of the events that are declared to amount to a development, but only from the conscious contemplation of the one who conceives the succession [of events] as a development.

The empiricist, who sees all law as a mere game of interests, and who distinguishes preponderant interests or interests that deserve protection, likewise hides the problem in indistinct ambiguities. The word interest contains an opposition to every norm and ought expressly to remain within the factual, the realm of experience. Where it enters into the definition of the law, it is meant to eliminate the norm that lies beyond all interests. The legal wrong [*das Unrecht*], which is defined as a damage to some interest, thereby appears as that which is primary. The ground of this primacy is said to follow from a purely empirical fact: an interest must first be damaged before humans can arrive at the thought of protecting it. For example, the damage to interest that lies in a murder must first itself have occurred, before one can say that life is a protected **[33]** interest and that there is a norm according to which murder is something reprehensible. The act of defending against an attack, in this view, becomes the prototype of every lawful action, and thus redeems and ennobles the savage's [*des Wilden*][xxxvi] instinctive addiction to revenge, by portraying it as a defence of society.[xxxvii] – This train of thought confuses the psychological occasion for becoming conscious of the norm with the [justifying] ground of its validity, and the theory turns into a causal explanation of the norm from the psychological fact of habituation. The notion of damage to interests, which guides such explications, and which alone is the cause of the appearance of simple comprehensibility, nevertheless invariably contains a normative element, one that is found either in the 'interest' or in the 'damage'. Not everyone is a fitting subject of an interest; the law does not treat it as a damaging of the interests of the animal when it is slaughtered. Accordingly, the question arises, who decides[xxxviii] whether a damage to interests has occurred, the one putatively damaged or a higher instance. If one conceives of the human being as a member of a community and if one then claims that, in a concrete case, there is a damage to interests, one to which the community reacts, then the judgment is taken away from the damaged individual. The community, however, does not judge its own interest or the subjective interests of the individual damaged in the concrete case, it never portrays itself as a judge in its own affairs. It appeals, rather, to an 'objective' norm.[xxxix] There is no way in the world through which it would it be possible for the interests to distil out of themselves the norm by which they could be balanced and classified. The comparison, frequently invoked, with the Baron Münchhausen, who drew himself out of the bog by the pigtail, does not hit the one who desires to make the norm independent of the interest, but rather the one who derives the norm from the very interest that he subordinates to the norm. [34] If the interest of the community or of the collectivity merely as such, merely as the stronger, were determinative, then the present collision of interests would likewise be one that involved the collectivity; the latter would have to decide about it as a party and its right would then, in truth, be nothing but power, it would insert itself as a participant, when the interests of the individual have been damaged, and would make its own interest prevail. This approach would have the merit of consistency. But if the interests of this collectivity, or such as are protected by it, are the only ones worthy of being labelled as interests, then the collectivity's interests are more important than those of individuals. It is self-evident, then, that the former stand higher than the latter, that it is a misfortune if they are overgrown by individual interests and that the ground of the superiority of the interests of the collective cannot be deduced from the mere [notion of] interest. Here, too, the [notion of] interest, strictly speaking, refers to a justified interest, the discussion is no longer about the naked fact.

The theory, which explains the law as fact, sees itself ever again pushed back to the point where it must distinguish between a power that is capable of becoming law and one that is not capable of this, between an enlightened egoism and a dumb egoism, between an egoism capable of development and an egoism incapable of development. 'Capable', in this context, simply means 'valuable', the juxtaposition of individual and collective interests, likewise, contains evaluations that make it possible to 'elevate' power into law. The definition of the law begins where power becomes irrelevant; no counter-argument can be derived from the fact that one hesitates to draw the consequences up to the point where the irreconcilability becomes striking. In every negation of the justification of the law, as it is contained in the definition as power, one finds, instead, the hidden undertaking to argue for the justification of power; [35] the definition does not lower the law; it elevates power. It was possible only because power had already been conceived as law. The perplexity caused by the attempt to mix the empirical facts referred to by talking about power in a circle determined by norms, such as the law, finds an illumin-ating illustration in the fact that one can respond to the assertion that law is only ever power by putting forward the opposite claim, that power is only ever law, without running any risk of being refuted.

If there is to be a law, it must not be derived from power, as the difference between law and power is altogether unbridgeable. No one will call the opinion of an individual human a norm; it pertains to the essence of the norm that it is valid independently of the individual (in the philosophic sense). For the norm, there is no individual who could constitute it by virtue of perceiving it, whether it is logical or legal correctness that stands in question. If the mere opining of an individ-ual is incapable of grounding a norm, then that of ten or one hundred thousand individuals must be equally incapable of doing so, because the sum is not capable of elevating itself above the type [Art] of that which is summed up.[xl] It is close at hand, precisely in this context, to say that there is a point at which quantity turns into quality. In the cases, however, in which it might appear that a metamorphosis of this kind is indeed taking place, the reason for this is always that the expansion of quantity is taken to be a form of the appearance, a symbol or an index of a quality. The impression that the great or imposing mass makes upon the observer refers to something extra-worldly, extra-human and timeless. The psychological effect of great spaces and temporal expanses, the sublimity of colossal buildings, are examples of such representation [36] of quality by quantity. Nothing essential, however, has changed therewith, since the senseless can never grow up into a sense, that which is alien to value can never grow up into a value. A gradual transition is wholly unthinkable; to appeal to it so as to ground legal or ethical values would be to confuse the question of the genesis of a reality with the question concerning the symptoms of a value, which the expansion of quantity can frequently be held to stand in for. If the *diuturnitas*,[xli] the *longum tempus*,[xlii] is a sign that something has found recognition as [a] value, and if this recognition implies a *praesumptio facti*[xliii] for the groundedness of this value, then the grounding of the value [still] does not amount to a mere investigation of facts, not even if recourse is made to the con-venient evasion of the gradualness of a factual sequence of events playing itself out in infinite temporal spaces, one that is ascertainable, in its individual stages, only in rough outline. The dripstone needs centuries and millennia to take on a salient shape, but the minerals out of which it forms itself must always have been there, and no dripstone could form out of a pure compound of oxygen and hydrogen, even in a million years.

'Eternity does not overtake itself on its own ladder'[xliv] (Däubler, *Das Nordlicht* II, p. 533). The observation of nature, to which the common life of humans also belongs, insofar as it is only a matter for the descriptive and explanatory social sciences, cannot yield any law. The establishment of a norm alone is capable of grounding the distinction between lawful and unlawful, but not nature. The sun shines upon the just and the unjust.

If the law can be derived from facts, then there is no law. Both worlds stand [37] juxtaposed; that the proposition that all law *is only*[xlv] power can be precisely inverted into the thesis that all power is only law does not prove any mutual relation and derivation, but the incompatibility [of law and power]. If the law now receives its own rhythm, if its norms must be valid independently of any empirical fact, in a closure without gaps, it will also follow that an empirical fact as such can never be made subject to the law's judgment, that is, in the law there are only matters of fact and elements of the crime, not, however, individual facts as such. Even the word, which occurs in a positive statutory application, transforms the real process, which is given for legal qualification, into a matter of fact, of the kind presupposed by the law; [in this transformation,] it might transpire that the matter of fact is not given, in which case the legal evaluation will likewise immediately end and the 'case' will no longer come into consideration. The 'given state of affairs' is never judged by the judge as merely given; the logical relation, here, has its empirical-psychological reflex: the judge cannot recognize any matter of fact [in the legal sense] [*Tatbestand*] unless he already 'envisions' the statutes that are to find application or unless he is already more or less conscious of them. Any presentation of processes and events, any material report [of the facts that might bear on a case], even if it strenuously avoids any question of law, can be given only after exhaustive clarity about the possibilities of legal judgment has been achieved. The matter of fact thus already amounts to the result of a specification, by which a new construction has been created, and it is this matter of fact alone with which the jurist is concerned. The perfect closure of the world of legal norms is therewith secured.

In order to express the conflict of opinions in a concise formulation, one might say that the [38] notion of the law as a means to other purposes faces off against the other notion that sees in the law a final purpose. The notion of purpose, however, is to be understood, in these two cases, in two fundamentally different ways, because a final purpose that pretends to be a final purpose according to the concept, and not merely in the concrete case is something essentially other than a purpose that takes its place in the endless mechanism of purpose and means. The opposition does not lie in the psychological, in the realm of human opinion. If it did, it would signify no more than the fact that there are humans, on the one hand, who employ the law (that is, the beliefs that humans hold about the law) as a means, while on the other side there are those, by contrast, who consider the law to be the purpose of their power as a means. Therewith, the matter would have become an historical one and its decision been made dependent upon what humans, in a concrete situation, hold to be most important or feign to be most significant. If, however, the purpose as final purpose, as absolute purpose, is to be elevated out of this nexus of the factual, then it ceases to be the purpose of concrete humans, while there emerges a series of constructed subjects of this 'purpose' who are unable, though, to make use of any 'means' unless they are conceived as effective realities. Whoever indeed, puts forward the proposition that power is only [a] means of law, against the thesis that the law is only [a] means of power, sees in law a supra-empirical power that makes the empirical serviceable to its purposes. If the law, then, is the purpose and power a means of realizing it, the law can proceed from power if the proposition that power is [the] means of the law makes power into a material[xlvi] out of which law is formed. If, however, the law as absolute purpose is to have nothing in common with the means, then no **[39]** means can ever correspond to the purpose and there is no reason to think that [the notion of] purpose should be drawn into the definition of the law. Purpose therefore does not belong in the definition of the law.

Purpose is defined as something that ought to be achieved. The whole antagonism between Is and Ought is still contained, in an unexplained form, in the turn of phrase 'ought to be achieved'. The phrase may, for one, say that someone, a concrete subject, wants to achieve something, something that, seen from his vantage point, is a purpose, namely that which ought to be achieved: thus, for instance, satiation is the purpose of eating, in the individual case and in general; – or else the 'Ought' expresses a recognition, so that, in this explanation of the phrase, the purpose is something of which one must demand that it be achieved. In this distinction, what is unsatisfactory in the definition of the law as a desire, as a purpose, becomes manifest to the eyes. The normative, which is embedded in the words 'ought to be realized', contains nothing more than a reference back to the law and asserts nothing more than: the law

[Recht] is something that ought to be realized with right [mit Recht]. The emphasis is upon the normative, upon the justification of the purpose. What matters, hence, is not the purpose, but rather the norm. To add the notion of purpose signifies bringing the realization of the law into its definition, whereby a moment of reality and, to use the formulation of the antithesis, a moment of power enters into the definition of a pure norm independent of every fact and experience. The norm can bear no will, no purpose; the bearer of a purpose can only be a reality, perhaps one that sees its task in the 'realization' of the law, but which, precisely on that account, must be strictly separated, conceptually, from the law as long as that purpose is at issue. The question of the purpose is not the [40] question of the essence of law, but rather that of the subject of the ethos to be found in the law. The norm stands above the mechanism of means and purpose, but the empirical world can be a means of the law, in the sense of a medium, insofar as a condition ought to be realized within it which must be labelled as rightful and by a power that is itself rightful. To define the law as purpose or will, however, amounts to nothing other than to allow entry to the thought of security, in its most material significance. While this does not turn the law into a mere means, as demanded by the unadulterated theory of power, it does turn law into a purpose – one that, in the last analysis, is still methodologically homogeneous with the means as the power theory understands it. This holds, in particular, where security, for its part, is held to provide the 'external conditions' for a moral life of individuals and where the law, as the epitome of these external conditions, is to become the means to this purpose.

In every reference to a will, to something that ought to be realized, there lies a breach of the boundary that separates the law from reality, an inconsistency that confuses and obscures. As the will, here, can only signify a phenomenon that pertains not to the law, but rather to being. The law, as a will that ought to be realized, means nothing other than a norm that ought to become a fact and which therefore ceases to be [a] norm in order to be received by the empirical volition of humans. Since there is no other world for the law than that of the law and since the expansive force of legal evaluation grasps every object that is brought into relation with the law [Recht], in order to make it into an object of legal judgment, if it cannot ignore it, the law cannot have a will to realize itself out of itself. As long as the focus is on this world of the [41] law alone, the proposition holds, in truth, that there is no lawless space within the law, a proposition that one often hears misapplied to the positive statute, as a result of a layman's confusion [of the idea of law with positive statute].

this significance of language and regards it merely as a fact, akin to every other fact.[1] [47]

Should such a method that does no more than determine linguistic usage, for example, come to the result that the territory belongs to the concept of the state, then this need not be false; it is, however, neither grounded nor capable of a grounding other than the reference to the constantly changing usage of the language. In place of the reference to territory, the space, a reference to time could just as well be included in the concept of the state, which would demand a continuity for which space only serves as a means, in order to implement it and to render it secure. Should the fact that there is no empirical state that does not have a territory be offered as a reason for the essentiality of the territory, then every concept of an object of the bodily world would have to include this embodiedness, even though precisely this does not constitute what is specific to it. Empirical states that persist next to one another must self-evidently persist next to one another in space. But if the conceptual requirement of a territory is to distinguish the state from other constructs of human mutual belonging that also display a continuity, for example from a church, then the claim [that a state must have a territory] marks only the beginning of the real inquiry into the state, as it will then be required to give material reasons for regarding territoriality as an essential characteristic of the state, and these reasons must have a deeper significance than the mere purpose of avoiding a confusion of the state with other things. 'Exact' observation can indeed offer a ground but not a grounding, it can heap together all possible 'characteristics' and therewith provide the presuppositions of a terminological investigation, but even the explanation of the requirement of a territory out of the argumentation that the state is precisely not a Church, even though it remains negative and without immediate epistemic value, would no longer be an exclusively descriptive account, because it repudiates a Church's claim [48] to a territory and claims that there is an essential and not merely an accidental or concrete difference between Church and state. It would be very instructive to raise the question whether the requirement of a territory would still have to be retained if the entire

---

[1] *Leibniz*: 'Doctrina juris ex earum numero est, quae non ab experimentis, sed definitionibus nec a sensuum sed ratiocinis demonstrationibus pendet et sunt, ut ita dicam, juris non facti.' (8th draft out of the Nachlaß, published by Mollat, Leipzig 1885). (trans. Doctrines of the law of which it is the case that they depend not upon and exist not from experience, but from definitions[,] nor from the senses but from reasoned demonstrations, and thus I say, [they are doctrines] of law and not of fact.)

Earth had once been subjugated to a single state. This condition, after all, is within the domain of empirical possibility, the question is therefore not unjustified or nonsensical. The 'exact' method is nevertheless unable to answer it, it is unable even to decide whether the conceptual requirement of a territory ascertained by it follows from the mere fact of the persisting next to each other of multiple states, or from the particular kind of power that specifically distinguishes the rule of the state from that of a Church or of another association.

Does a 'future state', once realized, remain a state? The answer is difficult on account of the fact that every state that is to be consciously erected by humans, according to some state-ideal, in general has the tendency to spread itself over the entire Earth, to become 'catholic' in this sense. The comportment of the French Republic at the time of the great revolution offers an example of this, as does the ambition of the Holy Alliance to implement the idea of 'legitimacy'. This tendency is based on the thoroughly correct thought that there can be only One Truth,[liv] but that there can also only be One highest Power.[lv] Now, the concept of the state attained on the inductive path, by 'exact determination', invariably proposes, alongside the attribute of a territory, that of a highest power. As a result, it is forever exposed to the objection that, accordingly, there must be several hundred highest powers upon the Earth. The extent to which this objection is more than an empty puzzle is shown by its importance for the judgment of the relation between state and Church, in which [context] the impotence of the aforementioned exact **[49]** method may be recognized with particular clarity. The Roman Catholic doctrine proceeds in its handling of the legal relations with the state with a definiteness and clarity, which is already worthy [*wert*] of the most careful attention of legal philosophers on the ground that here the practical importance of a consistent theory thereby becomes manifest. The Church lays claim to Catholicity over and against the state; in unison, the Catholic teachers of Canon Law [*Kirchenrecht*] emphasize that the state as such nowhere exists, that, in [empirical] reality, there are only individual states which are mere products of history. The state, Walter says in his textbook of Canon Law [*Kirchenrecht*] (13th edition 1861, p. 89, note 2, as well as Schulte, 2nd edition 1868, p. 133 inter alia), is an 'abstraction, out of which one can make and has made everything possible in legal philosophy'. The Church, by contrast, which according to its own doctrine is the only Church and can recognize no other Church next to it, which thus itself represents the realization of an ideal, enjoys an infinite advantage, precisely for this reason, over the individual state, which recognizes, alongside itself, one hundred other states as equal in their rights and does not even pretend to a superiority over the relativity of the temporal. With the question concerning the ideal state, which can only ever be One, the concrete state constantly allows itself to be compared with the empirical, while the Church, for which ideal and reality, according to its own doctrine, go together, appears in the role of the ideal state, of the *civitas Dei*,[lvi] so that it can deploy every argument that forms part of the philosophic grounding of the ideal state for itself and against the concrete state at the same time. If there is only One Church,[lvii] then the Church is necessarily perfect; if there are one hundred states, then the individual concrete state is necessarily imperfect. [50]

The concept attained via an abstraction from one hundred imperfect things cannot yield the concept of a perfect thing, not 'the' concept of the state, which must form the basis of philosophic considerations. An inquiry into the state that aims to do more than to gather material for occasional questions of expediency must not rest content with the 'inductive', 'exact' procedure; for [such an inquiry] the concept of the state can only be ascertained by assigning the state a position in a system of values, one from which its authority follows. The state that is to be something other than the cumulative effect, conceived as independent essence, of the actions of individual humans, a point of intersection of causes and effects, [that is to be] more than a senseless power, is drawn into the rhythm of evaluations, becomes the member of a world that does not rest upon it, but in which it receives a significance, which it does not determine but that, rather, determines it. The state owes its dignity to its conformity to a norm [*Gesetzlichkeit*] which is not derived from the state – one in the face of which the state's own authority remains derivative. This means that, since that conformity to a norm [*Gesetzlichkeit*] can only be found in the law, the law is not to be defined from the state but rather the state from the law, the state is not the creator of the law, but rather the law is the creator of the state: the law precedes the state.

The thesis that only that which is proclaimed as statute by an empirical concrete state, in a determinate form, merits being regarded as 'law' has never yet been able to give a ground for this necessary connection of the law with the state, and neither does it lose its arbitrariness if it becomes a ruling opinion. There must be a conceptual kinship between law and state, if the law can only proceed out of the state, and both stand in a relation to one another [51] that is so intimate that, as a result, it is not even possible to say anything about the priority of the one before the other.[lviii] Such an essential kinship can, however, never be proven by way of purely factual determinations. No empirical observation can establish that something which the state commands in a definite form is law, and only because it is the state that commands. Nothing is explained here with an image or a word like organism, as nothing is made clear by the transference of a purely empirical relation to methodologically heterogenous relations and the correctness of a method cannot be proven by an image. The presupposition of the applicability of an image would be that it was the empirical relation of law and state that is sought, which is precisely not the case.

Unless a transcendental pre-established harmony is supposed, from which it follows that what the state commands is always law, then the only argumentation that remains is that the elevated position of the state as the *highest* power within a particular territory can lend to the expressions of its will the quality of legal propositions. The assertion that a power is the highest, given an empirical perspective, is a factual and concrete ascertainment, [and] no [factual] power may be designated, without heavy methodical inconsistency, as 'not further derivable'. For the purely factual observation, there is no other 'highest' power than that one that is highest in the given moment. As a result, there is no power, for such an observation, that is 'not further derivable' in the authentic sense, because every power, like every fact, can be investigated for the ground of its existence and be derived from it. The law, which can only proceed from the highest power, presupposes a highest power according to its concept. What power is the highest is, in turn, not determined by a [52] fact, but rather by an evaluation, that is, according to the norms of a legal observation. The highest power, which constitutes the state, is, according to its essence, a unity that can only be attained via evaluative criteria. *The proposition that the law can only proceed from the highest power thus inverts itself against the power theory and receives the content that only that which proceeds from the law can be a highest power.* The law is not in the state, rather, the state is in the law.

Therewith the primacy of the law is grounded. The merely factual power is incapable, at any point, of raising itself to any justification, without presupposing a norm by which the justification is legitimized. For a merely factual power there are only concrete individual cases, but not a will combined into rational unity; only punctual expressions of a blind power, but not a continuity.

The inquiry which, in truth, may be called a purely empirical one is never justified in foisting a rational sense on the merely strongest power.

What is more, the mass of positive statutory laws can never be something which is accessible to a systematic treatment. The nothing-but-factually strongest power is incapable of expressing anything other, from case to case, than an equally factual will. With this opinion, any interpretation which desires to do more than establish facts has reached its end; just as, on the other side, an interpretation which presupposes that the legislator always wants something rational proceeds from an opposition between factual and justified power, in order to affirm the one against the other.[2] Any interpretation, any scientific [53] treatment, of statutory law therewith has as its fundamental premise the precedence of the law to the state qua mere power. Even the proposition, evident and therefore particularly important for a philosophic investigation, that only a determination enacted under definite formalities and to be repealed under corresponding formalities is to be regarded as a statute law [Gesetz] in the precise sense contains as its core the negation of mere factuality in the law, a protest against the senselessness of a determination which only has an existential ground and the postulate of a rational calculability, that results as soon as the carrying out of external business is placed under a norm. The most elementary points of departure of all juristic intellectual activity, the mere possibility of a statute or of an interpretation – involve the recognition of a mutual relation, they demand a legitimation which cannot be given by a fact but only by a norm, and they place the law before the state, as is already implied by the word 'legitimation'. [54]

The term 'rule-of-law state' [Rechtsstaat] likewise indicates the primacy of the law, since it signifies a state, for a legal-philosophic inquiry,

---

[2] Today, in the time of the 'free law movement', everyone knows that the legislator or the author of the statute cannot possibly have anticipated all of the cases which are decided by appeal to the statute and, accordingly, could no more have intended the concrete decision. Science and practice take control of the statute and impose upon it a rational sense until it is acceptable. It is now one of the most interesting contradictions of intellectual history that precisely those who most loudly refer to the insufficiency of the factually expressed will of the statute law gladly label their method as 'factual jurisprudence' and thus make a bitterly serious programme out of a witty [geistreich] paradox, while in truth their presupposition is that that which rationally ought to be the case, given a certain state of affairs, must take priority to that which can offer as its sole ground of validity that it is indeed the factually expressed will. The free law movement, accordingly, is not a matter of 'factual' jurisprudence, but rather, in order to formulate the antithesis, of a jurisprudence of norms. Since there is little prospect, of course, precisely in this methodological dispute, that the participants will become aware of its premises, and since the advertising force of error will always remain greater than that of the truth, since many, indeed, do not even shy away from seeing an argument in the force of advertising, there is thus little hope for clarity at hand and the discussion becomes all the more tumultuous the more unfruitful it is.

that lets the law be the measure for the state, as a principle which has antecedent validity. The constitutive elements of the concept of the state can only be derived from the law, as the labelling as a 'rule-of-law state' does not signify the confirmation of a mere accidental agreement of the factual state of affairs in an empirical state with a complex of legal norms; rather, in combining the state with the law, the state is wholly seized and determined by the law, completely raised into the sphere of the law. The predicate of being a rule-of-law state is not one to be affixed externally to some entity obtained by way of some other method, such as the afore-mentioned 'inductive' one, on the condition that this entity is adminis-tered, incidentally, in such a way that its dependable regularity justifies its designation as a 'rule-of-law state'. Thus a state of beavers or ants can never be a rule-of-law state. A rule-of-law state, rather, is a state that wants wholly to become a function of the law, and which, although it formulates the norms to which it subjugates itself, does not declare them to be legal norms merely because it articulates them. By contrast, it expressly recognizes that it only articulates them because they are law and that it subjugates itself to them only upon precisely this ground. The understanding of law that takes the will of the state to be the only source of law cannot explain such a process and must ignore it, since the will and its expression as statute, [from this perspective], turn into a brute fact. The current consensus opinion, if one collates the expressions of opinion on the matter that are made in different disciplines, although often in isolation and wholly without any method, is that the factually valid will of the state, as a foundation, is held to carry a sphere closed within itself, namely, that of the [55] positive law, within which one argues according to [the rules of] juristic construction. For the clarification of this view, one might as well refer to the analogy of the Kantian primacy of practical reason or to the predominance of the will over the intellect, which predominance, according to a view held by significant philosophers, does not touch upon the independence and closure of logical rules.[lix] Still, the dominant opinion amongst jurists on the will of statute, which is supposed to be the criterion of interpretation, would [seem to] stand in lively tension with this analogy, at least if the will that founds the law [*Recht*] – as the 'rational' sense, as the 'objective thought content', as the 'true' will, or however one might refer to it – may be set against the merely factual will of the originator of the statute. By way of this under-standing of interpretation, which is the only possible one, the law as norm receives a position, *vis-à-vis* the will as mere fact, which is thoroughly analogous to that of the independent judge over and against any intervention buttressed by mere external superiority. The independent judge, as a civil servant of the state, is subjected to the state, but he is nonetheless subjected only to 'statute' – that is, according to the dominant opinion, to the will of the state; this is possible and conceivable in virtue of the fact that the 'will of the state' is itself subjected to an evaluation – one that annexes to the 'statute' an element that goes beyond the factuality of a powerful will.

Neither a conceptual construction that transcends an aggregation of undisciplined associations, nor an explanation of the meaning of elementary processes of legal life is conceivable without the primacy of the law to the state. The state is thus to be derived from the law and that which is essential to it is to be seen in its particular position towards the law. [56] The significance that pertains, in this context, to the statute enacted by the state will have to result from the explanation of the state, as will the structure of values into which law, state and individual are arranged by the predominance of the law, taken as the most general foundation.

In the middle of this tripartition stands the state. The state's position as the point of transition from one world to the other follows from the juxtaposition of the norm and the real empirical world. In the state, as a point of construction, the law as pure thought becomes the law as earthly phenomenon. *The state is accordingly the legal construct, whose sense consists exclusively in the task of realizing law*, of bringing about a condition of the external world that, as far as possible, corresponds to the requirements which allow themselves to be derived from legal thought for the behaviour of individual humans and for the organization of the external world.

It is particularly important that this definition, which makes the state depend upon the law, integrates the purpose [*Zweck*] into the conceptual determination of the state and that it sees in the state an instrument of the influence of the law on reality. But the state, even though it is the sole construction of the law that admits a purpose into its concept, does not cease to be a construction of the law. This purpose is not an accidental, individual one, but rather the law itself, which wholly fills in the concept of the state and transforms the state into a function of the law. The purpose, which, in the introductory discussions, was recognized as inimical to every norm and thus also to every juristic construction, does not signify an inimical element here. Every subjectivity of the purpose is here excluded; the purpose, which makes up the state, is not a goal set by the state for itself; it is the law, [57] rather, that, in the very same moment in which it is to become a purpose, posits the state as the bearer of this purpose. The state thus does not have the purpose; it is the purpose, rather, that fulfils the state and defines it. The direction of purpose does not give the law any new content, but rather constitutes a special construct: the state. The law is for the state, to make use of an expression of St Augustine (*de civ. Dei* II. 11. c. 24), *origo, informatio, beatitudo*.[lx] For this reason, there is no state other than the rule-of-law state and every empirical state receives its legitimation as the first servant of the law. In return, however, it is also the only legal subject in the eminent sense, as it is the only bearer of the ethos to be found in the law.

For a philosophic inquiry, the state is neither an apparatus that, under the observance of certain formalities, issues forth commands which humans accept as statutes not to be further derived, nor a power complex that compels its factual recognition and that is otherwise rational to no higher degree than any other superior power. The state, according to its idea [the idea of the state], becomes the bearer of a task, its grandeur rests in the fact that it is nothing other than this task, its dignity is derived from the law and consists in the exclusivity with which it is seized and suffused by the law.

Ruled by the law in every element, the state can only ever will [the realization of] the law. It would relinquish and surrender itself if it were to call upon its mere power. It would amount to a perfect contradiction for an authority to base itself upon a concrete state of affairs rather than a norm. There has never yet been a state, in history, that has done this, and in the case of which [state] the moment of objectivity against itself, the reference to a third, imagined in whatever shape, by appeal to which the power in question legitimated itself as the highest and deserved, would have been **[58]** altogether lacking. One must not ignore this important fact, that every power justifies itself with reasons and therewith at least 'officially' recognizes a duty of responsibility. It bespeaks an impressive sensitivity[lxi] to the fact that the reference to a concrete, merely factually strongest power would contain an infinite regress of empirical dependencies, one that would push aside the state as person, and through the recognition of which the state would disavow[lxii] itself. The incorporation of a definite territory into the concept of the state likewise emerges from the desire to move from a mere enumeration of accidental, transitory individual conditions to a closed continuity. The conceptual continuity of the state, however, is gained only once every attempt to establish continuity through an empirical sequence, which is only mechanically connected by [relations of] cause and effect, is abandoned, and conceptual continuity is seen to consist in the state becoming completely one with a norm. Thus the characteristics that have been posited by a concept of the state derived from concrete appearances attain their foundation and conceptual clarity. The requirement of a territory signifies only a preliminary rooting in something empirical, something the manifest constancy of which was particularly suitable to serve as an apt expression of the independence of the state from all that is individual and transitory as well as a symbol of the state's position in the 'mid'-point between the realms of the law and of reality. The sense of the state, accordingly, consists in its task of realizing law in the world and of working upon the world in this direction. Why it is the *highest* power follows from this task; why it has to be the highest *power* is explained by the orientation of its task, since to have an effect on the world of phenomena presupposes a factual power. The concept of the state thus occupies a position, for the law, that is precisely analogous to the position that the [59] concept of God, which emerges from the necessity of realizing morality in the real world, assumes for ethics.

The state first brings the imperative into the law. An effect upon something, an action in any direction, is foreign to the legal norm itself, according to its concept alone. The legal character of a norm therefore has nothing to do with its enforceability or with a tendency to enforceability. The [law's] coercion and the tendency to it refer to the real, empirical world, to being, they have a concrete state of affairs in reality in view, the bringing about of which by real means is their purpose. Since the purpose, in the sense of such making-real, is essentially foreign to the law as norm, the tendency to coercion does not belong on the side of the law, but on the side of the state as the means of the law. How things look in the world, as a matter of fact, makes no difference to the content, form or correctness of the legal norm. The [law's] coercion or its enforceability do not touch the essence of the norm, as they only concern the coerced – that which is made to correspond to the norm by coercive means. Hence, they can also not be the distinguishing characteristic of the legal norm compared with other complexes of norms. That which is specific to the norm cannot be defined by reference to the real effects related to it, no more than the essence of a judicial judgment can be defined by reference to the effects of its legal force or its easily attributed 'tendency' to be executed. As of the legal norm, it may be said of every norm that it has a tendency to be enforceable. This means no more than that there are humans to be found who provide the norm with factual recognition, if necessary, by the use of coercive means of some kind, because they hold

the norm to be important enough. Such a psychological effect upon **[60]**
human beings, however, merely indicates a factual success of the representation of the norm, it does not concern the norm itself.

The distinction of law from ethics, recognized by great men and
transmitted as a general opinion, is so definitely opposed, however, to
these remarks that it becomes necessary at this point to clarify the view
presented here and to secure it against doubts by way of an engagement with the legal theory of Kant and his successors. A legal duty can,
according to Kantian terminology, only be an 'external' duty, that is,
an obligation to [perform] some 'external action'. For Kant, this results
from the fact that the distinction between ethics and the law concerns
the different [form of] 'legislation', which is an internal one in ethics
and an external one in law. The difference between external and
internal legislation consists in the difference of the incentives
[*Triebfedern*],[lxiii] of the psychological motives for dutiful action, and
the specificity of the legal duty in the fact that an incentive other than
the pure representation of duty is taken up into the statute, in that the
law derives its incentives[lxiv] from the 'pathological determining
grounds of choice, inclinations and aversions', and, amongst these,
again from the last, from the aversions, 'for it is a lawgiving, which
constrains, not an allurement, which invites' (*Metaphysische
Anfangsgründe der Rechtslehre*, first ed. 1797 Intr. p. XV, as well as
the 2ⁿᵈ ed. 1798).[lxv] When, however, Kant perceives that which is
distinctive in the legal duty not in its content or in its authority, but
rather in a psychological motive, he makes his division of moral duties
into those of the law and those of ethics or morality impossible in the
more narrow sense, since in logical immediacy, without a *divisio per
saltum*,[lxvi] if in truth the motive ought to constitute the *differentia
specifica*,[lxvii] **[61]** this would result in a division in which duties, which
according to their essence exclude every other motive than the obliga-
tory character of the action to be performed, are juxtaposed with other
duties whose essence is compatible with another motive, one that
consists, for instance, in coercion or in a reward in the eudaimonistic
sense. Why the duties of this latter kind are legal duties and why they
cannot be legislated by some instance other than the state, why it is not
possible, in other words, for every association or romantically minded
band of robbers to posit duties of this kind, by the use of the factual
power accessible to it and the motives that result from it, cannot be
derived from the Kantian division, although this would have to be
possible if the division were oriented towards a consideration of the

essential [aspects of the] relation [of law and morality]. For Kant, after all, this division amounts to the fundamental distinction in his *Metaphysics of Morals*.[lxviii]

If legal duties are duties such that an incentive distinct from the representation of the mere duty does not in any way contradict the idea of a legal duty, and if, by contrast, the authority of ethical duty consists in the fact that it binds human beings *a priori* and unconditionally, through their own reason, the authority of the legal duty can, nevertheless, likewise stem from its reasonableness; the addition of coercion will then appear as accidental. Should coercion become something essential, and that is the case in Kant, because he concludes from this that a legal duty can only ever demand an external action – then coercion must result from the essence of legal duty, which means that a legal duty is a duty that, according to its essence, presses toward enforcement. However, this pressing, this tendency, would, since coercion can only refer to the external, empirical world, have a direction [62] towards the empirical – towards that which accords with experience. Coercion could thus result only from the empirical, concrete content of the norm, but to utilize this content for the characterization of the legal norm must be regarded as one of the 'grossest and most pernicious errors'.[lxix] If the law, in truth, belongs to the species of norms that, where their concept is in question, cannot be learned from experience, if the postulate of purity is taken seriously, then every relation to coercion and the tendency to enforceability is lowered to the *accidentale*,[lxx] it turns out to be an incidental epiphenomenon; what coercion and enforceability are can only be learned from experience; only a being of experience can a have a tendency to coerciveness, but not a pure norm.

A further point needs to be added. The definition which the law is given by the Kantian juxtaposition with ethics leaves the most important questions unanswered, in particular concerning the justification of legal coercion; it does not even indicate whether anyone may attach any form of coercion whatsoever to some reasonable prescription and whether the norm will thereby become a legal norm. The question is naturally negated by Kant. Not everyone may coerce another to fulfil his duties and thereby confer a legal character on duties that would otherwise be ethical: if the noble brigand compels the rich man to help a starving third person, then the action of the rich does not amount to the fulfilment of a legal duty. Only the *justified*[lxxi] attachment of coercion, thus, makes the duty into a legal duty, the emphasis is on the justification, not on the [moment of] coercion; the justification itself cannot again be explained by reference to coercion, since it would then cease to correspond to a norm and be a mere efflux of factual relations. It is not at all self-evident, [63] what is more, that the incentive the use of which constitutes the species of duty must, in all cases, be contained in coercion and not in some other effect on the will. Kant brushes this point aside and claims (Introduction, p. xv): 'It is clear that in the latter case this incentive which is something other than the idea of duty must be drawn from pathological determining grounds of choice, inclinations and aversions, and among these, from aversions; for it is a lawgiving, which constrains, not an allurement, which invites.' But although it is self-evident to us that, in empirical legal life, one works with measures of coercion and not with compensations and enticements, the reference to this self-evidence is still no argument, least of all for Kant; it does not result from Kant's legal-philosophic system; it is brought in from outside and aids in bridging a gaping cleft.

The contemporary scholars who have attained great merit in the working out and further development of Kantian ideas in legal theory, in particular *Stammler*, *Natorp* and *Cohen*, place the main weight upon the unity of ethical and legal legislation, which must, [according to their view], both derive from the same practical reason. They thus distinguish law and morality as two principles that, despite their differences, can be traced back to the same form of [practical] law [*Gesetzlichkeit*]. Due to the thorough and encompassing discussions that Stammler in particular has put forward, and which, in addition, are dedicated to the special interests of legal philosophy, the distinction between internal and external dutifulness could have attained a univocal clarity and therewith have displayed its fundamental correctness. This, however, has not taken place. For Stammler, the law is, according to its [64] concept, an autonomous, inviolable, binding will; its specific difference to morality, which determines itself, like the law, according to the thought-form of purpose and means, not of cause and effect, consists in the fact that the internal order, namely that of morality, refers only to the wishing will and to humans conceived as individuals, whereas the law concerns the acting will and binds the purposes of different human beings together into the form of a pursuit of common purposes. The law as a binding will does not thereby have a real independence, is no mystical collective entity above the individual, but rather only the logical condition of the joint action of the multiple wills that it binds together, which latter are thereby defined as 'means for one another' (*Theorie der Rechtswissenschaft*,[lxxii] 1911, p. 75). The will that binds together independently faces the bound will and first makes the latter logically possible. The opposition between wishing, as willing without means, and acting as, so to speak, a capable willing, signifies an opposition that corresponds to that between disposition and deed, between internality and externality and, since one may demand the strictest consistency of a work that pretends to do nothing less than to give a critical foundation of the whole of legal science, finally also the opposition between individual and plural willing. The external regulation, after all, concerns the purposes of humans, the internal regulation can only ever touch the individual. The marker of distinction of the law as opposed to morality thus ends, despite all protest-ations that it would be a misunderstanding to think that the 'bound willing' signifies [no more than] the combination of multiple wills in a numerical sense, in the opposition between one and several human beings (as a purely numerical combination that remains within the world of real [65] appear-ance), and this stamps the[lxxiii] protestations as a wish which has remained unfulfilled. A law which, as a will that binds together, 'determines a plurality of wills as means for one another', while the several will-contents that are bound together must be distributed over several persons (p. 78), and the willing that binds together exists independently from the one that is bound, is robbed of any criterion for this conjunction [of individual wills]. Since the 'determination [of individual wills] as means for one another' cannot be found in the consciousness of the willing humans – as the view would then be no categorial determination, but rather a mere recording of psychological facts – all interest of science concentrates itself on the specification of this 'determination' and on the specifically legal criterion of the drawing together. A summation in pure thought of conceivable contents of whatever sort is possible from many perspec-tives and purposes; observed from an infinitely high and trans-temporal perch, we may all work in secret agreement with the world of animals and plants, or even with lifeless nature, perhaps we are all tools of a most highly rational will. But if the law is to remain restricted to humans, then Stammler may not understand the human being as the homo sapiens of natural history or as [that which falls under] any biological category. He must understand it, rather, as a rational being, one that comes into consideration only because it has reason and only insofar as it has reason, in other words, he must understand it no longer as the real individual, but rather as the [legal] construction. In that case, however, the logical impossibility of the proposition of the bound will of several, opposed to the wishes of the individual, becomes evident. Stammler's ethics likewise addresses itself to the [individual] human being, and again only to the rational individual who, despite the fact that he is nothing other than rational, nevertheless has an internality and an externality, who [66] can wish and knows how to employ means, which latter, since the specific difference between wishing and willing is to consist in the relationship to the means, can only be external means, that is, such as belong to the real world of phenomena, just as the [external] act and the realization [of purposes] more generally, both of which play such a decisive role in Stammler, have solely empirical content. If the antithesis 'internal-external' is to have a sense, then it must concern the same human being in every case. If it is the separated will of the individual for itself (p. 450 ff.) [that is at issue] in ethics, the law will then [be concerned with] a multiplicity of wills in the numerical sense. Any unity of law and morality is lacking if both are reduced to the juxtaposition of internality and externality, of individual and plural, so that the individual with its internality appears, in ethics, as the real empirical individual, while the several individuals whom the law determines, in their willing, as means for one another suddenly emerge in an altogether different sphere which is pure of everything empirical. Stammler, in the most extensive explicitness, has put forward his protest against the objection that his legal subject signifies an individual in the empirical sense, the legal subject, rather, is to be a purely methodological concept (p. 200). The contradiction is striking, since the question now arises: what, then, do internal and external mean?

For *Natorp*, who did not fail to notice this difficulty, the distinction between internal and external, which for him runs parallel to that between autonomy and heteronomy, contains only two different directions of the same original lawfulness [*Gesetzlichkeit*] (*Kantstudien*[lxxiv] XVIII. p. 1 ff.). The law strives from heteronomy towards the autonomy of morality, the morality of autonomy strives towards the heteronomy of the law, as from the centre of a circle to the periphery, while the law [67] pursues the opposite path. In this way, it is then explicitly said, heteronomy ought to be sublimated into autonomy. A similar thought is indeed not foreign to Stammler, who likewise assumes a segue of the law into morality and does not admit any contradiction of the correct law with the latter. But the unity, therewith, simply perishes if the oppositional pairs internal-external; autonomous-heteronomous; and even abstract-concrete (p. 39) are taken strictly. A sublimation of the external into the internal cannot be made understandable by [appeal to] the fact that it proceeds gradually; why the centre is of greater value than the periphery is not self-evident to a presuppositionless ethics, as little as is the superiority of the internal to the external. Natorp says that the same harmony of purposes is demanded by the law 'from without' that morality requires 'from within', when the same, in terms of content, is demanded in both cases. The law creates the external conditions for internal morality. All this can only mean that the law establishes a peaceful life for the human and provides him with the necessary security for more important things, it thus relates to morality no otherwise, in the case of individual humans, than a suitable diet or hygienic care relate to the achievements performed by a human who is in possession of his unhindered bodily functions. The thought that the law creates the external conditions for ethics, both methodologically as well as in its psychological emergence and in its concrete content, is nothing other than the continuation of the opposition between spiritual and worldly authority, of which the worldly authority is only there on account of evil and bad humans who will leave the good in peace to live their blessed [*gottseligen*] lives only as a result of coercion. **[68]** The state and the law then reduce to police functions, as is articulated with particular clarity by Luther and Zwingli. And yet, an ethics which remains conscious of its autonomy and calls itself 'pure' with reflection would have to let the ethical value of the human be wholly independent of the external accidents which might strike him. It can recognize no accident at all that signifies a hindrance to the moral value or a furtherance thereto; the moral value of a truly moral human in the age of security, in the twentieth century, is not *eo ipso* a higher one than in the age of the Condottieri or of the *Völkerwanderung*. The dignity and sublimity of the categorical imperative, with the fullest justification, is found precisely in the fact that it maintains its exceptionless authority independently of any external situation and its effect upon humans. *Si fractus illabatur orbis* . . .[lxxv] The role which pertains to the 'external conditions of morality' in a pure ethics, accordingly, becomes ever more unclear. Morality is independent of external culture, ethical culture can only ever be the affair of the individual. Strictly speaking, all external conditions are irrelevant, the rules of law, so understood,[lxxvi] no less than those of medicine or of public hygiene [*Volkshygiene*].

Heteronomy can in no way be united with autonomy, nor externality with internality, the Nothing cannot sublimate itself into Something, the concrete does not 'aim' at the abstract. No circumlocution, no imagery, helps to surmount the incompatibility. The individual, to whom Kantian ethics addresses itself, and the many, who play a role in the law, cannot be wedged under a unified overarching concept, not even with the help of the indeterminate will, borne by no consciousness, or of a **[69]** fuzzy concept of purpose, which has wreaked havoc everywhere in jurisprudence, but particularly in the theory of interpretation.

In *Stahl*[lxxvii] it is an ever-recurring argument that only the individual thinks, and that the contrast between the historical and the rationalist theory of law consists in the fact that the living individual comes to be restored in his rights by the historical theory. But Stahl fails to realize that, even though the psychological process of thinking as a concrete phenomenon can only ever be observed in individual humans, correct thinking does not ask for concrete processes in the psyche of the individual. For juristic thought, the individual can at most be an 'object', it is not to be confused with the subject of juristic thinking, with the transcendental unity of juristic apperception. Such a confusion is more understandable in Stahl than in Stammler, although Stahl, too, as much as the Kantians, reaches a unity of autonomy and heteronomy. All philosophy that aims to lead law and morality back to one and the same principle ought at least to be aware of the consequence that state and God will then relate to one another not otherwise than law and morality, and that both are thus to be regarded, with the same necessity and in the same sense, as divine. The commingling of the two domains of law and of morality leads to an indescribable confusion of the views about the state, to which one must, given a fusion of law and morality, attribute a divine character. Stahl has drawn this consequence, by demonstrating the state to be an institution of a personal God, a result which is based exclusively upon the thought that law and morality may not be separated, that heteronomy and autonomy are identical in the end. [70]

Law and morality, which Feuerbach and Fichte had already separated as two forms of judgment opposed to one another by reason, are thus not to be derived from the same principle. They cannot come into contradiction with one another because they have nothing to do with one another. The relation of the law to morality is unlikely to be that of an external precondition, because the law itself, according to its essence, is [a] norm and a norm cannot become the executrix of another norm, the sword in the hand of another norm. Leaving aside the methodological impossibility of such an assumption, it would differ from the two-swords-theory, which is the only consistent formation of the premise of a unity of a law and morality, only in formulation and terminology. The opposition between law and morality is not that between power and norm. The role of the sword – therein a remarkable methodological superiority of this medieval theory[3] displays

---

[3] Petrus Damiani Sermo 69: Felix, si gladium regni cum gladio iungat sacerdotii, ut gladius sacerdotis mitiget gladium regis et gladius regis gladium acuat sacerdotis. [tr. Peter

itself – could only be played by the state, as the real power. And it is therefore also more than something that sets 'external conditions', because it wholly merges into the law. The debasement of the law which is implied by the theory of the external conditions cannot be emphasized enough; in such a view, the law becomes a maid,[lxxviii] perhaps the ideal housewife,[lxxix] who, by way of her circumspection and noiselessness, keeps the house in order and therewith fulfils the external conditions for the undisturbed professional activity of her husband.[lxxx]

The legal norm never enters into a liaison with reality [and] thus coerciveness or [71] enforceability[lxxxi] cannot be attributed to the legal norm as a conceptual marker. The correct place in which coercion and its effect belong is the state as the mediator of the law, whose meaning lies in realizing law. Power thus belongs to the concept of the state, so that only that empirical appearance may be called a state which displays such power. Power as such does not thereby become a state; it is only said that an instance that explicitly renounces influence upon the visible world and coercion may not be called a state. The authority of the state none-theless does not lie in power, but rather in the law that it brings to implementation. The superiority of the law follows precisely from the fact that the state executes it, in the same sense in which the judging judge appears, in contemporary empirical legal life, as higher and more valuable than the executing civil servant, with a definiteness that is great and significant even if it is seldom recognized. No one will deduce the opposite from the circumstance that the judge is help- and powerless, given the limits of his competence under existing statutes, without the executing civil servant and that his sentence first attains factual effectiveness and richness of influence in virtue of the activity of another. Only the judg-ment is juristically interesting, not the execution.[lxxxii] The most correct judgment is not that which is executed most thoroughly; a decision whose fitting justification and justice is admirable can be worthless for the practical needs of the party for the paltry ground that the adversary is exempt, without this damaging the juristic dignity of the judgment. Given the evidence of the antithesis between the correctness of the knowledge and of the fruitfulness of the execution, a confusion of the methodological relations is not to be feared. The inferiority of the factual over and against

Damian (Petrus Damiani), Sermon 69: It is felicitous if the sword of the realm is conjoined with the sacerdotal sword, so that the sacerdotal sword mitigates the sword of the king and the sword of the king sharpens the sacerdotal sword.] (Cited according to Mirbt, *Quellen zur Geschichte des Papsttums* [tr. *Sources for the History of the Papacy*] 3rd ed. Number 234).

that which is called 'knowledge' has even found its expression in the gradations [72] of the civil service hierarchy, in which the independent judge stands in a higher sphere, one wholly different in kind [*ganz anders gearteten*], than the huissier.[lxxxiii] The relation of subordination, as long as it was not recognized as the emanation of the purely intellectual relation of superiority of the judge over power, had therefore to be noted with a certain astonishment, because the organ of execution also partakes in the state's competence, an *imperium*,[lxxxiv] so that an actual ground of inferiority cannot be given. This astonishment articulates itself markedly in a decision of the United Civil Senate of the Reich Court [*Vereinigte Zivilsenate des Reichsgerichts*] (*Entscheidungen in Zivilsachen*,[lxxxv] vol. 16, p. 408), where it is said: 'According to the prescriptions of the Code of Civil Procedure, the execution likewise represents itself as an act of the executive power of the state, as an efflux of the state's sovereign power, although the act of execution no longer lies in the hands of the court, but rather, for the most part, takes place, at the instigation of the party, through subordinate, non-judicial organs of the administration of justice, the bailiffs of the court.' Thus, although the execution [of a judicial decision] is an act of the state and, just like adjudication, is placed in the hands of state officials without the judge deciding the case at hand being the bailiff's superior in some closed hierarchy of ranks, the bailiff nonetheless remains the subordinate. Self-evidently, this fact might be explained historically, but historical data that are incapable, in particular, of grounding the *justification* of the evaluation do not suffice for a legal-philosophic interpretation. The meaning of this difference in rank [between the judge and the bailiff] results from the fact alone that the relation of the judicial finding to its execution or realization leads, in its further interpretation, to the priority of the norm to the empirical. [73]

There is no domain of legal life that does not receive a deeper significance via this fundamental principle. The elementary taken-for-grantedness with which every citizen and every party demands the independence of the judge has already been emphasized above as an important indication. Its importance is independent of the concrete historical formulation in which the demand is presented and which today employs the juxtaposition of the judiciary and the administration. The thought has been effective at all times in which there has been a judicature and it has the independence of the law from the state qua mere power for its content. The confusing explanation that the law is precisely the will of the state and that the state is capable, at all times, of creating another law overlooks that which is decisive – namely, the limitation under which the powerful will of the state finds itself when it presents itself as law; the self-subordination under the will once articulated, which ought to hold as it is proclaimed, unaffected by the fluctuating factuality of the will. Only once the state becomes the sole bearer of the juristic norm, its sole addressee, the sole entity that is duty-bound in the legal sense, does the continuity of the legal norm become explicable by appeal to the concept of the state, together with the identity of the state itself, even throughout political alterations, which latter would otherwise be inexplicable transfers of power-competences to another, so that the endurance of the hitherto existing statutes up to their formal repeal could be made comprehensible only via an insupportable fiction. The relative irrelevance of the real relations of power for the designation of a power-complex as a state thus likewise receives a satisfying interpretation and has a precise analogy in the equality of the parties before the statute or in the juridical irrelevance of the economic value of the object of contestation at trial. [74]

In order now[lxxxvi] to turn back to the independence of the judge, it is likewise based on the priority of the law to the state as power and does not cease to have a legal-philosophic significance because it was for centuries a political postulate and still is one today as well. When the demand for the separation of the judiciary and the administration was raised in the eighteenth century it went along with a strengthened emphasis on the subjection of the judge to statutory law, out of an impulse to avoid the misunderstanding that one power was to be set against the other. The personality of the judge, everything that hung together with his empirical individuality, was negated in the sharpest way, the judge, as the well-known phrase goes, was to be nothing more than '*la bouche qui prononce les paroles de la loi*'.[lxxxvii] It had to become evident, however, that the statute whose mouth the judge was to be could not be identified with the manifest content of concrete prescriptions issued by the state. If the judge was subordinated to the state's statute as an expression of mere factual arbitrariness, then he remained the functionary of a power, it was only that the distance between the power and the subordinated judge was now greater, that the mutual relation via an intermediate link had become more complicated. Modern sociologists, to whom the state is only the product of the super- and sub-ordination of two classes, have traced out the mutual relation and discovered that, in truth, every judicial decision is a confirmation of the factually valid power in the state. The elucidation of the highly plausible error of this conception becomes possible only via the clarification in principle of the distinction between causal (sociological) and juristic observation. Only thereby does the sense of [judicial] 'independence' become recognizable as well. The proposition that the judge is the mouth of the *statute*[lxxxviii] was also soon recognized as incorrect by practice. [75] It could not be ignored that the course of the application of statute is influenced by numerous extra-statutory factors, like precedents [*Präjudizien*], arguments drawn from the moral value judgments of the time and of the people, the interests of legal intercourse, etc. Where the 'personality' of the judge was then pushed into the foreground, in response to the insight into the incompleteness of the statute, against the imperative of the strictest subjection of the judge to the law, this solution of the problem still remained under the spell of a falsely adopted antithesis. Even today the whole independence of the judge from every arbitrary power consists in the judge's absolute dependence upon the *law*[lxxxix] alone. The [judge's] 'personality' may find consideration, in this context, only insofar as[xc] this word is understood to refer to such characterological qualities as offer a guarantee that the [judge's] devotion to the law is exclusive and complete. If the word 'statute' [*Gesetz*], in the proposition according to which the judge is the mouth of the statute, receives the significance of 'law' [*Recht*], then it is still valid today and it asserts that, according to the idea, the judge is a function of the law. Therein lies his dignity and his true independence, and it is difficult to grasp how a degradation of the judge can be found in the fact that one wants to hear the reason of the law that has come to articulated consciousness speak through him. –

By virtue of the fact, however, that the state creates the connection between the law and the empirical world, a moment of the empirical flows into the legal norm proclaimed by the state, which norm has gone through the state as a medium and has thus suffered a specific modification. The whole realm of empirical law, as a result, disintegrates into two complexes. The state, the mediator of the law, enters acting into the world and must there accommodate itself to the world's mechanism of means and end. [76] In the same moment in which it uses the empirical world, in order to make something determinate out of it, the world acts back upon the state, with a power akin to that of the power which the material has over the artist, or that which the attributes of the servant have over the master. The world places the state in the nexus of its relations and brings it about that the state, in order to act upon the world, must itself bring forth expressions of a merely empirical will.[4] If an effect is to occur in the empirical world, there is a need

---

[4] *Harnack*, in his critique of *Sohm's* treatise 'Wesen und Ursprung des Katholizismus' ['Essence and Origin of Catholicism'] (Abhandlungen der Philol.-histor. Klasse der K.

for empirical means, and coercion comes into consideration as the strongest of these. The norm that, according to its concept, is extra-empirical does not know this boundedness; the tendency to enforceability is something which is[xci] brought into the law by the state.

On the one hand, accordingly, there stands the law that was there before the state and which, as a thought, is independent of the state, [77] a law which, in its relation to the state, can be described as ruling, originary law, and in its relation to the concrete expressions of will which are its reflection in the empirical world as abstract law; on the other hand, there stands the law of the state, as serving, purpose-determined, mediating law, which does not stand to the originary law in the relation of means and end, whose purposiveness, rather, consists in its inclusion of the empirical world as the field of its effects. This opposition of both laws, however, is not of the type that two self-enclosed masses of definite propositions stand against one another; the separation, rather, is to be made within each empirical legal proposition. That which determines the legal proposition and distinguishes it, for example, from a police ordinance derives from the element of originary, non-state law, the further determination of which is not the task of this treatise and of which (in order to be concise, for once, at the risk of paradox) we wish to say no more than that it must emerge as a natural law without naturalism.

The fundamental dualism in the law that pervades every realm of legal science and which expresses itself in the distinction between criminal and police injustice [*Unrecht*], which appears anew again and again, in the juxtaposition of *jus divinum*[xcii] and *jus humanum*[xciii] based upon a

---

Sächischen Gesellschaft der Wiss. vol. 27. 1909), *Urchristentum und Katholizismus* [*Originary Christianity and Catholicism*], Leipzig 1910, p. 136, note 2, has cited a proposition of Goethe on the realization of the idea, which pertains to this context: the idea 'always enters into manifestation as a foreign guest.' – Harnack sees 'the main failure of Sohm's treatment' (according to which any canon law [*Kirchenrecht*] stands in contradiction to the essence of the Church) in the fact that Sohm overlooks the necessity with which the inclusion of the idea in the temporal takes place, if it ought to be realized. Harnack claims that only Catholic canon law, which wills the legal regulation of all that is spiritual, stands in contradiction with the concept of the Church as an ideal magnitude, but not that canon law which rules the Church as an external association ([ibid.,] pp. 185/6). But it seems to me that the question is precisely whether such an external law stands in any relation at all with the essence of the Church, one that would justify using the label 'canon law', and that Sohm's treatment (the correctness of the content of which can remain another matter), when the 'essence' of the Church is being discussed, refers precisely to the idea alone that ought to be realized and which itself cannot define the statutes and rules of its realization in time, since these rules pertain wholly to temporality.

commingling of law and ethics, in that of legal propositions that are coercive according to their 'nature' and those that are dispositive, or in the oppositions between statutes that are to be extensively and restrictively interpreted, between alienable and inalienable legal goods, or between higher and lower prerogatives, etc. thereby first receives its systematic foundation. The treatment of such oppositions, in particular of that between criminal and police [78] injustice, most often proceeds from the false endeavour to postulate as criteria two different norm-contents or purposes, whereas it would be correct to perform the separation of the legal thought from the moments that relate to its realization and implementation within each and every enactment of the state. The indication of the punishment and of its level within the individual penal statute belongs to this complex of means which is not immediately affected by the pure norm. The distinction thus leads to *Binding's* ingenious theory of norms, even though it took its point of departure from wholly different interests. Now, there are statutory prescriptions whose significance is altogether exhausted by such a mediating position, which have, so to speak, no light of their own, in the sense of a legal thought, and which merely refer to one that is positioned outside themselves. Since such prescriptions, which are essentially determined by considerations of enforceability and expediency, appear as subordinate in contrast to others, and since this classification is based upon the correct distinction between a legal norm and its realization in concrete circumstances, the separation between criminal and police injustice is to be recognized as correct in principle. The details of its implementation do not belong in the present context.

The importance of the distinction [that is to be drawn] within the statute enacted by the state for interpretation and its theory can likewise only be intimated here. It concerns the question, which would require a special investigation, of the place of the concept of purpose in interpretation, a question that has entered a new stage of scientific interest as a result of the meritorious and significant work of *Kelsen*. The area of the justified use of the notion of purpose overlaps with the domain of [79] the element in the state's law that exclusively concerns the relation of ends and means. New legal thoughts, accordingly, cannot be grounded by appeal to the purpose of a statute, but the purpose can help to identify new means of the realization of such thoughts. Here, too, the endogenous dualism of the law comes to light in the bifurcations of scientific (Thöl, Otto Bähr) and subaltern (Sternberg) or instructional (Kohler) law, between statute and equity or common law (Schmölder) etc., whose constant repetition in ever new formulations in itself already merits the greatest attention.

Just as the judicial decision always makes reference to a statute and brings the concrete case under general principles that necessarily go beyond the interest of the concrete case, while the execution, by contrast, is always something concrete and itself again makes reference to a concrete decision, so as to hang together only mediately with the domain of the more general statute, so the abstract legal thought takes form in a positive state statute. The closure that results therefrom within the world of the law, in which even everyday processes reflect the great fundamental relations, itself again contains an argument for the interpretation found here and clarifies it. The legal thought that is to be executed in the world, and to which external obedience is to be enforced, is in need of a recognition of reality in the fact that it is formulated with a precise content, whereby the precision of the content (not of the form) stands in functional dependence on the distance from the execution. The legal thought, which is to serve as a yardstick for the transformation of reality, must become positive, that is, its content is *set*[xciv] by an act of sovereign decision, it becomes a statute and is articulated in a concrete **[80]** version. Therewith the abstractness of the legal thought does not signify something attained out of concrete legal propositions via omission – such a method could not yield anything noteworthy – but rather the detachedness from every empirical appearance. Between everything concrete and everything abstract there lies an insurmountable cleft that cannot be closed by any gradual transition. It is therefore necessary that this moment of mere fixity, according to which it may turn out to be more important *that*[xcv] something becomes a positive determination than what concrete content it has, will make itself felt in every positive statute. This indifference with regard to content – and this gives the connection to the discussions in my treatise *Statute and Judgment* – results from the state's striving for realization [of the law]. Its significance for the individual judicial decision is more manifest and more evident, because here the distance between insight and execution is not so great, but its influence is no smaller in the formulation of a positive statute. The judgment must concern a concrete case in order to be executed, the statute is in need of concretization in the judgment before its enforceability becomes a fact, the abstract legal thought must become positive statute before the state can be active for its realization, that is, before it sets its apparatus of coercion in motion – in order to bring about a state of affairs that corresponds to the norm. *Sohm* (*Kirchenrecht*, p. 2) put forward the important propositions: 'The statute, inversely, depends fundamentally on the form (summum jus, summa injuria) and it must in the first instance depend on the form, as it is in this way alone that the statute is capable of arriving at the decision that stands above the parties, that imposes itself on both parts as just, despite their conflicting interests, that emanates not from the influences of the moment, but from fixed, traditional, commonly valid [81] principles. The fact that the law, though it does not conceptually demand coercion, nevertheless strives toward coercive realization is connected to this.' In this context, the statement of *how* [these facts are] connected stands in need of being rendered more precise: because the law is to be coercively realized by the state as its exactor, all state law must be exactly 'formulated' and 'determined', in order to be capable of concrete realization. At this point, moreover, one ought not to omit to point out that for *Hegel* (*Naturrecht* § 5, § 15 note), the will is a *definite* realized content and the possibility of another content presenting itself to the imagination.[5]

The giving up of timeless correctness and the reception of a moment of indifference with regard to content are the consequence of the ἐνανθρώπησις[xcvi] of the law, the sacrifice that must be offered because a pact was made with the powers of the real world of appearances. The proposition 'respect your neighbour' is no positive statute and can never become one. Should able and brave men succeed in making it the direction point of state legislation, in definite historical circumstances, then it becomes a paragraph, it enters into another sphere and the impression that it will henceforth make on the minds of those who see the paragraph as the mortal enemy of life will also be different.

At the end of this chapter, attention is to be drawn to a phenomenon whose examination forms a suitable conclusion of the disquisitions on state and law: as soon as a striving for a realization of thoughts, for a rendering visible and a secularization, emerges somewhere, [82] there immediately arises – alongside the need for a concrete decision, which, above all, and even at the expense of the thought, must be determinate – the striving for an instance, one that is determinate and infallible in the same way, that is to give this formulation. Here, too, the Catholic Church with its doctrine offers an example in typical purity. Once the thought of a visible Church, organized constitutionally by a legal order, and therewith of a *jus divinum*[xcvii],

---

[5] The statute must, 'so that it is a statute, not a mere command, be defined in itself'. (*Grundlinien der Philosophie des Rechts* [*Fundaments of the Philosophy of Law*] 1821, p. 307, § 291.)

which is a true *jus*^{xcviii} and not an ethics – had come to be accepted, there
was a need of such concrete formulations for doubtful cases. If consideration
is given, for once, to the human being in its corporeality, one must also give
consideration to the fact that these weaklings must know, above all, and
want to know, where they stand. If they are subject to a superior who
appears in corporeal form, then the latter's directives will have the same
concrete corporeality. He, thereby, fulfils the law [*Gesetz*] in virtue of which
he came to exist in the first place. The consequence of the infallibility of
decisions *ex cathedra*^{xcix} is patently obvious, and whoever admits the premise of a *jus divinum*^c and a legal order of the Church will not be able to
withhold his admiration of this consequence. There remains only the
alternative, after all, to either recognize the Catholic doctrine as justified,
or to adopt Luther's standpoint, as *Sohm* (*Kirchenrecht* p. 460 ff.) and *Stutz*
(*Kirchenrecht* in particular § 44 p. 883) have presented it, and to regard all
law as incompatible with the essence of the Church.

But the Catholic Church has erected one further doctrine that is of
extraordinary importance for the methodology of legal science. If the
dualism in the law is admitted and recognized, it will appear proximate to
subject the process of the realization of law, that is, of its transformation into
directives enacted by the state, to [some kind of] control, so as to protect the
abstract norm. [83] This grounds the basis of the Catholic doctrine of the
Pope, as the infallible interpreter of the natural moral law [*natürliches
Sittengesetz*] and of the content of revelation, who receives the competence
to declare state statutes that stand in contradiction with the natural moral
law or with the *jus divino-naturale*^{ci} to be non-obligatory in conscience. The
exercise of his *potestas indirecta*,^{cii} which is regarded as an act of jurisdiction,
and which is held, by many canonists, to be determinative [not merely of its
moral bindingness but also] of a statute's validity in state law – contains a
real *vis coactiva*,^{ciii} even where the expression *potestas directiva* is employed
in place of *potestas indirecta*^{civ} (Suarez, *de fide cath.* 3.22.1).^{cv} So as to put
this doctrine into the context of the disquisitions of this chapter, leaving
aside its religious significance, it may be said that it inserts an additional
instance in between the law and the state, in order to protect the law from
power. It is interesting how this thought, too, emerges in ever new costumes,
from the philosophers in Plato's State^{cvi} to Fichte's demand for an ephorate,
which, in a case of emergency where the basic statutes of the state have been
violated, can announce a state interdict, suspend the power of government
and hold the executors accountable. The fear of an abuse of the actual power
of the state, a distrust of the factual evil or weakness of human beings, as well
as the attempt to counter it are at the basis of all such proposals. However,

the methodological error, likewise, is always the same. No statute can execute itself; only human beings can ever be set up as guardians of the statutes and it is no help to whomever does not trust the guardians to subject them to new guardians in turn. Here, too, the insurmountable cleft between the pure norm and its realization cannot be filled up by however many intermediate links. **[84]** The valiant defender of judicial independence Heinrich Simon claimed (1845), quite strikingly: 'The statutes only articulate what ought or ought not to occur; they give no surety that what is commanded really occurs, and that what is forbidden really is refrained from.' There is a point at which what is correct can no longer be compelled. The distrust of the force of the good and the correct, which force, to be sure, may not be made dependent on the insight of individual humans, because it would then be lost, this distrust wears itself out and falls into groundlessness [*ins Bodenlose*], like all negation that has not been preceded by a position. Beyond that, admittedly, any argument ceases, and neither the trust in the power of the good and the just nor the political question concerning the technique of concrete enforcement belongs to legal philosophy.[cvii]

Chapter 3

The Individual

The thought that the law, in its essence, is power has its last roots in the conviction that all law can come only from the state as the highest earthly power and the strongest reality that a human being may face. Before it – before the encompassing, compact power with its impersonal mechanism and its destructive factuality – any appeal to another instance, any critique, appears to be a futile *raisonnement*.[cviii] In view of the [state's] enormous achievement of having embanked and rendered harmless, at least externally, a sea of unbridled and narrow-minded egoism and of the rawest instincts, and having forced even the influential evildoer at least to [engage in] hypocrisy, any critique might perhaps even be held, by some, to amount to an unjust and frivolous doctrinarianism. Indeed, whoever observes human beings individually or en masse with discerning glance and sees how they aspire only, 'full of haste, to save their individual happiness' (Däubler),[cix] will be moved by the fact that it was possible to bring an order into these interests, as they wildly scatter apart – an order on whose regular functioning one may rely with some security.

Now, whether the astonishment about this achievement gives credit to the state[cx] or whether it expresses a trusting happiness about the reasonableness and ultimate goodness of human beings, what is impressive about the state always lies in the fact that the organization of factual forces stands above any subjectivity [86] and, in its totality, uses every individual as its tool, even the most powerful despot, because the organization of factual forces far transcends him. Such an astonishment – which, in any case, has other psychological grounds than the hand-rubbing cosiness of the undisturbed enjoyment of a rent – derives, then, from the insight into the state as a supra-individual, not an inter-individual instance: one that does not owe its dignity to any shield-raising on the part of individuals, but confronts them with original authority. Through the recognition of a transpersonal dignity of the state, however, and accordingly in any philosophic notion, for which the state signifies neither a security establishment nor a welfare institution, the singular, concrete individual disappears.

Indeed, the state is either a servant of the individual or of the law. Since the latter view alone is correct, the state, like the law before it, is prior to the individual and, as the continuity of the state derives from the law alone, so the continuity of the individual living in the state flows only from the state. The state, as has been said in the previous chapter, is the only subject of the legal ethos – the only one that has a duty to the law in the eminent sense; the concrete individual, by contrast, is compelled by the state, and its duties, like its entitlements, are only the reflex of a coercive force. The antithesis is that of law and state, and not that of law and individual, and the *Hegelian*[cxi] proposition that the law is the unity between the impersonal rule and the individual is to be modified, in light of our discussion, to the effect that the positive law is the unity between the impersonal, supra-empirical rule and the state. The empirical individual drops out altogether; it is the state as power and thus as non-law that stands face to face with the law in order to realize it. **[87]**

It follows from the concept of the state as a task that the significance of the individual within the state, likewise, can be measured only by reference to a task. For the state, the individual as such is the accidental bearer of the only essential task, of the determinate function that it has to fulfil. In principle, the state can therefore hold no one to be irreplaceable or unrepresentable and the meaning of the state could be given a much deeper explanation from the vantage point of this general phenomenon of the functionary, of the fungible personality, of the civil servant, than through its degradation into the *negotiorum gestor*[cxii] of the 'personality' that alone is [held to be] important.

For the discussion of the significance of the individual, it is instructive to begin with the reminder how precisely the maxim 'be yourself' tersely juxtaposes the difference between a concrete being and a demand that is to be fulfilled, and therewith the two different subjects, constituted in different spheres, which it contains.[6] Plato

---

[6] The abuse, which many have made of 'be yourself', who draw out of the sublime, super-human [*übermenschlich*] principle of an autonomous ethics the open letter for an indolent or narcissistic sufficiency, self-evidently cannot be spoken of in this treatise.

had already conclusively explicated this: Τὴν τοῦ ἑτέρου[cxiii] φύσιν[cxiv] ἀποδείξαντες οὖσάν τε, καὶ κατακεκερματισμένην ἐπὶ πάντα τὰ ὄντα πρὸς ἄλληλα, τὸ πρὸς τὸ ὂν ἑκάστου[cxv] μόριον αὐτῆς ἀντιτιθέμενον, ἐτολμήσαμεν εἰπεῖν ὡς αὐτὸ τοῦτό ἐστι[cxvi] ὄντως τὸ μὴ ὄν[cxvii] (Sophista 258 D).[cxviii] (Cum[cxix] enim ostenderemus alterius ipsius naturam esse, pérque[cxx] omnia entia divisam atque dispersam invicem, tunc partem ejus oppositam ei quod cujusque ens est; esse ipsum re vera non ens asseruimus. Thus the translation of the Greek-Latin Complete Edition with the Commentaries of Marsilius Ficinus,[cxxi] Frankfurt 1602, pp. 180–1.)[cxxii] [88]

Even the proposition *cogito ergo sum*[cxxiii] not only permits an interpretation that moves away from the singular empirical individual and points towards a normative construction, but goes so far as to suggest that interpretation. It has been objected against the proposition, from the psychological side, that it does not matter from which activity existence is inferred,[cxxiv] so that the incorrectness [of the proof] lies in the fact that it focuses specifically on thinking, although it might have spoken about any random occupation. The objection is correct insofar as the conclusion of the empirical existence of my individuality cannot be drawn from the empirics of my own thinking. But what is essential here is that conscious thought involves the devotion to the laws [*Gesetze*] and values of correct thinking, whereby the accidental singular individual disappears, in order to partake in an extra-individual value that alone merits the predicate 'being', taken in an evaluative sense. Lichtenberg's remark that it is perhaps more correct to say 'it thinks in me' than to say 'I think'[7] likewise permits of an interpretation that finds in it an expression of the supra-individual validity of every correct norm and of the insignificance of the individual in comparison to it. The thought that we 'die and become', as a result, has never disappeared.[cxxv] The self in the highest sense is an ethical construct,

---

[7] I have chosen this example because the language critic Mauthner likes to refer to it. Without any great hesitation, the language critic undertakes to define the supra-individual, 'epistemological' subject, which is the problem of Lichtenberg's saying, by locating the subject of thought in language, as a fact that is easy to ascertain, and he thus transforms the supra-individual into the inter-individual. [Tr. In the 2004 German edition, perhaps drawn from a faulty printing scan of the 1914 German edition, 'Mauthner' (1914; 1917, p. 87, note 1) is printed as 'Mautliner' (2004, p. 88, note 7), which is corrected in the 2015 German edition. The 2011 Spanish translation and the 2013 Italian translation, both based upon the 2004 German edition, print 'Mautliner'. See Schmitt (2011), 61 note 2; Schmitt (2013), 83 note 2. Schmitt appears to make reference here to Fritz Mauthner, author of *Beiträge zu einer Kritik der Sprache*, as well as studies of Spinoza and Aristotle.]

not [to be identified with] the individual human being. Thus it was possible that Fichte, in his appeal to the public, could undertake the demonstration [that] the belief in the 'I' is first the true belief in God and the only way of **[89]** getting free of the temporal. Thus the subject of autonomy in Kantian ethics, likewise, cannot be the empirical, accidental individual that belongs to the world of the senses, because that subject is not bound to the law [*Gesetz*] by any interest, and its capability to become the subject of autonomy does not result from empirical facts but from its reason. It has autonomy only insofar as it is a rational being, only thus is its will generally legislative. What, however, a rational being which is thus required is cannot be determined by empirical moments. It consists, rather, in a value that is constituted by a norm or, as Kant would say, by a law [*Gesetz*]. To fulfil the objectively valid norm means, seen from the vantage of the individual, negating one's own subjective empirical reality. The sovereignty of the transcendental unity of apperception over the concrete consciousness as psychological fact, translated into legal philosophy, signifies only the irrelevance of the individual. It has already been explained in the course of the review of Stammler's legal theory in the previous chapter, in a different context, that the individual human being as fact has no significance, but must become something that lies in another sphere. The Kantian demand, that a human being always be [treated as] an end in itself, and never be permitted to become a means, is valid, therefore, only as long as the presupposition of autonomy is fulfilled, that is, only for a human being which has become a purely rational being, not for the [mere] exemplar of some biological genus.

The singular[cxxvi] empirical, concrete individual similarly is irrelevant in the state. The doubt that, with this, a bureaucratic schematizing, a culture-inimical *chinoiserie*,[cxxvii] is being advocated, may indeed be raised here, but it is based upon a misunderstanding, namely on the errant confusion of the state with what **[90]** day-to-day politics understands by 'government'. Even the riposte that precisely the great personalities led the state to flourish, and that even the best form of state would decay without great personalities, fails to escape from the overestimation of the concrete and the material. The discussion here does not concern political things. The 'flourishing of the state', the 'decay of the state', these are all historical processes which pertain to the world of experience alone, and if these latter are tagged with an evaluation, as it is implied by the attributes of flourishing or decay, they are measured by reference to arbitrary impressions and objects of comparison which, to this day, have never been precisely analysed. The state of Tamerlane, if that is what one wants to call his power-complex, was more powerful than the Athenian state was at any time; it is incomprehensible why anything ought to follow from this for legal-philosophic inquiry. The worry, however, that personality is [unduly] diminished, and that it would do an injustice to great men to assign them as well the position of a mere functionary in the state, does not directly strike the state, but rather those human beings who, not content to fulfil their duty, also want to be significant. If the individual functions which the human ought to discharge are regarded as stations that not everyone can fulfil and should it turn out, in the course of history, that individual humans were especially suited to these functions, then this merits awe and admiration. But the greatness of these men consists in the greatness of their task and its fulfilment; it would be ridiculous to say of any great statesman, irrespective of the motives that drove them, to say of Caesar, the great Friedrich or of Bismarck, that they saw their goal in the 'harmonious development of their personality'. Only the identification with the task, the measureless submission to the matter at hand, the immersion in the task, the pride of being the servant of the state and therewith of a [91] task, the self-forgetfulness, with which they were *projectissimi ad rem*,^{cxxviii} that alone makes up the great moments of their lives, those that are worthy of admiration. The value lay in the 'matter' that they had and by which they were grasped, not in what Hegel, with strong expressions against Jacobi, described as the boredom and feebleness of empty being, indeed as 'bawdiness^{cxxix} with oneself'. This value, in truth, is also the only one that humans recognize. Even at that level of abstraction from the empirical individuum, which is accessible even to the human of the normal empirical type, in 'business', the significance of the individual has the following value structure: the capitalist, as Marx and Sombart have portrayed him, who places nothing on his personal needs, everything on the augmentation of his capital, whose soul is the soul of his capital, turns into the servant [*Diener*] of a task and, in this sense, into a functionary [*Beamter*], and the goal of his striving goes far beyond his ephemeral individual existence, at least in the case of the typical capitalist, who is concerned with more than a commodious evening of life or the means for costly passions. Thereby he is precisely as great and imposing in making money as he is ridiculous and contemptible as an enjoyer, in money-dispensing. The further explication of the characterological side of the issue, however, is forbidden by the boundaries to be drawn from the object of our investigation.

Whoever today deploys the proposition that the individual is significant only to the extent that he is a functionary [Beamter],[8] exposes himself to the associations of the masses, to the incomprehension of those [92] of whom Roger Bacon says that they *mechanici omnes praecedunt et negotiantur sicut bruta et sicut inanimata.*[cxxx] But there is no point in having discussions with human beings who, in a legal- and state-philosophic discussion, want to add jokes about their letter carriers or about their entitlement to a pension. What is contemptible in a subaltern pettiness and pedantry, in the 'duty gnomes' (Däubler),[cxxxi] is precisely the incapacity to become one with a great matter, the incapacity for abstraction, and the consequent confusion of what is here referred to as the state and its task with the 'higher administrative agency' and the concrete humans who are its organs. If, on average, humans become civil servants in order to have a secure livelihood and a social position, then this is as insignificant for the idea of the state and the evaluation of the individual in the state, as it is irrelevant to art what its managers make of it.

It is admittedly one from China,[cxxxii] Lao Tzu, who found the deepest words for the significance of the state, and it is true, furthermore, that also in Plato's ideal state every one becomes a civil servant and of his particular importance nothing remains, all his dignity rather depends upon his giving himself over to the state. The more complete and the more conscious this giving over is, the higher he stands in the state, where everyone must perform the function that is assigned to him,[cxxxiii] but is not permitted to seek his own utility. Such a subsumption of the individual may be uncomfortable, it may appear to a swooning romanticism as an unbearable austerity, but it does not signify a degradation. The ancient philosophers separated humanity into two halves, into masters and slaves, those capable and those incapable of bearing rights, and thus projected the contrast between ruling and serving, spirit and matter, onto two groups of human beings, and the different functions again onto different castes and classes. Today, we take pride [93] in the fact that we no longer recognize such external differences and that we make no distinction between persons before the law [Gesetz]. But we should know that the point of our general human freedom can only be that of working out the dualism with the greatest dispassion, unperturbed by the given social group- and power-relations, so that external accidents are not decisive.[cxxxiv]

---

[8] It is repeatedly to be recalled that only the significance of the individual in the state is being spoken of, not somehow of religious things.

Every value that can be linked with the individual human consists in the submission to the supra-individual rhythm of a lawfulness [*Gesetzlichkeit*]. In the world of the state, this basic principle of all manifestation of value has become deed in the clearest way. However, it holds no less for the great scholar or philosopher or artist, and nothing is more symptomatic of the level of the opinion ruling today than that the words of Schiller, that the singer ought to walk with the king,^{cxxxv} are hardly understood any longer today and, in the best case, are conceived as an appeal to the state, which ought to 'do' something for art, whereas the sense of these words is that both, the king as well as the great artist, according to the idea, have a task in the highest sense, and that the empirical accidents of their personal life must therefore be irrelevant to them.

Thus the state is not a construction that humans have made for themselves. It is the state, on the contrary, that makes every human being into a construction. The great, transpersonal organization is not created by individuals as their handiwork; it does not fit into any sequence of means and ends of however many human beings; it is inconceivable that the egoism of human beings, rising above itself on its own, could have erected this more-than-human entity as a means for its ends, only to then be immediately thrown back into the Nothing by its sublimity. The purpose is as little the creator of the law or of the state as the sun is to be defined **[94]** as a fire lit by freezing savages^{cxxxvi} to warm their limbs with it.

The state takes hold of the individual and integrates it into its rhythm.^{cxxxvii} Even if a self-confident ruler were to utter the sentence, *l'état c'est moi*,^{cxxxviii} the state, and thus the law, would prove to be superior, because whatever could, with some justification, identify itself with the state, would, without remainder, have to have become a function of the state, in which case even this haughty utterance would receive the sense that the prince is only the first servant of the state, *le premier serviteur et le premier magistrat de l'Etat*,^{cxxxix} it is meaningful only as long as the prince – who, if he undertakes to turn the state into a means of his personal purposes, becomes 'broken iron'[9] – remains an

---

[9] That the prince is the organ of the state, does not stand over or outside of the state, is also in need of no further grounding for contemporary state theory and is recognized. The question, whether the ruling house has a 'right to the throne' and whether this right is originary or derived from the state, answers itself via the demonstrations of the text itself. It is otherwise with the question, whether the appointment in the service of the state is based upon a 'contract', as the presently ruling opinion supposes, which question is no longer immediately touched via legal philosophic demonstrations, because the contractual 'will' can itself again be conceived as a juristic construction.

instrument. In all such cases, one is faced with a re-melting of the individual, with a re-creation in a [different] sphere, not with an abstraction from mere particularities of the individual, and also not with a 'limitation' of the natural person or a 'liberty within the bounds of the statute', a seal to be impressed upon some content that is 'naturally' given. It may be that, when it was said of the Spanish king, in the time of the founding of his absolutism, that he is the living statute, the statute become flesh, *ley viba e animada en las tierras*,^{cxl} humans turned the matter on its head, in that they behaved [95] as though the caprice and the 'plaisir'^{cxli} of a human could be a law [*Gesetz*]; the correct thought, which alone was able to lend historical durability to absolutism, is the inverse: the absolute ruler is superior to all relativity of the temporal, he does not even come into consideration anymore as a human, he no longer has moods and delectations, he is altogether one with the 'law' [*Gesetz*]; he does not stand above the law, as little as he stands above grammar. Again it is the doctrine of the Roman Catholic Church that has attained the greatest methodological clarity here and, as a result, also the strongest historical durability: the infallible Pope, who is the most absolute which it is possible to conceive upon Earth,¹⁰ is nothing for his person; [he] is only instrument – placeholder of Christ on earth,^{cxlii} *servus servorum Dei*.^{cxliii/11} The will of the absolute ruler can be law [*Gesetz*] only because, in the exercise of his office, he can will nothing more than what is right [*Recht*]. The historical deformations, the revolting events that are to be traced back to the absolute rulers of the 17th and 18th centuries, are not thereby 'beautified'. It is only necessary to see them in another perspective, to abstract from the individual, to know how much a philosopher must, indeed, remain indifferent to the fact that precisely these concrete persons indulged their individual perversities and that, *sub specie*^{cxliv} of such an [96] understanding, the prince as an individual and concrete human being is every bit as irrelevant as any other individual in the state. The dignity to which he lays claim and which is attributed to him attaches only to his office, not to the mortal

---

¹⁰ The most interesting compilation of expressions and decisions, out of which the position of the Pope in the Catholic Church is derived, is found in Justinus Febronius, *de Stato Ecclesiae* (ed. altera, 1765, p. 215 ff.), of which the citation out of the *Decisiones S. Rotae Romanae*, Clementis Merlini, 1662, Dec. 577, n. 26, an. 1638 is particularly important: 'Papa est supra omne jus positivum' ['The Pope is above all positive law'].

¹¹ It should be repeated that the discussion is not about the individual Popes and not about that which individual Popes have thought and done, but rather of the idea of the Papacy [*Idee des Papsttums*], to which one does not do justice with such 'cultural-historical' anecdotes.

human being. In virtue of the kind of similitude to the deity that the absolute monarch exhibits as the 'living law' [*lebendiges Gesetz*], he is immediately subjected to the law, just as the God of theology, whose omnipotent will can will nothing evil, nothing unreasonable.[12]

If the individual accordingly disappears within the state, it might seem all the more as though every critique of the state were an empty *raisonnement.*[cxlv] But the discussion here was not about the concrete state, about one of the many empirical states. If the insight into the essence of the state is pursued consistently, then the individual, and what it becomes in the state, indeed appears as a new construction, but the latter does not therefore float in the air and is no arbitrary act of the state. The state is itself the result of a lawfulness [*Gesetzmäßigkeit*], itself a construction, and the construction into which the individual turns results, in the last consequence, from the state's own [con-onstruction]. The individual does not become the state's plaything, the state does not confer dignities on arbitrary grounds, but only ever in the fulfilment of the laws [*Gesetze*], upon which its own dignity is [97] based. Its authority is not a fact, before whose awe-inspiring inexplicability one would have to stand terrified, but rather a meaning that can become known and made conscious. The admiration of the state is based on the insight that, here, a great idea appears and even rules the masses, and precisely not on fear or on swooning interjections. A test of how far the idea has become a fact therefore always remains possible and therewith also a rational critique. Only about ourselves ought we to be silent. The complaints that proceed from an egocentric standpoint merit no respect.

They are also not respected as such. For the evaluation of humans, it is very important that everything they give out as a reason, or that they pretend is a reason, in public, is indeed a reason, not the mere indication of a motive. This, indeed, is the argumentation of every critique which is taken up by humans in public, and even when greater groups of humans raise their demands, then they always appeal to the justification of their claims, not to their power. Should the objection be made against them that they are led by interests, then they seek to prove that the interests in question are justified.

---

[12] The arguments which *Stahl* brings forth for the personal God thus allow themselves to be offered equally well for the proof of the necessity and justification of an absolute monarch or of the infallibility of the Pope. One can even add further that the expressions of such an instance have the particular advantage that they are conveyed in a current language and are immediately comprehensible. But precisely the individual, the concrete, personal, which for Stahl is that which is decisive in the personal God, the consideration of life, of history, of development, necessarily becomes an *abstractum* again in the treatment of the question concerning the law.

Everyone defends himself most vigorously against the charge of personal interest, as if it were an insult, although it is conceivable, after all, that someone might strive for something good and justified out of self-seeking motives. Perhaps this is even the rule, although the mechanism by which it comes about that the individual, despite his egocentricity, turns into a collaborator in a great work of which he hardly understands a sentence, is only of secondary interest to the philosopher. Nonetheless, however, human beings experience it as a slight when one accuses them of being led by their interests [98] and not by the matter at hand. It is striking, however, that the distinction between psychological motive and substantive argument, which everyone understands so well in the practice of political striving, the strict rejection of all 'immaterial', 'personal' critique, the recognition that the individual and his personality do not matter, is suddenly forgotten in doing theory. Even the individual that is turned into the epicentre of value by some state theory must still legitimate itself with its value, since nothing has a value by 'nature', there is no other value than that 'which the law determines for it' (Kant, *Grundlegung zur Metaphysik zur Sitten* 2nd ed., p. 79).[cxlvi] The focus on the issue at hand, whose recognition amounts to a recognition of objectivity, results from the norm alone; it is therefore, as paradoxical as it may sound to many, the opposite of a mere facticity. The individual as a particular empirical entity, however, is initially nothing but a fact.[cxlvii] The law, of which it has been shown that it must precede power as mere fact, thus also precedes the individual and can, if this is so, only be an objective law; it does not have its origin in the opinions of the individual as such and it also does not address it to that individual; it knows no individuals at all. Although one should not fail to recognize the practical usefulness, for matters that arise in the administration of the state and in empirical legislation, of the formula that the statutory law exists for the sake of human beings, and not human beings for the sake of the statutory law, it still remains decisive that a norm that holds because it is good and right cannot hold for the sake of the interests of the sum of individual human beings. What is more important than that there are humans is that there are good and just humans.

To speak of a freedom of the individual that puts a limit on the [authority of the] state is bound to give rise to misunderstanding. The state [99] does not intervene in the sphere of the individual from outside, like a *deus ex machina*. What is a subject, a point of imputation, an individuality for the state becomes all of this as a result of an inescapable consequence to which the state itself is subordinate. Of the freedom of the individual, one can only speak if the state is not understood as the manifestation of the legal thought, but rather as a power complex, and the individual, in polysemous unclarity, as the bearer of justified demands, or perhaps also as a fact, like the state itself, so that it would be imprudent for the latter to risk a trial of strength. The freedom of the individual would then be the formula for concrete political demands, demands which presuppose that the state against which they are directed is not a pure rule-of-law state, but a means for material purposes, one that keeps to individual rules, but only 'pourvu qu'il ne soit pas contraire aux principes du gouvernement'^{cxlviii} (Montesquieu). But as long as the subject is that of the legal philosophic construction of the state or of the individual these issues are to be abstracted from, and only the ideal state, the state that has wholly become a rule-of-law state, comes into consideration. A right of the individual to freedom, in the sense that the empirical individual could lay claim, in all cases, to certain purely material advantages – like decent housing or the chicken in the pot – is neither a juristic right, nor a problem for the solution of which philosophy would be competent.

To be sure, the objection will be made by the individuals, again and again, that individual human beings are the 'presupposition' of all goods, of all activity, of all fulfilment of duties, that the concrete, bodily human being must be there before anything else can be spoken of. This is, for instance, the last and most important argument that *Stahl* puts forward so as to ground his 'historical' legal [100] philosophy, and the weightiest objection that he leads into the field against Kant appears to him to be that Kant, when he speaks of duties and rights of the sovereign towards those who obey, no longer has real human beings before his eyes (*Philosophie des Rechts*, vol. I. 1st ed., p. 148). What can already be taken away from the discussions up to this point, however, is that this is precisely what the correctness of the Kantian thoughts consists in and that Kant is hit more by the charge of not having emphasized this consequence with sufficient clarity. Stahl's objection ignores the opposition and the incompatibility of the abstract and the concrete and, moreover, commits the logical error of allowing empirical 'presuppositions' to decide about the value or, in other words, the error of the crassest materialism, for which the brain is 'more important' than the thought, because there is no thought without the brain, [a line of argument] that can then be extended, into infinite regress, to other 'presuppositions', such as good digestion and its 'presuppositions', such as the supply of a definite quantity of nutrients, which in turn has its presuppositions. A *value* can never be obtained in this way, least of all for the state or the individual. If, by contrast, the problem is discussed from the perspective of value, then the state is capable of conferring a value on the individual from no other point of view than according to the norms that ground its own value. For the state, the essence and value of anything that is subjected to it can only be contained in a task and in its fulfilment. There is an autonomy in law, but its bearer is the state alone, as the sole subject of the 'ethos in law'. The law, in its mere capacity as law, addresses itself only to the state. Only of the state does the law demand to be fulfilled, and not of the individual, to whom the historical development [of the law] has therefore left only the 'right of necessity', which is not to be discussed in more detail here, [101] whereas all other coercive force has devolved to the state. Autonomy means something else in law than it does in ethics, where the individual is regarded as its possessor. To bring this last type of autonomy into any proximity of kinship with that of the law is to take one's departure from false antitheses, namely those of law and individual, or the very ancient one of state and individual, while the individual must, correctly, be cut out, and the law and the state confront one another alone. No individual has autonomy in the state. It is not thinkable that a foreign essence should come and jump into the world of the law and appeal to values and dignities resting only in itself, in its purely empirical uniqueness, values whose acceptance would amount to the silent assertion of the most inexplicable of all *generationes aequivocae*.[cxlix] The embodied concrete individual, as long as the view does not elevate itself above material corporeality, is a wholly accidental unity, a wafted-together heap of atoms, whose figure, individuality and uniqueness are none other than that of the dust that has been spun into a column by a whirlwind. If, however, the view goes beyond the material, the criterion of individuality will consist in a value that is drawn from a norm. The value in the law, and in the mediator of law, in the state, is to be measured, therefore, according to the norms of the law alone, not according to things that are endogenous to the individual.

The history of the dogmas of legal science provides sufficient examples of the sovereignty with which legal opinions have behaved towards the merely factual. The whole great domain of fictions, which play a role in legal life for other than merely 'editorial' reasons, is to be mentioned here, since the fiction arises only once the [102] 'fact' is given a hearing and employed for purposes of comparison, although without receiving an independent significance.[13] The most illuminating example, however, which shows up in any civil service legislation in some form or other, is provided here as well by the doctrine of the Roman Catholic Church,

---

[13] The authentic fiction in the law is thus not a 'consciously false assumption' and therewith *no* fiction in Vaihinger's sense (*die Philosophie des Als ob*, Berlin 2nd ed. 1913); that which is 'untrue' is first inserted into it via naturalism.

with its constituting of the *charisma veritatis*^{cl} by the mere bestowal of office, whereby the office is no longer based on charisma, but the bestowal, rather, becomes constitutive of the charisma. This thought, which, by the way, belongs to the *jus divinum*^{cli} of the Church, is juristic (and anti-individualistic) in the most eminent sense: the concrete personal, characteristics of the concrete person that administers an office may not be invoked against the authority of the office, and the proposition, that God gives the necessary understanding to the one to whom he gives the office, is not only of sociological but also of juristic interest and is recognized everywhere. The examples of such antinaturalism in the law could be multiplied many times over: the independence of the 'will' of the statute from any actually existing will has already been mentioned in another connection, it becomes yet more probative via the comparison with the 'contractual will' of the parties in legal transactions of the civil law, where the will that is to be assumed [to exist], according to the standards of 'good faith',^{clii} takes precedence over the uncontrollable individual processes, as they play out in the soul of the contracting parties, and where the legally relevant fact carries the day against the accidental fact. The clearest case, however, is the kind of immortality that the law has created through the legal institution of inheritance and which, in this most elementary [103] phenomenon of legal life, allows [the law's] superiority over natural historical or biological categories to step into the light almost demonstratively. The testament, which derives from adoption, and which finds its sense in the continuation of the legal personality of the testator into infinity, signifies the greatest abstraction from empirical embodiment.[14] It fits both the testator and the heir into legal constructions, and thus makes one 'juristic' person of them. Even masses of assets and corporative associations as such can become 'juristic persons'

---

[14] As evidence for how every truly philosophic treatment of the right of inheritance attains to this abstraction, the following sentences from Lassalle's *System der erworbenen Rechte* [*System of Acquired Rights*] may be emphasized: 'As essential as it is, ... to grasp the affirmative moment that the Roman idea of the testament represents, and which precisely consists in having transferred the essence and the infinity of subjectivity into the pure internality of the will freed from the confines of natural and historical *immediacy* ...' (2nd ed. 1880; vol. II. p. 22). 'The will, as the ideal subjective *juxtaposed* to the real external world, must show this its speculative nature also in the heir, in that it contrasts the latter with the reality of the object of wealth, thus using him to manifest the fissure' (ibid., p. 209). Lassalle closes his work with a sentence from Leibniz, which he cites in the highest admiration: 'Testamenta vero mero jure nullius essent momenti, nisi anima esset immortalis' [Latin in Schmitt's German original: 'Testaments would be in true undiluted law of no moment [null and void], if the soul were not immortal'] (Nova Methodus Jurisprud. pars spec. § 20).

of this kind. The misunderstanding to which the word 'fiction' fell victim has created confusion and unclarity in all these questions. The word fiction contains only the reference to a comparison with the external world and does not declare the juristic person to be a construct of lies and arbitrariness, as though the individual human individuum were the only 'true' legal subject. This signification of the word 'fiction' would indeed offer no explanation, but would amount, rather, to the confession of a confusion of the empirical individual with the point of imputation for legal norms. [104] The explanation of the juristic person as a fiction, as offered by Savigny and Puchta, nonetheless shows a greater understanding of juristic method than the numerous attempts to establish the *real*[cliii] bearers of rights and duties. While the employment of fiction still remains conscious of the renunciation of the empirical external world, the striving to discover the palpable reality that 'wears' the rights or duties like a gown or a wallet completely drowns in the factual and forgets that the juristic construction 'legal subject', in all cases, whether it is a matter of a real human being or of a company with limited liability, is necessarily always only a 'juristic' unity and person. Only the confounding of the factual [as such] with [the fact] that has been turned into the element of a case [*Tatbestandsmerkmal*] has hindered a clear insight. It is to be hoped, given the inspirations that are owed to the investigations by *Vaihinger* on fiction, that the importance of fictions like those here drawn upon as examples for the structure of juristic concepts and notions will no longer be overlooked. The 'fictive' juristic person is the archetypal image of all personality in the law. If the practical significance of the juristic person has first become a reality in contemporary economic life, in such encompassing dimensions, and if the [need for] conscious juristic treatment of the problem thereby psychologically suggests itself, then this merely fulfils the natural law [*Naturgesetz*] that the most simple logical relations are the last, in historical development, to enter into consciousness.

The theories that, at the time of the great French Revolution were brought into validity, contained, in the type and mode in which they expressed themselves, the typical confusion of norm and factuality. Thus Robespierre, for instance, stood upon the ground [*Boden*] of the theory of the *volonté* [105] *générale*. Although he conceived of it wholly naturalistically, and consequently was of the opinion that the people must exercise its sovereignty through the greatest possible number of elections, so that the shortest possible legislative periods were the best way, in general, for the exercise of its sovereignty – a thought that, in its compelling correctness from the standpoint of this naturalism, shows how this 'will' annihilates itself in its mindless atomism – he nevertheless resisted the appeal to the original electors proposed by the Gironde,^{cliv} in the trial against the King, with the argument that even the sovereign people must not be allowed to strive for the abolition of the republic, 'since the republic is virtue'. The politician will be able to recognize the usefulness of such inconsistencies of a fanatic of virtue, for whom virtue was a mere consequence of the Rousseauean natural law, for the methodically observant philosopher, however, the proof of an inconsistency is the only objection that he can make. A clear alternative, therefore, arises in the case of this example mentioned last: either to recognize the mere factual 'will' of the people without reservation, or else to ignore it altogether, since it is 'virtue' that is decisive, and if the will of the people agrees with virtue, its expression is superfluous, while the people's vote is irrelevant if it opposes virtue. If only the rational will merits respect, then reason decides and not the will. If the state is to be grounded upon a contract and if it is supposed to have 'emerged' from the fact that multiple individuals banded together and bound themselves into a collectivity that represents an independent, common will, a *volonté générale*, then such a 'contract' refers to a legal order that is already presupposed. The individuals, of whom it is said that they founded the state via contract, do not appear as random **[106]** individual human beings but rather as contractors within the frame of a legal order, so that the process of the founding of the state by contract no longer signifies an historical but rather a juristic event. The error of contract theory, therefore, was not the construction of a contract; rather, it was to assume empirical individuals as parties to the contract. –

The critique of the importance of the empirical individual human can confirm no value and no significance of the individual as such. No one may appeal to a mere fact, neither the ruler nor the subject, as an individual neither of them is important. A fundamental law [*Gesetz*] of 'respect' is not thereby violated. The human being does not merit respect because it is a human being; it is the human being who is good and worthy of respect, rather, that merits respect. The political-practical need to emphasize that no human being takes precedence over any other arises from concrete historical circumstances in which it is necessary to set oneself against the arbitrariness of power and thus has the greatest practical significance. The philosopher, however, must remain conscious of the fact that the human being, in this case, is not to be understood as a natural-historical or biological category, and that it does not merit respect merely in virtue of its birth from human beings. The politician, for his part, will concede that to him too the condition will seem 'ideal' in which everyone – without regard to 'accidents' that, at any rate, cannot exist in natural history – is respected according to merit, and not merely because it so happens that he is there, and that all the difficulty of politics consists in the ascertainment of merit and in its realization under concrete temporal conditions. The attribution of the value of the individual to his task and its fulfilment, thus, does not annihilate the dignity of the individual; rather, it shows the way, in the first place, to a justified dignity. [107] The annihilation of the individual, to which the objection here to be expected refers, does not come from the law and from the state that is wholly taken up in the realization of the law, but rather from the state qua power-complex, from a factuality that is to be met with a battle of power against power. The question of how the empirical individual can here be given help is no longer a legal-philosophic one, as little as the question of how it can be brought about that the holders of power always comply with the law. All that legal philosophy can do is to point out how all power without law is meaningless, and that even the most powerful individual is irrelevant as such. What goes beyond this are in part psychological and characterological, in part pedagogical and purely technical questions of politics. –

There are times of mediacy and times of immediacy. In the latter, the giving over of the individual to the idea is something taken for granted by human beings; there is no need for a penally organized state in order to help the law to recognition, indeed, the state seems, according to the saying of Angelus Silesius, to stand like a wall before the light. In times of mediacy, by contrast, human beings mistake the means for the essence and the state for that which is most important, and they know no other law than that which is mediated by the state. In a rhythm that spreads over the ages of humanity and which subjects the individual to its great momentum – here, too, the individual does not matter and resembles, in its uniqueness, with its cares about personal aims, the wave of the storm, which knows not whither it flows and yet is firmly spellbound into a gesture of most zealous determination – in indefatigable repetition, the two extremes replace one another, and make themselves felt in every area of spiritual life, in a form that, in particular, allows the plea for [108] the particular civilization and culture to alternate with the accusations of a physiocratism based on natural law that appears in ever-changing garb. Even in the most important expression that the distinction between immediacy and mediacy can find, in the juxtaposition of intuitive and discursive thought, the opposition remains the same, and the most significant manifesto for a conceptual, developmental thinking that wants to attain to truth progressively, through the stepwise refutation of its own objections, namely the Preface and Introduction of the *Phenomenology of Spirit*,^{clv} is owed to Hegel, who (now it will be permitted to say: consequently) also perceives in the state the highest moral instance. But before one thinks about levelling out or bridging over the distinction, one ought to come to know it in all its strictness and importance. Perhaps one will then realize that there is nothing more to refute and to prove here. So as to stick with the image, one might add that the advocate of mediacy could refer to the fact that only springs that emerge far from the sea and must seek their way through hindrances can become majestic currents; the advocate of immediacy,^{clvi} by contrast, sees only that all waters, the imposing currents, as much as the little brooks, finally end in the sea, in order to find their rest in its infinity.

Notes

ⁱ   *Zuerst ist das Gebot, die Menschen kommen später.*

ⁱⁱ   *autoritätsfeindliche*: literally, 'authority-hostile'; more colloquially, perhaps, 'anti-authoritarian'.

ⁱⁱⁱ Rathenau (1912). Schmitt omits the first word of Rathenau's title (*Zur*, meaning 'towards a', 'for a') in his reference to the work above. Rathenau (1867–1922), who would later be assassinated as foreign minister in the Weimar Republic, was Schmitt's political target in Schmitt's 1913 pseudonymously published satire poems, *Schattenrisse*, as a 'Nicht-Deutsche', in Schmitt's understanding of this term. See Villinger (1995), 14.

^{iv}   *per antiphrasin*: 'by antiphrasis'. Schmitt here seems to claim that the age can be called an individualistic one only should 'individualistic' have a polar opposite meaning to that which it is usually taken to have.

^v   *geformter Reichtum*: literally, 'formed richness' or 'formed wealth', i.e. wealth that has been formed into good manners and good taste.

^{vi}   Here, Schmitt seems to refer to Matthew 5:3, which, in the King James version, reads: 'Blessed are the poor in spirit: for theirs is the kingdom of heaven.'

^{vii} According to the editor of the 2015 German edition, at this point in his personal copy (*Handexemplar*) of *Der Wert des Staates*, Schmitt here marked a wish for an additional paragraph break, writing 'Textabsatz' in the margin. See Schmitt (2015), 110, note [2].

^{viii} Latin in Schmitt's German original: 'on the threshold', 'at the outside'.

^{ix}   Here, Schmitt may make reference to a quote from one of Schiller's shorter works, 'The Philosophers' [*Die Philosophen*], in which a student [*Lehrling*] seeks a fertile or abundant maxim or proposition. In answer to this, an eighth interlocutor tells the student that the practical maxim still holds that 'If you can, then you should!' ['Du kannst, denn du sollst!']. See Schiller (1838), vol. 1, 432.

^x   The 2015 German edition here introduces a note to indicate that Schmitt's annotations in his personal copy of the book indicate that Schmitt would cut this paragraph off at this point and begin a new paragraph. See Schmitt (2015), 110, note [3].

^{xi}   In Schmitt's personal copy of the book, he here expanded the sentence with the note, 'und keine Praxis' ['and no practice']. See Schmitt (2015), 110, note [4].

^{xii}   Schmitt's annotations to his personal copy here indicate that he would introduce a new sentence, ending the prior sentence at the point of the semi-colon. See Schmitt (2015), 110, note [5].

^{xiii}   Greek in Schmitt's German original: 'of itself'.

^{xiv}   Greek in Schmitt's German original: 'participation', 'partaking in'.

^{xv}   Schmitt here seems to refer to Feuerbach (1796).

^{xvi}   Latin and unitalicized in Schmitt's German original: 'the good father of the family'.

^{xvii}   Latin and unitalicized in Schmitt's German original: 'in an embrace', 'in a grasp', 'in a complex'.

^{xviii}   In a note in his personal copy, Schmitt here replaces 'wenn' with 'was'. See Schmitt (2015), 110, note [6].

^{xix}   In a note written into his personal copy, Schmitt here indicates that he would change this comma to a period and here begin a new sentence. See Schmitt (2015), 110, note [7].

^{xx}   Sandrine Baume here renders the German as 'la plus grossière de toutes les erreurs' ['the grossest of all errors']: Schmitt (2003), 70. Celestino Pardo opts for 'el más monstruoso de todos los defectos' ['the most monstrous of all the defects']: Schmitt (2011), 12. Perhaps most accurately, Furio Ferraresi, renders the German as 'la più mostruosa di tutte le gradualità' ['the most monstrous of all the graduality']: Schmitt (2013), 29.

^{xxi}   The 1914 edition (p. 14) reads 'fruchtbare Bathos', while the 2004 and 2015 editions (p. 21) read 'fruchtbare Pathos'. The translation for the later editions would be 'fruitful pathos'.

^{xxii}   For further discussion of Mozart's *Don Giovanni* in Schmitt's early work, see Schmitt's letter to his sister, Auguste Schmitt, dated 3 December, 1905: 'For the time being play only *Mozart!* . . . You don't believe it, how beautiful he is, one must learn to understand him, and that is not so difficult. But he signifies the same for music which Goethe does for poetry: he possesses a clear, pure, childish beauty; he is a Greek – In the vacation I will bring piano excerpts out of *Don Juan* and *The Magic Flute*, then we shall attempt to see and to enjoy his beauty together.' See Schmitt (2000), 40.

^{xxiii}   In the 1914 edition, a dash follows this paragraph, which has been dropped in the 2004 and 2015 editions.

^{xxiv}   Here, Schmitt appears to make reference to a famous discussion in Spinoza's posthumously published *Tractatus politicus*.

^{xxv}   Alternatively, 'right of rights' [*Nach dem Rechte des Rechts*].

^{xxvi}   Latin and unitalicized in Schmitt's German original: 'he is reasoning from his chains', 'he is reasoning out of his chains'.

^{xxvii}   Latin and unitalicized in Schmitt's German original: 'It is not possible to detract quantity from the law.'

^{xxviii}   Latin and unitalicized in Schmitt's German original: 'argument from utility', 'argument from use'.

^{xxix}   More literally, 'although now' [*Obwohl nun*].

^{xxx}   In the 2003 French translation, this clause is taken out of its concessive framing and made a sentence on its own: 'Seul celui saisit une conception dans ses conséquences ultimes, est apte à la comprendre correctement' ['Only one who knows a conception in its ultimate consequences is apt to understand it correctly']. See Schmitt (2003), 78.

xxxi   The title, On the power of the Pope, is given in Latin and unitalicized in
        Schmitt's German original. As Sandrine Baume notes in her edition, the full
        title of the work is *Resolutio lutheriana super propositione sua decima tertia de
        potestate papae.*

xxxii   Latin and unitalicized in Schmitt's German original: 'The first thing that moves
        me to believe that the Roman pontiff is superior to all others is the will of God,
        which we see in the fact (that the Roman pontiff is recognized to be superior to
        others). Without the will of God it would not have been possible for the Roman
        pontiff ever to attain this monarchy.'

xxxiii The 1914 and 1917 editions here print 'geworden ist', while the 2004 and 2015
        editions print 'geworden sind'. See Schmitt (1914), 24; Schmitt (1917), 24;
        Schmitt (2004), 30; Schmitt (2015), 30.

xxxiv   'Races' renders Schmitt's German term *Rassen*. See Schmitt (2015), 30; Schmitt
        (2004), 30.

xxxv   Latin and unitalicized in Schmitt's German original: 'a contradiction in the
        adjective'. Schmitt here seems to claim that 'goalless' (*ziellos*) and 'development'
        (*Entwicklung*) are two terms that mutually exclude and contradict each other.

xxxvi   Here, 'of a savage' renders Schmitt's German term *des Wilden*.

xxxvii As noted in the 2015 German edition, Schmitt's notes to his personal copy
        indicate that he would here introduce a paragraph break. Introducing the note
        about the paragraph break, the 2015 German edition omits a dash present in all
        prior editions, which the editors read as a transcription error. See Schmitt (1914),
        27; Schmitt (1917), 27; Schmitt (2004), 33; Schmitt (2015), 33; 110, note [8].

xxxviii Schmitt's German here is *wer darüber entscheidet* – a version of the question *quis
        judicabit*?

xxxix   As noted in the 2015 German edition, in Schmitt's personal copy, his marginalia
        indicate that he would here introduce a new paragraph. See Schmitt (2015), 110,
        note [9].

xl   As noted in the 2015 German edition, the hand-written corrections in Schmitt's
        personal copy of *The Value of the State* indicate that he would here begin a new
        paragraph. See Schmitt (2015), 110.

xli   Latin and unitalicized in Schmitt's German original: 'longevity', '*longue durée*',
        'long duration'.

xlii   Latin and unitalicized in Schmitt's German original: 'long time'.

xliii   Latin and unitalicized in Schmitt's German original: 'presumption of fact'.

xliv   '*Die Ewigkeit ereilt sich nicht auf eigener Leiter.*'

xlv   Schmitt's phrase 'is only' [*sei nur*] is italicized in the 2004 and 2015 editions, but
        not in the original 1914 and 1917 editions. See Schmitt (1914), 31; Schmitt (1917),
        31; Schmitt (2004), 37; Schmitt (2015), 37.

xlvi   Schmitt's apparent wordplay on the resonances between making and power, '*die
        Macht zu einem Stoffe macht*', is difficult to convey fully.

xlvii   Alternatively, 'every rogue', 'every villain' [*jeder Schurke*].

xlviii Compare Schmitt's later arguments in section 4 of *Staat, Bewegung, Volk: Die
        Dreigliederung der politischen Einheit*.

xlix   Greek in Schmitt's German original in all editions: 'a transformation into another
        kind', 'a transition into another type'.

l   Latin and unitalicized in Schmitt's German original in all editions: 'a great band
        of robbers', 'a great mercenary band'.

li   Latin and unitalicized in Schmitt's German original in all editions: 'according to general, but not universal, principles'.

lii *Strohdreschereien*: 'flailings at straw'; less literally, 'pitching at windmills'. In an article on Schmitt and Kierkegaard, Burkhard Conrad translates *Strohdrescherei* in this passage as 'a useless exercise'. See Conrad (2009), 145–171, at 157.

liii Latin and unitalicized in Schmitt's German original in all editions: literally, 'breathing voice', 'mere name'.

liv Schmitt's orthography here is *nur Eine Wahrheit* (in which 'Eine' is capitalized), here rendered correspondingly as 'One Truth'.

lv   Schmitt's orthography here is *nur Eine höchste Gewalt* (in which 'Eine' is capitalized), here rendered correspondingly as 'One highest Power.'

lvi Latin and unitalicized in Schmtt's German original in all editions: 'the city of God', 'the commonwealth of God'.

lvii Schmitt's orthography here is *Eine Kirche* (where 'Eine' is capitalized), here rendered correspondingly as 'One Church'.

lviii As noted by the editor of the 2015 German edition, in his personal copy (*Handexemplar*) of the book, Schmitt revised this sentence to read 'which ought to be so internal, that on account of it seemingly nothing even might be said to constitute the priority of the one before the other' in place of 'which is so internal, that on account of it nothing even may be said to constitute the priority of the one before the other'. See Schmitt (2015), 51; 111, note [13].

lix Here, amongst the *bedeutenden Philosophen*, Schmitt may have Vaihinger in view.

lx   Latin and unitalicized in Schmitt's German original: 'origin, content, blessedness'.

lxi Here, 'impressive' translates *imponierendes*, which, as noted by the editors of the 2015 German edition, in his personal copy, Schmitt has corrected to *bedeutsames* (meaning 'significant', 'meaningful'). With this change, the phrase would read 'here a significant feeling articulates itself'. See Schmitt (2015), 111, note [15].

lxii Here, 'disavow' renders *desavouieren*, which, as noted by the editors of the 2015 German edition, Schmitt has corrected in his personal copy to *aufheben* (meaning 'sublimate', 'dissolve'). With this alteration, Schmitt's phrase would read 'via the recognition of which the state would dissolve itself'. See Schmitt (2015), 111, note [16].

lxiii *Triebfedern* is a Kantian technical term, frequently rendered as 'incentives'. The notion might also be conveyed with 'drives'.

lxiv *Triebfedern* is divided into 'Trieb federn' in the 2015 German edition, in contra-distinction to earlier editions, which the editors read as the product of a faulty scan of 'Trieb-federn' from the 2004 edition. See Schmitt (2004), 60; Schmitt (2015), 60. The term is a technical term in Kant.

lxv Both parts of translation from: Kant (1996b), 353–603, at 383.

lxvi Latin in Schmitt's German original: 'division by leap'.

lxvii Latin in Schmitt's German original: 'specific difference', that which speciates one concept or idea from another.

lxviii The German text is unitalicized, but this sentence contains a reference to Kant's major work, *The Metaphysics of Morals*, as well as to the metaphysics of morals as theory or body of knowledge (which may or may not have been discovered by Kant and described in the book of that title).

lxix Schmitt is here offering a direct quotation from Kant (1996b), 370.

lxx   Latin and unitalicized in Schmitt's German original: 'accidental'.

lxxi   Schmitt's term *berechtigte* ('justified') is italicized in all four versions of the German original.

lxxii   Tr. *Theory of Legal Science*. As the editors of the 2015 German edition note, in Schmitt's personal copy of the book, he here corrected '*Theorie der Rechtswissenschaften*' to '*Theorie der Rechtswissenschaft*', so that the title of the work in translation would be *Theory of the Legal Science*. See Schmitt (2015), 64, 111.

lxxiii   As the editors of the 2015 German edition note, in Schmitt's personal copy of the book, he here replaced *die* ('the') with *jene* ('those'), so that the modified clause would read 'stamps those protestations'. See Schmitt (2015), 65; 111.

lxxiv   Tr. *Kant Studies*. The journal *Kantstudien* still exists and now publishes mostly in English, but under the original German title. It was in 1914 and remains one of the leading Kant journals.

lxxv   As Sandrine Baume notes, Schmitt here appears to make reference to Horace, *Carmina*, III.iii.7: 'If the world breaks and collapses . . . ' The line continues, '*impavidum ferient ruinae*' ('the ruins would leave him undaunted'). See Schmitt (2003), 110, note 27. No less, this Latin tag makes an appearance in Hegel's *Science of Logic*, in the context of a discussion of Kant.

lxxvi   Namely, as external conditions for the ethical life.

lxxvii   Friedrich Julius Stahl (1802–1861) was a German legal theorist and political thinker. Two of his main works are *The Philosophy of Law from the Historical Point of View* and *The Constitution of the Church according to the Teaching and Law of the Protestants*.

lxxviii   *Magd.*

lxxix   *zur idealen Hausfrau.*

lxxx   Alternatively, 'of her man' [*ihres Mannes*].

lxxxi   The German has *Erzwingbarkeit*. What is *erzwingbar* is something that *kann erzwungen werden*. The English is thus 'enforceable' or perhaps 'coercible'. Kant's claim that legal duties are external is tied to the notion of Erzwingbarkeit: external acts can be brought about through the threat of coercion, but such threats cannot make the motive of the act in question moral. Thus Kant concludes that it is an essential characteristic of legal duties to be enforceable (which is what Schmitt is concerned with denying).

lxxxii   Alternatively, 'the carrying out of a capital sentence' [*Hinrichtung*]. 'Execution' in English (and German) can refer to the implementation of any sentence, whereas Hinrichtung is always the execution of a capital punishment.

lxxxiii   Alternatively, 'than the bailiff'.

lxxxiv   Latin and unitalicized in Schmitt's German original: 'command', 'jurisdictional competence'.

lxxxv   Tr. *Decisions in Civil Matters*.

lxxxvi   As the editors of the 2015 German edition note, in his personal copy, Schmitt here adds 'noch kurz' ('yet briefly', 'still briefly') into the margin. See Schmitt (2015), 74; 111.

lxxxvii   French and unitalicized in Schmitt's German original: 'the mouth that pronounces the speeches of the statute'. In *Gesetz und Urteil*, Schmitt deploys the same quotation in French, which he there attributes to Montesquieu. For Schmitt's legal terminology, *droit* in French corresponds to Schmitt's usage of

Recht ('law', *ius*), whilst *loi* in French corresponds to his notion of *Gesetz* ('statute', *lex*). The reference is to Montesquieu, *De l'esprit des lois*, XI.vi. See Montesquieu (1979 [1748]), 301.

lxxxviii Schmitt's term *Gesetz* ('statute', 'statute law', *loi*, *lex*) is italicized in all German editions.

lxxxix Schmitt's term *Recht* ('law', *ius*, *droit*, *nomos*) is here italicized in all editions of the German original.

xc In the 2015 edition, uniquely, a comma is inserted following *unter* ('under'). There is no comma here in any of the three prior German editions and the editors read this comma as introduced by typographic error into the 2015 edition. Compare Schmitt (2015), 75; Schmitt (2004), 75; Schmitt (1917), 73; Schmitt (1914), 73.

xci As the editors of the 2015 German edition note, in his personal copy, Schmitt has here written *erst* ('first') as an addition to this sentence, so that clause would read 'the tendency to enforceability is something which is first brought into the law by the state'. See Schmitt (2015), 111, note [20].

xcii Latin and unitalicized in Schmitt's German original: 'divine law', 'divine right'.

xciii Latin and unitalicized in Schmitt's German original: 'human law', 'human right'.

xciv Schmitt's term here, *gesetzt* ('set'), which is cognate with the term translated as statute throughout, is italicized in all four German editions.

xcv Schmitt's term here, *daß* ('that'), is italicized in all four German editions.

xcvi Greek in Schmitt's German original: 'the becoming human', 'the becoming flesh'. Sandrine Baume translates the term in this passage as 'Incarnation': Schmitt (2003), 120 note 42. A typographic error, likely due to a faulty scan in the 2004 prints ἐναθρώπγ,σις in place of ἐνανθρώπησις. The error is retained in the 2015 German edition. See Schmitt (2015), 81; Schmitt (2004), 81; Schmitt (1917), 80; Schmitt (1914), 80. Cf. Schmitt (2013), 77.

xcvii Latin and unitalicized in Schmitt's German original: 'divine law', 'divine right'.

xcviii Latin and unitalicized in Schmitt's German original: 'law', 'right'.

xcix Latin and unitalicized in Schmitt's German original: 'from the (papal) throne'.

c Latin and unitalicized in Schmitt's German original: 'divine law', 'divine right'.

ci Latin and unitalicized in Schmitt's German original: 'divine-natural law', 'divine-natural right'.

cii Latin and unitalicized in Schmitt's German original: 'indirect power'.

ciii Latin and unitalicized in Schmitt's German original: 'coercive force'.

civ Latin and unitalicized in Schmitt's German original: 'directive power', 'direct power'.

cv As Sandrine Baume notes, Schmitt here appears to refer to Francisco Suarez, *Defensio fide Catholicae et Apostolicae* 3.22.1. See Schmitt (2003), 122 note 46.

cvi While the term is unitalicized in Schmitt's German original, it is perhaps worth noting in this connection that 'Der Staat' was Schleiermacher's German translation of Plato's *Politeia*, the work known in English as *The Republic*, in French as *La République* and in Italian as *La Repubblica*.

cvii As the editors of the 2015 German edition note, in his personal copy, Schmitt expands the sentence at this point, continuing, 'but rather in the concrete practical legal theory of the state'. See Schmitt (2015), 84; 111, note [21].

cviii *Räsonnement* is the Germanized French word for 'reasoning', given here in French and italics.

cix *voller Hast ihr Einzelglück zu retten.* Sandrine Baume marks this as a reference to 'Theodor Däubler, *Das Nordlicht III*, München, Florentiner Ausgabe, Müller, 1910' in her 2003 French edition of *La valeur de l'État et la signification de l'individu.* See Schmitt (2003), 125 note 1.

cx Alternatively, 'applies to the state'.

cxi The 1914, 1917 and 2004 German editions italicize the first part of this word in keeping with the orthographic italicization of proper names, but not the second half of the term (*Hegel*sche). In the 2015 German edition, the entirety of the word is italicized.

cxii Latin in Schmitt's German original: 'manager of business affairs'.

cxiii The *Oxford Classical Texts* edition of this passage renders this first τὴν τοῦ ἑτέρου as τὴν γὰρ θατέρου, offering no manuscript variations that support Schmitt's alternative rendering. Indeed, Schmitt's putative source for this citation, the 1602 Frankfurt edition of Ficino's Greek-Latin text, also prints γὰρ θατέρου in place of τοῦ ἑτέρου. See Plato (1602), 180. However, in the first volume of Arthur Schopenhauer's *The World as Will and Representation* (*Die Welt als Wille und Vorstellung*), Schopenhauer quotes precisely this passage of Plato's Greek followed by Ficino's translation, and Schopenhauer's text prints τοῦ ἑτέρου in place of θατέρου. This may lead the reader to suspect that Schmitt is deriving the quotation from Schopenhauer rather than from Ficino's translation of Plato. See Arthur Schopenhauer (1986), 555; Schopenhauer (1891), 484. The translator is thankful to Mark Fisher and Kinch Hoekstra for help with this reference and several references that follow.

cxiv Both the 2004 and 2015 German editions print ψύσιν in place of φύσιν ('nature'), which is present in the 1914 and 1917 editions. The editors read the later printings as a transcription error – perhaps the result of faulty scanning of the 1914 text with 'scan-to-print' technology. While the Italian and French translations omit the Greek entirely, Celestino Pardo's Spanish translation prints ψύσιν, deploying the 2004 German edition as its copy text. See Schmitt (2011), 61.

cxv The 2015 German edition omits the aspiration mark on ἑκάστου for εκάστου.

cxvi In Schmitt's putative source for this citation, the Greek reads ἐστιν. See Plato (1602), 181.

cxvii Nicholas P. White renders this passage of Plato's *Sophist* as follows: 'Since we showed that the nature of *the different* is, chopped up among all beings in relation to each other, we dared to say that *that which is not* really is just this, namely, each part of the nature of the different that's set over against *that which is*.' See Plato (1997), 282. Francis Cornford translates the passage as follows: 'We have shown that the nature of the Different has existence and is parcelled out over the whole field of existent things with reference to one another; and of every part of it that is set in contrast to "that which is" we have dared to say that precisely that is *really* "that which is not".' See Cornford (1935), 294–295. Seth Benardete interprets the passage to read: 'Once we had proved that the nature of the other both is and has been chopped into bits to extend over all "the things which are" in their mutual relations, we had the nerve to say that this very thing is in its being "that which is not" – a proper part of the nature of the other in its opposition to that which severally is'. Benjamin Jowett renders the passage as: '[F]or we have shown that the nature of the other exists, and is distributed over all things in their mutual relations, and when each part of the other is contrasted with being, that is precisely what we have ventured to call not-being.' See Jowett (1871), vol. III, 526.

cxviii   In Schmitt's putative source for this translation, the 1602 Frankfurt Latin-Greek edition, this passage appears at 258F–259A. See Plato (1602), 180. In Arthur Schopenhauer's *Die Welt als Wille und Vorstellung* I.iii.§ 71, the same passage of Plato's *Sophist*, cited above by Schmitt, is cited by Schopenhauer first in Greek, then Ficino's Latin translation with the reference, in some editions of Schopenhauer, given as '258 D'.

cxix   In the 1602 Ficino edition that Schmitt cites here, *Cum* is accented as *Cùm*. See Plato (1602), 180. The translator is thankful to Kinch Hoekstra for this reference.

cxx   The 2004 and 2015 German editions omit the accent mark on *pérque* that is present in the 1914 and 1917 editions. See Schmitt (2004), 87; Schmitt (2015), 87; cf. Schmitt (1914), 87, Schmitt (1917), 87. While Furio Ferraresi and Celestino Pardo omit the accent, their 2013 Italian and 2011 Spanish translations both respectively follow the 2004 German edition as a copy text; Sandrine Baume retains the accent in her 2003 French version, which uses the 1914 German edition as its copy text. See Schmitt (2013), 83; Schmitt (2011), 61; Schmitt (2003), 127.

cxxi   Marsilio Ficino, which Furio Ferraresi renders back into the vernacular in his translation of *Il valore dello Stato*. See Schmitt (2013), 83.

cxxii   Both the French and Italian translators of the work omit Schmitt's Greek quotation (present in all editions of the German original) from their versions. See Schmitt (2013), 83; Schmitt (2003), 127. The edition to which Schmitt here refers appears to be Plato (1602), 180–181.

cxxiii   Latin and unitalicized in Schmitt's German original in all editions: 'I think therefore I am,' See Descartes, *Discours de la méthode*.

cxxiv   Schmitt's point here seems to be that Descartes' proof of the reasoner's existence would work as well if the reasoner were to say to themselves, 'I laugh, therefore I am'. So the proof is indifferent what activity is chosen to run the proof – there is nothing special about thinking – although Descartes seems to argue that it is our awareness of our own thought, specifically, that gives evidence of our existence.

cxxv   Schmitt's implicit reference in the unsourced quotation here seems to be to Goethe's poem 'Selige Sehnsucht'.

cxxvi   As the editor of the 2015 German edition notes, in his personal copy of the text, Schmitt here added *einzelne* ('singular') before *empirische, konkrete Individuum* ('empirical, concrete individuum')

cxxvii   Here, 'culture-inimical *chinoiserie*' renders Schmitt's term *kulturfeindlichen Chinesentum*. Furio Ferraresi renders this as 'un elemento cinese anticulturale': Schmitt (2013), 84. Sandrine Baume, in her French version, opts for 'chinoiseries ennemis de la culture': Schmitt (2003), 128.

cxxviii   Latin and unitalicized in Schmitt's German original in all editions: 'most projected at the matter', 'most directed toward the matter'.

cxxix   *Unzucht*, here rendered as 'bawdiness' (alternatively, 'fornication'), could mean 'sodomy' in legal contexts, although in the present context *Unzucht mit sich selbst* would seem rather to imply self-pleasure.

cxxx   Latin in all three editions of Schmitt's German original: '[that they, the masses] precede all mechanics and trade just as brutes and just as inanimate ones [as persons without spirit or soul]'.

cxxxi   Here, Schmitt appears to refer to Theodor Däubler's poem *Das Nordlicht*.

cxxxii   Here, 'one from China' renders Schmitt's *ein Chinese*, which might more literally
           be rendered 'a Chinese', as Furio Ferraresi ('un cinese') and Sandrine Baume ('un
           Chinois') translate the term in their versions. See Schmitt (2013), 86; Schmitt
           (2003), 131.

cxxxiii   Alternatively, meaning 'mind one's own business'. Schmitt's phrase *das Seinige
           tun* may be a reference to the Socratic definition of justice as minding one's own
           business or doing one's own thing in Plato's *Republic*, Book IV, 433a.

cxxxiv   More literally, 'so that external accidents do not decide'.

cxxxv   See Friedrich Schiller, *Der Jungfrau von Orleans*, I.ii: '[König] Karl: Drum soll
           der Sänger mit dem König gehen,/sie beide wohnen auf der Menschheit Höhen'
           ['(King) Charles: There the singer should walk with the king,/they both dwell
           upon the heights of humanity'].

cxxxvi   Here, 'by freezing savages' translates Schmitt's *von frierenden Wilden*.

cxxxvii   Alternatively, '[t]he state grasps the individuum and infixes the individuum into
           the rhythm of the state'. In this sentence, however, the German pronouns avoid
           an ambiguity of cross-reference in a manner difficult to reproduce in English
           translation.

cxxxviii   French and unitalicized in Schmitt's German original: 'I am the state'; more
           literally, 'the state, it's me'.

cxxxix   French and unitalicized in Schmitt's German original: 'the first servant and the
           first magistrate of the State'. All schoolchildren (and adults) in Wilhelmine
           Germany would have known that this is how Frederick the Great liked to refer to
           himself.

cxl   Spanish and unitalicized in Schmitt's German original: 'living and animate law
           within the lands', 'living and animate law upon the land'.

cxli   French and unitalicized in Schmitt's German original: 'pleasure'. The quotations
           around the word are present in all four German editions.

cxlii   *Statthalter Christi auf Erden*. *Statthalter Christi* is German for 'vicarius Christi'.

cxliii   Latin and unitalicized in Schmitt's German original: 'servant of the servants
           of God'.

cxliv   Latin and unitalicized in Schmitt's German original: 'under the aspect'.

cxlv   Meaning 'reasoning'. Schmitt here uses a Germanicized version of the French
           word in his German original (*Räsonnement*).

cxlvi   Kant (1996a), 85.

cxlvii   For a rendering of this sentence that accords it a slightly different meaning, see
           Schmitt (2003), 135.

cxlviii   French and unitalicized in Schmitt's German original: 'provided that they are
           not contrary to the principles of government'. Schmitt's apparent source is
           Montesquieu, *De l'esprit des lois* (1748), XIX.5, where the full sentence might be
           rendered as: 'It is up to the legislator to follow the spirit of the nation [*l'esprit de
           la nation*], when it is not contrary to the principles of government, because we
           do nothing better than what we do freely, and in following our natural genius.'
           In his quotation, Schmitt has substituted 'pourvu qu'il' ('provided that') for
           'lorsqu'il' ('when it'). Montesquieu's example is France, and Montesquieu
           seems to be instructing those making laws to let France be and not try to make
           it something it is not. The translator is thankful to William Selinger for help
           with this reference.

cxlix   Latin and unitalicized in Schmitt's German original: 'equivocal generations', 'ambiguous procreations'.

cl   Latin and unitalicized in Schmitt's German original: 'charisma of the truth'.

cli   Latin and unitalicized in Schmitt's German original: 'divine law'.

clii   *Treu und Glauben*, less idiomatically rendered as 'trust and faith'.

cliii   Italics present in Schmitt's German original in all German editions (*realen*). See Schmitt (1914), 105; Schmitt (1917), 105; Schmitt (2004), 104; Schmitt (2015), 104.

cliv   The Girondins.

clv   Hegel's *Phänomenologie des Geistes*, presented in quotation marks and normal face typescript in all four editions of the German text.

clvi   Literally, 'the Immediate' [*der Unmittelbare*], which Furio Ferraresi renders as 'il sostenitore dell'immediatezza' ('the supporter of immediacy') in Schmitt (2013), 99.

BIBLIOGRAPHY

Anschütz, Gerhard (1933) *Die Verfassung des Deutschen Reiches vom 11. August 1919: Ein Kommentar für Wissenschaft und Praxis*, 14th edition (Berlin: Georg Stilke).

Aristotle (1995) *The Complete Works of Aristotle*, ed. Jonathan Barnes, vol. 2 (Princeton, NJ: Princeton University Press).

Austin, John (1911) *Lectures on Jurisprudence or the Philosophy of Positive Law*, 5th edition, ed. Robert Campbell, vol. II (London: John Murray).

Bacon, Francis (2004) '*Novum organum*', in Graham Rees and Maria Wakeley (eds.) *The Oxford Francis Bacon*, vol. 11 (Oxford: Oxford University Press).

Balakrishnan, Gopal (2000) *The Enemy: An Intellectual Portrait of Carl Schmitt* (London: Verso).

Baume, Sandrine (2003) 'Carl Schmitt, penseur de l'état', in Carl Schmitt, *La valeur de l'état et la signification de l'individu*, ed. and trans. Sandrine Baume (Geneva: Droz), 7–57.

Bendersky, Joseph W. (1983) *Carl Schmitt: Theorist for the Reich* (Princeton, NJ: Princeton University Press).

Berman, Russell A., and Zeitlin, Samuel Garrett (2018) 'Note on the Edition and Translation', in Carl Schmitt, *The Tyranny of Values and Other Texts*, eds. Russell A. Berman and Samuel Garrett Zeitlin, trans. Samuel Garrett Zeitlin (Candor, NY: Telos Press), xiii–xvii.

Berthold, Lutz (1999) *Carl Schmitt und der Staatsnotstandsplan am Ende der Weimarer Republik* (Berlin: Duncker & Humblot).

Caldwell, Peter C. (1997) *Popular Sovereignty and the Crisis of German Constitutional Law: The Theory and Practice of Weimar Constitutionalism* (Durham, NC: Duke University Press).

Cohen, Hermann (1904) *Ethik des reinen Willens* (Berlin: Bruno Cassirer).

Conrad, Burkhard (2009) 'Kierkegaard's Moment: Carl Schmitt and His Rhetorical Concept of Decision', in Kari Palonen (ed.) *Redescriptions: Yearbook of Political Thought, Conceptual History and Feminist Theory* (Berlin: LIT Verlag), 145–171.

Cornford, F. M. (1935) *Plato's Theory of Knowledge; The* Theaetetus *and the* Sophist *of Plato* (London: Kegan Paul, Trench, Trubner & Co.).

Cristi, Renato (1998) *Carl Schmitt and Authoritarian Liberalism: Strong State, Free Economy* (Cardiff: University of Wales Press).

Croce, Mariano, and Salvatore, Andrea (2013) *The Legal Theory of Carl Schmitt* (Abingdon: Routledge).

Delany, Joseph (1911) 'Occasions of Sin', in *The Catholic Encyclopedia*, vol. 11 (New York: Robert Appleton Co.). http://www.newadvent.org/cathen/11196a.htm.

De Wilde, Marc (2018) 'The Dark Side of Institutionalism: Carl Schmitt Reading Santi Romano', in *Ethics & Global Politics* 11, 12–24.

Düringer, Adalbert, and Hachenburg, Max (1908) *Das Handelsgesetzbuch vom 10. Mai 1897*, 2nd edition (Mannheim: J. Bensheimer).

Dyzenhaus, David (1997) *Legality and Legitimacy: Carl Schmitt, Hans Kelsen and Hermann Heller in Weimar* (Oxford: Oxford University Press).

Dyzenhaus, David (2001) 'Hobbes and the Legitimacy of Law', in *Law and Philosophy* 20, 461–498.

Endicott, Timothy A. O. (2000) *Vagueness in Law* (Oxford: Oxford University Press).

Evans, Richard J. (2004) *The Coming of the Third Reich* (London: Penguin).

Fetscher, Iring (1982) 'Lassalle, Ferdinand', in *Neue Deutsche Biographie*, vol. 13 (Berlin: Duncker & Humblot), 661–669.

Feuerbach, Paul Johann Anselm (1796) *Kritik des natürlichen Rechts als Propädeutik zu einer Wissenschaft der natürlichen Rechte* (Altona: bei der Verlagsgesellschaft).

Finnis, John (2011) *Natural Law and Natural Rights*, 2nd edition (Oxford: Oxford University Press).

Foulkes, Albert S. (1969) 'On the German Free Law School', in *Archiv für Rechts- und Sozialphilosophie* 55, 367–417.

Freund, Julien (2017) 'The Contemporaneity of Thomas Hobbes', in *Telos* 181, 40–47.

Fuller, Lon L. (1964) *The Morality of Law*, revised edition (New Haven, CT: Yale University Press).

Galli, Carlo (2013) 'Presentazione', in Carl Schmitt, *Il valore dello Stato e il significato dell'individuo*, ed. Carlo Galli, trans. Furio Ferraresi (Bologna: Il Mulino), 5–18.

Giese, Friedrich (1948), *Einführung in die Rechtswissenschaft* (Wiesbaden: Springer).

Gross, Raphael (2005) *Carl Schmitt und die Juden. Eine deutsche Rechtslehre*, 2nd edition (Frankfurt/Main: Suhrkamp).

Gusy, Christoph (1997) *Die Weimarer Reichsverfassung* (Tübingen: Mohr Siebeck).

Hart, H. L. A. (1958) 'Positivism and the Separation of Law and Morals', in *Harvard Law Review* 71, 593–629.

Hart, H. L. A. (1994) *The Concept of Law*, 2nd edition (Oxford: Oxford University Press).

Hegel, G. W. F. (1991) *Elements of the Philosophy of Right*, ed. Allen W. Wood, trans. H. B. Nisbet (Cambridge: Cambridge University Press).

Herget, James E., and Wallace, Stephen (1987) 'The German Free Law Movement as the Source of American Legal Realism', in *Virginia Law Review* 73, 399–455.

Hobbes, Thomas (1996) *Leviathan*, ed. Richard Tuck (Cambridge: Cambridge University Press).

Hofmann, Hasso (2002) *Legitimität gegen Legalität. Der Weg der politischen Philosophie Carl Schmitts*, 4th edition (Berlin: Duncker & Humblot).

Huber, Ernst Rudolf (1939) *Verfassungsrecht des Großdeutschen Reiches*, 2nd edition (Hamburg: Hanseatische Verlagsanstalt).

Jowett, B. (1871) *The Dialogues of Plato, Translated into English with Analyses and Introductions* (Oxford: Clarendon Press), 4 vols.

Kahn, Victoria (2003) 'Hamlet or Hecuba: Carl Schmitt's Decision', in *Representations* 83, 67–96.

Kahn, Victoria (2014) *The Future of Illusion: Political Theology and Early Modern Texts* (Chicago: University of Chicago Press).

Kalyvas, Andreas (2008) *Democracy and the Politics of the Extraordinary: Max Weber, Carl Schmitt, and Hannah Arendt* (New York: Cambridge University Press).

Kant, Immanuel (1996a). 'Groundwork of the Metaphysics of Morals (1785)', in *Practical Philosophy*, trans. Mary J. Gregor (Cambridge: Cambridge University Press), 37–108.

Kant, Immanuel (1996b). 'The Metaphysics of Morals (1797)', in *Practical Philosophy*, trans. Mary J. Gregor (Cambridge: Cambridge University Press), 353–604.

Kantorowicz, Hermann U. (Gnaeus Flavius) (1906), *Der Kampf um die Rechtswissenschaft* (Heidelberg: C. Winter).

Kantorowicz, Hermann U. (1911) *Rechtswissenschaft und Soziologie* (Tübingen: Mohr Siebeck).

Kaufmann, Matthias (1988) *Recht ohne Regel? Die philosophischen Prinzipien in Carl Schmitt's Staats- und Rechtslehre* (Freiburg: Karl Alber).

Kaufmann, Walter (2013) *Nietzsche: Philosopher, Psychologist, Antichrist* (Princeton, NJ: Princeton University Press).

Kelsen, Hans (1931) 'Who Ought to be the Guardian of the Constitution? Kelsen's reply to Schmitt', in *The Guardian of the Constitution: Hans Kelsen and Carl Schmitt on the Limits of Constitutional Law*, ed. and trans. Lars Vinx (Cambridge: Cambridge University Press, 2015), 174–221,

Kelsen, Hans (1934) *Introduction to the Problems of Legal Theory: A Translation of the First Edition of the* Reine Rechtslehre *or Pure Theory of Law*, trans. Bonnie Litschewski Paulson and Stanley L. Paulson (Oxford: Clarendon Press, 1992).

Kennedy, Ellen (2004) *Constitutional Failure: Carl Schmitt in Weimar* (Durham/London: Duke University Press).

Kletzer, Christoph (2018) *The Idea of a Pure Theory of Law* (Oxford: Hart).

Kiefer, Lorenz (1990) 'Begründung, Dezision und Politische Theologie. Zu drei frühen Schriften von Carl Schmitt', in *Archiv für Rechts- und Sozialphilosophie* 76, 479–499.

Kramer, Matthew H. (2018) *H. L. A. Hart* (Cambridge: Polity Press).

Landau, Peter (2007) 'Goethes verlorene juristische Dissertation und ihre Quellen. Versuch einer Rekonstruktion', in *Sitzungsberichte der Bayerischen Akademie der Wissenschaften. Philosophisch-Historische Klasse*, vol. 2 (Munich: C. H. Beck).

Leiter, Brian (2007) *Naturalizing Jurisprudence: Essays on American Legal Realism and Naturalism in Legal Philosophy* (Oxford: Oxford University Press).

Lenel, Otto (1902) 'Der Irrtum über wesentliche Eigenschaften', in *Jhering's Jahrbücher für die Dogmatik des bürgerlichen Rechts* 44, 1–30.

Loughlin, Martin (2010) *Foundations of Public Law* (Oxford: Oxford University Press).

Loughlin, Martin (2017) *Political Jurisprudence* (Oxford: Oxford University Press).

Löwith, Karl (1995) 'The Occasional Decisionism of Carl Schmitt', in *Martin Heidegger and European Nihilism*, ed. Richard Wolin, trans. Gary Steiner (New York: Columbia University Press), 137–158.

Maier, Clara (2019) 'The Weimar Origins of the West German *Rechtsstaat*, 1919–1969', in *The Historical Journal* 62, 1069–1091.

Mastnak, Tomaž (2015) 'Hobbes in Kiel, 1938: From Ferdinand Tönnies to Carl Schmitt', in *History of European Ideas* 41, 966–991.

Maus, Ingeborg (1980) *Bürgerliche Rechtstheorie und Faschismus. Zur sozialen Funktion und aktuellen Wirkung der Theorie Carl Schmitts* (Munich: Wilhelm Fink Verlag).

McCormick, John P. (1997) *Carl Schmitt's Critique of Liberalism: Against Politics as Technology* (Cambridge: Cambridge University Press).

Mehring, Reinhard (2009) *Carl Schmitt. Aufstieg und Fall* (Munich: C. H. Beck).

Meier, Heinrich (1994) *Die Lehre Carl Schmitts* (Stuttgart/Weimar: J. B. Metzler).

Meierhenrich, Jens (2018) *The Remnants of the Rechtsstaat: An Ethnography of Nazi Law* (Oxford: Oxford University Press).

Mieck, Ilja (1992) 'Preussen von 1807 bis 1850. Reformen, Restauration und Revolution', in Otto Büsch (ed.) *Handbuch der Preussischen Geschichte*, vol. 2 (Berlin: De Gruyter), 3–292.

Montesquieu, Charles de Secondat, Baron de (1979). *De l'esprit des lois*, ed. Victor Goldschmidt (Paris: Flammarion), 2 vols.

Montesquieu, Charles de Secondat, Baron de (1989) *The Spirit of the Laws*, eds. and trans. Anne M. Cohler, Basia C. Miller and Harold Stone (Cambridge: Cambridge University Press).

Mouffe, Chantal (1997) *The Return of the Political* (London: Verso).

Natorp, Paul (1913) 'Recht und Sittlichkeit. Ein Beitrag zur kategorialen Begründung der praktischen Philosophie', in *Kant-Studien* 18, 1–79

Neumann, Volker (2015) *Carl Schmitt als Jurist* (Tübingen: Mohr Siebeck).

Pauer-Studer, Herlinde (2014) 'Einleitung: Rechtfertigungen des Unrechts. Das Rechtsdenken im Nationalsozialismus', in Herlinde Pauer-Studer and Julian Fink (eds.), *Rechtfertigungen des Unrechts. Das Rechtsdenken im Nationalsozialismus in Originaltexten* (Berlin: Suhrkamp), 15–135.

Paulson, Stanley L. (1992) 'Introduction', in Hans Kelsen (1934) *Introduction to the Problems of Legal Theory. A Translation of the First Edition of the Reine Rechtslehre or Pure Theory of Law*, trans. Bonnie Litschewski Paulson and Stanley L. Paulson (Oxford: Clarendon Press), xvii-xlii.

Paulson, Stanley L. (2007) 'Statutory Positivism', in *Legisprudence* 1, 1–29.

Paulson, Stanley L. (2016) 'Hans Kelsen and Carl Schmitt: Growing Discord, Culminating in the "Guardian" Controversy of 1931', in Jens Meierhenrich and Oliver Simons (eds.), *The Oxford Handbook of Carl Schmitt* (Oxford: Oxford University Press), 510–546.

Paulson, Stanley L. (2019) 'Hans Kelsen on Legal Interpretation, Legal Cognition, and Legal Science', in *Jurisprudence* 10, 188–221.

Plato (1602) *Divini Platonis Opera Omnia Quæ Exstant. Marsilio Ficino Interprete* (Frankfurt: Apud Claudium Marnium, & hæredes Ioannis Aubrii).

Plato (1986) *Plato's Sophist, Part II of the Being of the Beautiful*, trans. Seth Benardete (Chicago: University of Chicago Press).

Plato (1990) *Plato's Sophist*, trans. William S. Cobb (Savage, MD: Rowman & Littlefield).

Plato (1993) *Sophist*, trans. Nicholas P. White (Indianapolis: Hackett).

Plato (1996) *Plato's Sophist, or the Professor of Wisdom*, trans. Eva Brann, Peter Kalkavage and Eric Salem (Newburyport, MA: Focus).

Plato (1997) *Complete Works*, eds. J. M. Cooper and D. S. Hutchinson (Indianapolis: Hackett).

Pliny the Younger (1969) *Letters*, vol. I, books 1–7 (Loeb Classical Library 55), trans. Betty Radice (Harvard, MA: Harvard University Press).

Rasch, William (2016) 'Carl Schmitt's Defense of Democracy', in Jens Meierhenrich and Oliver Simons (eds.), *The Oxford Handbook of Carl Schmitt* (Oxford: Oxford University Press), 312–337.

Rathenau, Walther (1912) *Zur Kritik der Zeit* (Berlin: Fischer).

Raz, Joseph (1999) *Practical Reason and Norms* (Oxford: Oxford University Press).

Rubinelli, Lucia (2020) *Constituent Power: A History* (Cambridge: Cambridge University Press).

Rüthers, Bernd (2017) *Die unbegrenzte Auslegung. Zum Wandel der Privatrechtsordnung im Nationalsozialismus*, 8th edition (Tübingen: Mohr Siebeck).

Scheuerman, William E. (1996) 'Legal Indeterminacy and the Origins of Nazi Legal Thought: The Case of Carl Schmitt', in *History of Political Thought* 17, 571–590.

Scheuerman, William E. (2020) *The End of Law: Carl Schmitt in the Twenty-First Century*, 2nd edition (London: Rowman & Littlefield).

Schiller, Friedrich (1838) *Sämtliche Werke in zwölf Bänden* (Stuttgart und Tübingen: J. G. Cotta'sche Buchhandlung).

Schmitt, Carl (1912) *Gesetz und Urteil. Eine Untersuchung zum Problem der Rechtspraxis*, 2nd edition (Munich: C. H. Beck, 1969).

Schmitt, Carl (1914) *Der Wert des Staates und die Bedeutung des Einzelnen* (Tübingen: J. C. B. Mohr).

Schmitt, Carl (1917) *Der Wert des Staates und die Bedeutung des Einzelnen* (Hellerau: Hellerauer Verlag-Jakob Hegner).

Schmitt, Carl (1921) *Dictatorship: From the Origin of the Modern Concept of Sovereignty to Proletarian Class Struggle*, trans. Michael Hoelzl and Graham Ward (Cambridge: Polity Press, 2014).

Schmitt, Carl (1922) *Political Theology: Four Chapters on the Concept of Sovereignty*, trans. George Schwab (Chicago: University of Chicago Press, 2005).

Schmitt, Carl (1927) *Volksentscheid und Volksbegehren. Ein Beitrag zur Auslegung der Weimarer Verfassung und zur Lehre von der unmittelbaren Demokratie* (Berlin: Duncker & Humblot, 2014).

Schmitt, Carl (1928) *Constitutional Theory*, ed. and trans. Jeffrey Seitzer (Durham, NC: Duke University Press, 2008).

Schmitt, Carl (1931) 'The Guardian of the Constitution', in *The Guardian of the Constitution: Hans Kelsen and Carl Schmitt on the Limits of Constitutional Law*, ed. and trans. Lars Vinx (Cambridge: Cambridge University Press, 2015), 79–173.

Schmitt, Carl (1932a) *Legality and Legitimacy*, trans. Jeffrey Seitzer (Durham, NC: Duke University Press, 2004).

Schmitt, Carl (1932b) *The Concept of the Political*, expanded edition, trans. George Schwab (Chicago: University of Chicago Press, 2007).

Schmitt, Carl (1933) *Staat, Bewegung, Volk. Die Dreigliederung der politischen Einheit*, 2nd edition (Hamburg: Hanseatische Verlagsanstalt).

Schmitt, Carl (1934) *Über die drei Arten des rechtswissenschaftlichen Denkens*, 2nd edition (Berlin: Duncker & Humblot, 1993).

Schmitt, Carl (1936) 'Schlußwort des Reichsgruppenwalters Staatsrat Prof. Dr. Carl Schmitt', in *Das Judentum in der Rechtswissenschaft. Ansprachen, Vorträge und Ergebnisse der Tagung der Reichsgruppe Hochschullehrer des NSRB am 3. Und 4. Oktober 1936, vol. 1: Die deutsche Rechtswissenschaft im Kampf gegen den jüdischen Geist* (Berlin: Deutscher Rechts-Verlag), 28–34.

Schmitt, Carl (1938) *The Leviathan in the State Theory of Thomas Hobbes: Meaning and Failure of a Political Symbol*, trans. George Schwab and Erna Hilfstein (Chicago: University of Chicago Press, 2008).

Schmitt, Carl (1942) *Land and Sea: A World-Historical Meditation*, eds. Russell A. Berman and Samuel Garrett Zeitlin, trans. Samuel Garrett Zeitlin (Candor, NY: Telos Press, 2015).

Schmitt, Carl (1950a) 'Das Problem der Legalität', in *Verfassungsrechtliche Aufsätze aus den Jahren 1924–1954. Materialien zu einer Verfassungslehre* (Berlin: Duncker & Humblot, 1958), 440–451.

Schmitt, Carl (1950b) *The Nomos of the Earth in the International Law of the Jus Publicum Europaeum*, trans. Gary L. Ulmen (New York: Telos Press, 2006).

Schmitt, Carl (1954) *Dialogues on Power and Space*, eds. Federico Finchelstein and Andreas Kalyvas, trans. Samuel Garrett Zeitlin (Cambridge: Polity Press, 2015).

Schmitt, Carl (1967) 'The Tyranny of Values', in *The Tyranny of Values and Other Texts*, eds. Russell A. Berman and Samuel Garrett Zeitlin, trans. Samuel Garrett Zeitlin (Candor, NY: Telos Press, 2018), 26–41.

Schmitt, Carl (1970) 'On the TV-Democracy', in *The Tyranny of Values and Other Texts*, eds. Russell A. Berman and Samuel Garrett Zeitlin, trans. Samuel Garrett Zeitlin (Candor, NY: Telos Press, 2018), 200–205.

Schmitt, Carl (1995) *Briefwechsel mit einem seiner Schüler*, eds. Armin Mohler, Irmgard Huhn and Piet Tommissen (Berin: Akademie Verlag).

Schmitt, Carl (1996) *Politische Theologie. Vier Kapitel zur Lehre von der Souveränität*, 7th edition (Berlin: Duncker & Humblot).

Schmitt, Carl (2000) *Jugendbriefe: Briefschaften an seine Schwester Auguste 1905 bis 1913*, ed. Ernst Hüsmert (Berlin: Akademie Verlag).

Schmitt, Carl (2003) *La valeur de l'état et la signification de l'individu*, trans. Sandrine Baume (Geneva: Droz).

Schmitt, Carl (2004) *Der Wert des Staates und die Bedeutung des Einzelnen* (Berlin: Duncker & Humblot).

Schmitt, Carl (2003) *Tagebücher, Oktober 1912 bis Februar 1915*, ed. Ernst Hüsmert, 2nd edition (Berlin: Akademie Verlag, 2005).

Schmitt, Carl (2011) *El valor del Estado y el significado del individuo*, ed. Celestino Pardo (Madrid: Centro de Estudios Políticos e Constitucionales).

Schmitt, Carl (2013) *Il valore dello Stato e il significato dell'individuo*, ed. Carlo Galli, trans. Furio Ferraresi (Bologna: Il Mulino).

Schmitt, Carl (2015) *Der Wert des Staates und die Bedeutung des Einzelnen*, ed. Gerd Giesler (Berlin: Duncker & Humblot).

Schopenhauer, Arthur (1891) *Sämmtliche Werke*, vol. II, ed. Julius Frauenstädt (Leipzig: Brockhaus).

Schopenhauer, Arthur (1986) *Die Welt als Wille und Vorstellung*, vol. I, ed. Wolfgang Frhr. Von Löhneysen (Frankfurt am Main: Suhrkamp).

Schupmann, Benjamin (2017) *Carl Schmitt's State and Constitutional Theory* (Oxford: Oxford University Press).

Schwab, George (1989) *The Challenge of the Exception: An Introduction to the Political Ideas of Carl Schmitt between 1921 and 1936*, 2nd edition (Westport, CT: Greenwood Press).

Seiberth, Gabriel (2001) *Carl Schmitt und der Prozess 'Preussen contra Reich' vor dem Staatsgerichtshof* (Berlin: Duncker & Humblot).

Shapiro, Scott J. (2011) *Legality* (Cambridge, MA: Harvard University Press).

Smeltzer, Joshua (2018). '"Germany's Salvation": Carl Schmitt's Teleological History of the Second Reich', in *History of European Ideas* 44, 590–604.

Stammler, Rudolf (1911) *Theorie der Rechtswissenschaft* (Halle an der Saale: Buchhandlung des Waisenhauses).

Stanton, Timothy (2011) 'Hobbes and Schmitt', in *History of European Ideas* 37, 160–167.

Sternberg, Theodor (1904) *Allgemeine Rechtslehre*, vol. 1 (Leipzig: G. J. Göschen).

Taubes, Jacob (1987) *Ad Carl Schmitt: Gegenstrebige Fügung* (Berlin: Merve Verlag).

Taubes, Jacob (2017) 'Leviathan as Mortal God: On the Contemporaneity of Thomas Hobbes', in *Telos* 181, 48–64.

Tuori, Kaius (2004) 'The *ius respondendi* and the Freedom of Roman Jurisprudence', in *Revue internationale des droits de l'antiquité* 51, 295–337.

Van Calker, Fritz (1898) *Politik als Wissenschaft. Rede zur Feier des Geburtstages seiner Majestät des Kaisers am 27. Januar 1898* (Straßburg: Heitz).

Villinger, Ingeborg (1995) *Carl Schmitts Kulturkritik der Moderne: Text, Kommentar und Analyse der Schattenrisse des Johannes Negelinus* (Berlin: Akademie Verlag).

Vinx, Lars (2013) 'Carl Schmitt and the Analogy between Constitutional and International Law: Are Constitutional and International Law Inherently Political?', in *Global Constitutionalism* 2, 91–124.

Vinx, Lars (2015) 'Carl Schmitt's Defence of Sovereignty', in David Dyzenhaus and Thomas Poole (eds.), *Law, Liberty and State. Oakeshott, Hayek and Schmitt on the Rule of Law* (Cambridge: Cambridge University Press), 96–122.

Vinx, Lars (2019a) 'Carl Schmitt', in Edward N. Zalta (ed.) *The Stanford Encyclopedia of Philosophy*. https://plato.stanford.edu/archives/fall2019/entries/schmitt/.

Vinx, Lars (2019b) 'Ernst-Wolfgang Böckenförde and the Politics of Constituent Power', in *Jurisprudence* 10, 15–38.

Von Zeiller, Franz Edlen (1811) *Commentar über das allgemeine bürgerliche Gesetzbuch für die gesammten deutschen Erbländer der Österreichischen Monarchie*, vol. I (Vienna: Geistinger).

Wieacker, Franz (1952) *Privatrechtsgeschichte der Neuzeit unter besonderer Berücksichtigung der deutschen Entwicklung*, 3rd edition (Göttingen: Vandenhoeck & Ruprecht).

Zeitlin, Samuel Garrett (2015) 'Propaganda and Critique: An Introduction to *Land and Sea*', in Carl Schmitt, *Land and Sea: A World-Historical Meditation*, eds. R. A. Berman and S. G. Zeitlin (Candor, NY: Telos Press), xxxi–lxix.

Zeitlin, Samuel Garrett (2017) 'Interpretation and Critique: Jacob Taubes, Julien Freund and the Interpretation of Hobbes', in *Telos* 181, 9–39.

Zeitlin, Samuel Garrett (2018) 'Propaganda und Kritik: Eine Einführung in Carl Schmitt's *Land und Meer*', in *Politisches Denken. Jahrbuch 2017*, 27, 115–143.

Zeitlin, Samuel Garrett (2020) 'Indirection and the Rhetoric of Tyranny: Carl Schmitt's *The Tyranny of Values 1960–1967*', in *Modern Intellectual History*.

INDEX

Lightning Source UK Ltd.
Milton Keynes UK
UKHW021931190622
404667UK00004B/164

9 781108 494489